AID AS PEACEMAKER

Canadian Development Assistance and Third World Conflict

AID AS PEACEMAKER

Canadian Development Assistance and Third World Conflict

Edited by
ROBERT MILLER

Carleton University Press
Ottawa, Canada
1992

©Carleton University Press Inc. 1992

ISBN 0-88629-177-1 (paperback)
ISBN 0-88629-176-3 (casebound)

Printed and bound in Canada

Carleton Public Policy Series #11

Canadian Cataloguing in Publication Data

Main entry under title:
Aid as peacemaker: Canadian development assistance and Third World conflict

(Carleton public policy series; 11)

Includes bibliographical references.
ISBN 0-88629-176-3 (bound) – ISBN 0-88629-177-1 (pbk.)

1. Economic assistance, Canadian—Developing countries—Political aspects.
2. Economic assistance, Canadian —Developing countries. I. Miller Robert, 1941–.
II. Series.

HC59.72.E44A43 1992   338.9´17101724   C92-090657-5

Distributed by: Oxford University Press Canada,
                    70 Wynford Drive,
                    Don Mills, Ontario,
                    Canada. M3C 1J9
                    (416) 441-2941

Cover design: Aerographics Ottawa

Acknowledgements

Carleton University Press gratefully acknowledges the support extended to its publishing programme by the Canada Council and the Ontario Arts Council.

Contents

*Bernard Wood was formerly Chief Executive Officer,
Canadian Institute for International Peace and Security.

Part III: New Forms of Assistance

Acknowledgements

There are many people who contributed to the genesis and development of this book, some of whom appear within its covers as contributors. I would like to thank three people in particular, who helped move the book from the realm of good intentions to reality.

Roger Hill, when Research Director of the Canadian Institute for International Peace and Security (CIIPS), was enthusiastic about the project right from the beginning and provided invaluable help in defining the subject and obtaining CIIPS support. To both Roger and the Institute, I am grateful. I would also like to express my thanks to John Watson, the executive director of CARE, who saw the merits of the book and recommended that CARE provide the publishing grant which finally allowed *Aid As Peacemaker* to see the light of day. As my secretary at the Parliamentary Centre, Debrah Taylor did her usual fine job by transforming the pile of papers that arrived in the mail into a clean manuscript which could be turned over to Carleton University Press. Both Phil Rourke and Karen McBride gave the project enthusiastic and effective pushes when they were most needed. To all, my thanks.

Foreword

Linking aid and peacemaking is a multidimensional and multilayered challenge for advocates, analysts, and policymakers. Thus the attempt in the collection to explore so many facets of the linkage is as courageous and risky as it is timely and necessary.

At the most fundamental level, a sweeping linkage was made in the 1960s by Pope John XXIII when he said; "Development is the new name for peace." Many articles here are focused, at least in part, on tracing the roots of conflict in the systematic injustice which so often is part of underdevelopment and mal-development, and is increasingly irrepressible in the global village. The consciousness of this linkage of course must lead to serious analysis of the relationships among different kinds of "aid" and "development," and this challenge too is attacked here from many different angles.

At a less abstract level, there is also ample room to explore the various linkages between aid and peacemaking through case studies of particular conflicts and diverse channels and forms of assistance, as is done in the major sections of the book. There are hard practical and moral issues involved in the use of aid as an incentive or disincentive, about its targeting, and about the capacities of governments, nongovernmental organizations (NGOs), other institutions, and even military and civilian peacekeepers to contribute to peacekeeping through various types of assistance.

As should be expected in such an innovative exercise dealing with profound conflicts which inevitably produce conflicting interpretations, some of the treatments here will be controversial. The debates, however, are well launched and well advanced by these articles, and many of the themes are certain to attract increasing attention from official and nonofficial actors and analysts in the post-Cold War environment of conflict and new security challenges.

This project, so innovatively conceived and ably coordinated by Robert Miller, was financially supported by the Canadian Institute for International Peace and Security both before and during my tenure as director of that institution. It has been a good example of the kind of research, policy ideas and proposals, and public discussion which the Institute was created by the Parliament of Canada to encourage.

Bernard Wood

Aid as Peacemaker: Introduction

Robert Miller
Parliamentary Centre for Foreign Affairs and Foreign Trade

During a trip to Central America in the spring of 1988, the House of Commons Special Committee on the Peace Process in Central America came face to face with the damage and suffering caused by the civil wars which have marked that region's history. The statistics of people tortured, maimed, and killed were cited time after time until they lost the power to shock; the evidence of economies ruined and societies ripped apart finally induced feelings of hopelessness. It was only when members of the committee visited a prosthetics workshop in Managua that the full horror and absurdity of the situation hit them.

The workshop was supported in part by a small grant from the Canadian International Development Agency. The Committee members made a quick tour of inspection, as MPs have inspected hundreds of aid projects around the world. Everything was spic and span. There were fine examples of the workshop's products for the visitors to inspect. They were told that the facility employed ten young men and women and that there was a training program for apprentice workers. The workshop seemed an ideal grass roots project, just the sort that appeals to Canadian Members of Parliament, but then they came face to face with the reason for the workshop: men, women, and children who had had their arms or legs, or both, blown off by land mines or bullets. The patients walked about unsteadily or sat under shade trees with the preoccupied air of people who had just been fitted with wooden limbs.

The situation amounted to this: Canada was providing assistance for a model workshop serving the victims of a civil war which was destroying the development prospects of Nicaragua. The waste, suffering, and destruction mocked the rhetoric of development and seemed to render Canada's modest development assistance programs utterly irrelevant.

It was obvious to the MPs that in Nicaragua, and Central America as a whole, the prospects for development were tied to the prospects for peace and vice versa. Central American leaders as otherwise different in their ideologies as Daniel Ortega and Oscar Arias were in agreement on that point. Arias told the committee that a viable peace process was a prerequisite for development; Ortega argued that development, and specifically international development assistance, could serve as a vital stimulus for the peace process. In its July 1988 report, *Supporting the Five*, the committee concluded that outside assistance should be designed and employed in ways that would support the search for peace. "Programs of international economic assistance and the peace process should move together in tandem and reinforce one another at every step along the way."[1] Following the committee's work, it occurred to the author that this proposition might apply to Canada's aid programs in many parts of the world, and so the thesis behind this book emerged: where possible and appropriate, Canadian development assistance should be used to help avert, ameliorate, or reduce large scale violent conflict in recipient countries. In reflecting further on the proposition, it became apparent there were many difficult questions to be answered, some operational and some philosophical. How precisely would one go about using the Canadian aid program to promote peace? For that matter, *should* it always be used to promote peace? Are there not readily imaginable circumstances in which aid would be put to better use as a supporter of conflict? In any case, what does it mean to *promote* peace?

Considering the large number of developing countries which experience intense, prolonged conflict—and the tough problems this poses for Canadian development assistance—it seemed that pursuing the answers to these and other questions would be a useful undertaking. Fortunately, the Canadian Institute for International Peace and Security (CIIPS) agreed. It awarded the author two grants: the first of these made possible an exploratory workshop in February 1988 which recommended that the issues should be explored in greater depth; a second grant allowed the author to commission the papers in this volume and to organize a second workshop in November 1989 to review them.

The changing security scene

These papers should be presented in a historical context. The 1980s saw the most sweeping changes in international security concerns since World War II. For 40 years, East-West confrontation and the danger of nuclear war ranked as the greatest global security threat but, in a few years, all that has changed. Now the great worry is about economic collapse and anarchy in the East.

The threat of conflict in the late twentieth century has not so much receded as changed its nature and theatre of operations. In the first half of the century Europe led the world in war, but since World War II the vast majority of the estimated 22 million people who have been killed in armed conflict have lived in the third world. The grim statistics continue to appear year after year. In the years 1987 and 1988, there were twenty-three wars, which are defined as conflicts in which more than 1,000 people died during either year; of these, nine were in Africa, five were in Latin America, two were in the Middle East, and seven were in Asia. Depending on definitions, all or almost all were in the third world.

Despite their reassuring labels as "regional," "low intensity," or "local," these conflicts have exacted an enormous human cost and have crippled the development prospects of the countries involved. Lincoln Bloomfield has observed:

> For those in the Northern, developed world, "local" means a war taking place somewhere else. But for the people at risk, the human price can be enormous in casualties, refugee populations, and setbacks in the process of development. Nor does it follow that the passions involved, the intensity of commitment, or the ideological components are always minimal. What looks to outsiders like a brush fire may be a conflagration from the standpoint of the combatants.[2]

In one of the best hidden of these wars, South African de-stabilization of the frontline states in the 1980s cost the countries of the region as much as an estimated $10 billion annually or on the order of 40 percent of the region's Gross Domestic Product (GDP). The direct human costs have been far greater. It has been estimated that the "excess mortality" of children caused by the destruction of health services or war induced starvation amounted to some 800,000 during the period 1980 to 1988. When added to other war related deaths in the region, the total reached 1.5 million lives lost as a direct or indirect result of South Africa's strategy. In Mozambique, the most afflicted of the front line states, the death count attributable to de-stabilization was almost 900,000, or nearly 6 percent of the country's estimated population.[3]

The scale of destruction associated with conflict in Central America has likewise been enormous. In Nicaragua some forty-five thousand people were killed in the civil war that raged in the 1970s and 1980s; as a percentage of the country's total population of 2.3 million, this is a death rate equivalent to 450,000 Canadians or 4.5 million Americans. In El Salvador, the civil war took over sixty thousand lives out of a total population of some 5.6 million; the widespread use of land mines by both sides in the conflict produced a sizeable army of people maimed for life. Here too, there has been an intimate and tragic connection between civil war and the denial of basic human needs of the population. A report by the U.S. group Physicians for Human Rights chronicles violations of medical neutrality, human rights violations in the area of health care, and the denial of medicine and medical care as a weapon used against the population during years of civil conflict.[4]

While full scale civil war remains the exception in developing countries, persistent, intense, and large scale violent conflicts are common. Indeed they are now part of the stereotype of instability which attaches itself to many parts of the third world. In turn, they have contributed to the very dark assessment of development prospects in the 1990s. Bernard Wood has written that East-West detente has contributed to the resolution of some third world conflicts, but that "there are also major new dangers of regional instability, conflict, and war on the horizon."[5]

The 1989 report of the Arms Control and Foreign Policy Caucus of the United States Congress pointed to a similar conclusion based on what it sees as five key challenges that confront developing countries: economic stagnation, environmental deterioration, the power of the military, weapons proliferation, and the international drug trade. The report argues that these five challenges—to which one could easily add others such as the third-world population explosion—are emerging as a "potentially greater long-term threat to U.S. security than Soviet military power."[6] The events of the past 3 years have only confirmed this judgement.

Development wars

The so-called local and regional conflicts to which we refer are diverse in their origins, scale, and consequences, and we are far from possessing a single theory which would account for all of them. The subject has been extensively studied over the past twenty years, however, and various typologies have been developed to categorize and thereby highlight essential features of these conflicts.

The Massachusetts Institute of Technology (MIT) local conflicts project distinguishes among four types of conflict: interstate, internal with significant external involvement, primarily internal, and colonial.[7] Although the last of these types is now rapidly fading from the scene, the de-colonization of Namibia in 1989 is a conspicuous recent success of the international community in managing such conflict. The first of the types, interstate, is the traditional category of warfare between two sovereign states. It too seemed to be diminishing in frequency at one time, but it has made something of a comeback, most notably in the eight year war between Iran and Iraq and in Iraq's invasion of Kuwait.

The two categories of conflict which are of greatest interest to us in this study are the second and third: primarily internal and internal with significant external involvement. These conflicts are variously designated as revolution, civil war, insurrection, insurgency, and guerilla warfare; taken together, according to the MIT study, "they represent over one-third of the conflict agenda." Many such conflicts, and certainly the ones which have attracted the greatest international attention, have involved outside powers in one degree or other. The superpowers, in particular, have engaged in a global geo-political rivalry which features third world conflicts as the killing fields.

It was argued that once the East-West rivalry came to an end, many of these conflicts would resolve themselves, and the past few years have shown there is some truth to this assertion. Some formerly intractable conflicts, such as Namibia, Afghanistan, Cambodia, and Central America, have become resolvable or at least more containable. Even these examples, however, demonstrate that many third world conflicts have deep roots and were not just East-West side shows. These durable conflicts often involve long-standing socio-economic inequities, oppression of ethnic minorities, and the wide spread violation of human rights. Moreover, they reveal that the process of development itself is conflict ridden and conflict producing. The acceleration or the attempt to accelerate economic, social, and political change often intensifies the historic tensions among different groups in society.

For this reason, we refer to these types of conflicts as "development wars." We should not get carried away with the explanatory power of the term, but it helps to convey the fact that many violent conflicts are only an intensification of the struggle for power inherent in the process of economic, social, and political development. What is striking about the current situation is the apparent ease, frequency, and destructive power with which such tensions escalate out of control, even in countries with comparatively peaceful histories. The July 1990 insurrection in Trinidad and Tobago is only one example of violence which seems to have caught a country and the international community unawares. In the words of a former Trinidad journalist, "For Trinidadians, long accustomed to a pastoral political culture insulated from third world strife, it was a rude introduction to violent dissent."[8]

In the 1990s it would seem that many developing countries are dry tinder waiting to burst into flames. Our current sense of the volatility of development contrasts with an earlier confidence that economic growth and social and political change would reduce the causes of conflict and enhance the state's ability to manage what conflict occurred. In 1969 the Pearson commission report, *Partners in Development*, had this to say about the connection between conflict and development.

> The drive towards modernization inevitably creates conflicts between guardians of tradition and those who seek change. The controversies take on different complexions in different parts of the world, but underlying all is the demand for a more equitable sharing among individuals and nations of the benefits of progress. Pressures to this end put a premium on the adaptability of political and social structures. Resulting conflicts have been difficult, but, on the whole, surprisingly manageable as political structures in developing countries have improved in flexibility and responsiveness."[9]

Today those same "controversies" in the third world are neither as explicable nor as manageable as described in the report. While it remains true that the inequitable sharing of the benefits of development is a crucial underlying issue in many conflicts, it is by no means a sufficient explanation of why large scale violent conflict occurs. Ethnic, religious, and regional tensions are among the many other factors that make countries susceptible to conflict and sustain it when it occurs. New types of conflict are also beginning to appear, related to the drug trade in Latin America and to accelerating environmental damage in many parts of Africa. In these cases, the rise of violence is associated with a collapse in the government's ability to manage, let alone solve, fundamental problems. The record of third world governments in managing conflict has generally been both more brutal and less effective than was suggested by the Pearson commission. This problem arises, paradoxically, from the very weakness of many states in the third world and from a domestic environment which one author has described as "extraordinarily unstable."[10] Unfortunately, there is every reason to believe that the environment of many of these states will only grow more unstable in the 1990s.

It may strike the reader as self-evident that there is an intimate connection between development and conflict, and yet the tendency in the past has been to separate consideration of the two. Conflict has been the preserve of "security specialists" who have focused their attention on armies, police forces and weaponry. As for development authorities, they have tended to view conflict as a series of extraneous disasters unrelated to the processes of economic and social change. A United Nations study on de-stabilization and development in Southern Africa makes the following point: "There has been a post-war tendency of economics, both theoretical and applied, not to treat war as integral to economic processes. War has not been taken into account either as a variable or as an exogenous shock (like global terms of trade or national drought) whose impact on each social and economic sector, on overall macroeconomic levels, rates of exchange and balance of payments, requires serious attention."[11]

The management of third world debt by the International Monetary Fund (IMF) would appear to be a case of this intellectual infirmity in action. Characteristically, the fund has prescribed bitter medicine to cure economic illness, while ignoring the fact that the patient suffered from chronic or incipient instability. As a result, this branch of applied economics has invented its own form of violent third world conflict—the IMF riot.

This tendency to divorce economic development from broader considerations of human well-being has been convincingly documented by the United Nations Development Program (UNDP) in its first *Human Development Report 1990*. Noting the almost exclusive preoccupation of development with Gross National Product (GNP) growth, the authors observe that "human development is a process of enlarging people's choices," which include the desires for long and healthy lives, for education, for the resources needed for a decent standard of living, and for political freedom, human rights, and personal self-respect. The report then goes on to say: "The process of development should at least create a conducive environment for people, individually and collectively, to develop their full potential and to have a reasonable chance of leading productive and creative lives in accord with their needs and interests. ... If the scales of human development fail to balance the formation and use of human capabilities, much human potential will be frustrated."[12]

There is no simple cause and effect relationship between the frustration of human potential and the rise of violent conflict, so that it can be said that the one is immediately and invariably followed by the other. It is clear, however, that the denial of basic human needs is the fertile soil in which violence roots, a fact which is as evident in the violent crime statistics in industrialized countries as in the developing countries' vulnerability to large scale violence. Indeed this is one of the few reliable generalizations about development which has been lost sight of through an overly narrow concern with economic growth.

Aid and conflict

Despite the past tendency to dissociate the two, one can now see some evidence of a merging or at least linking of development and security concerns. The frequency of violent conflict, its durability, and the enormous destruction associated with it, have forced students of economic development to confront the subject. Likewise, there has been a growing recognition among "security specialists" that conflict resolution is unlikely to be successful unless it addresses the underlying causes of conflict; i.e., promotes human development.

There has been a corresponding rise in interest and concern about the role played by international development assistance in third world conflicts. Aid has never been regarded as the primary means by which the international community has attempted to resolve conflicts in the South, although the promotion of international peace and security has always been part of the rationale of aid. Moreover, some donor countries, and the superpowers in particular, have long used aid as an element in the achievement of what were essentially security goals. These policies were based on the confident assumption, noted earlier, that economic development *per se* would progressively eliminate the causes of conflict. In light of the failure of that hope, the links between aid and conflict are now being reexamined. We would identify the following major streams of concern.

The militarization of development

Many aid agencies and developed country governments have had to grapple with the problems of becoming entangled in third world conflicts through their aid programs, particularly as the result of widespread human rights violations. This has contributed to a growing recognition over the past twenty years that economic development cannot be divorced from human rights and that international assistance must be concerned to promote political as well as economic development. The prolonged economic decline of Africa has forced to the surface questions of governance—the problem of corruption, the absence of accountability, and the widespread incidence of military rule.

It is now apparent that conflicts in the South have more than transitory consequences. Among their enduring legacies is the militarization of government and the resulting deformation of development. Once seen as an instrument of modernization and a force for stability in fragile states, the military is now seen as an enormous drain on the resources available for development which, in turn, reinforces the causes of conflict. The UNDP *Human Development Report*, referred to earlier, documents the fact that "the rapid rise of military spending in the third world during the last three decades is one of the most alarming, and least talked about, issues."[13] In developing countries as a whole, expenditure on the military is more than that for education and health combined and, even in the least developed countries, military expenditures match the resources devoted to these basic human needs.

Given the scarcity of resources for development, the reallocation of expenditures from the military to human development ranks as one of the major issues facing developing countries and aid donors in the 1990s. It focuses attention on the arms export and military assistance programs of developed countries and poses other challenges for development policy makers. For example, it would seem more than coincidental that Costa Rica, which deliberately decided in the late 1940s to abolish its standing army, has since become the most economically and politically stable country in Central America. Granted the many differences between Costa Rica and its neighbours, one is still bound to ask how demilitarization can be made a normal feature of Central American development and indeed of development in the South generally?

Unnatural disasters

A second stream of concern focusing attention on the connections between aid and conflict comes from the rising incidence of so-called natural disasters which, upon closer examination, have a strong ingredient of human causation about them. The recurrence of famine in the Horn of Africa is a case in point. While it is generally agreed that the first great famine in the mid-1980s was related closely to adverse environmental changes and prolonged drought, it is also recognized that the second famine in 1989–90 was intimately connected to the wars in Ethiopia and the Sudan.

This fact has forced the issue of conflict resolution onto the agendas of donor governments and nongovernmental organizations (NGOs) alike: if famine is at least partially the product of war, then famine relief must be concerned to end war. For the NGO community, conflict in the Horn and elsewhere has raised difficult questions about the provision of humanitarian assistance in an age of conflict. As the result of what it saw as an escalating level of violence world wide, the International Committee of the Red Cross launched *An Appeal for Humanity* in 1985. Many other agencies involved in providing humanitarian assistance found that the need for their services was growing rapidly at the same time as the supposedly universal rules of international law in conflict situations were breaking down; aid workers and masses of civilians were coming under the gun to an unprecedented degree.[14] In Canada, the Canadian Council for International Cooperation (CCIC) embarked on a study of the problems facing its member agencies in situations of violent conflict. In the spring of 1988, it sponsored a conference on *Conflict and Development in the Horn of Africa* to explore such concepts as "even handedness" and to help develop an international protocol of neutrality for humanitarian organizations.[15]

Aid as peacemaker

As governments and nongovernmental organizations throughout the world were forced to confront the connections between aid and conflict, another stream of thought—regional conflict analysis—was creating an opening for aid as peacemaker.

Until recently, the substantial and rapidly expanding body of literature on regional conflicts has focused on the role of third parties in the institutionalization of the peace process and the development of formal mechanisms for managing what are called "security regimes" between adversaries in local or regional conflicts. As Hampson and Mandell note in an article, much of this literature has dealt only with the negotiation phase of conflict resolution and has little to say about the broader aspects of the process, such as confidence-building measures, the end of military assistance and domestic economic and political reforms. They conclude that "there is a need to fill this lacuna by examining the potential contribution of third parties to the development of more durable and lasting peace settlements."[16]

Development assistance is one of the means which may be used to contribute to durable settlements. An example is International Alert, one of a relatively new breed of NGOs which seeks to help resolve conflict by developing peacemaking proposals that combine conflict resolution elements, political and economic reform, and international development assistance. In cooperation with the International Peace Research Institute in Oslo, International Alert has organized international conferences and study sessions on internal conflicts around the world, with the objective of building consensus on a range of conflict-resolving policies and programs. The approach is conveyed in their 1989 report on Uganda. Pointing to the background of conflict and hostilities which has divided that country for decades, the report concludes: "Stability and peace cannot come overnight, nor can they be bought and sold in a marketplace. Instead, peace is the slow accumulation of confidence, the retreat of fear and the advance of human rights: political, economic, social and cultural."[17]

We have coined the term *aid as peacemaker* to describe this or other deliberate use of development assistance to help avert or resolve violent conflicts in the South; the aid may either be part of a conflict resolution package or simply attempt to address the conditions giving rise to conflict. Clearly the term is more suggestive than scientific, helping to focus our attention on the values underlying development and the means available for promoting them. That the term is most assuredly not a way of escaping difficult choices is made plain by pointing to the very different purposes it can be made to serve. The approach of International Alert seeks to avoid all use of violence in the settlement of conflicts and sees development assistance as a means of extending the reach of pacific dispute settlements. By contrast, the United States Commission on Integrated Long-Term Strategy, which reported to former President Ronald Reagan in 1988, betrayed no such hopes. In its report, *Discriminate Deterrence*, it concluded that in the coming decades the United States would need to be better prepared to deal with "low intensity conflicts" in the South. The commission made a series of recommendations to improve the design and targeting of military assistance to third world countries, but it observed along the way that conflicts of this sort are not just a problem for the Department of Defense. "In many situations, the United States will need not just DoD personnel and materiel, but diplomats and information specialists, agricultural chemists, bankers and economists, hydrologists, criminologists, meteorologists and scores of other professionals."[18]

These two quite different approaches to the use of aid in conflict situations suggest that the various streams flowing into aid as peacemaker are not likely to form a smooth flowing river of international cooperation. This diversity, taken together with the likelihood that violent third world conflicts may occur even more frequently in the future, leads to a simple conclusion: all those responsible for international aid policies and programs would be well advised to spend more time addressing these issues. The following papers have been prepared to that end.

Canadian aid as peacemaker: the papers

In common with other donor countries, Canada has long seen its aid programs as contributing in a general way to the promotion of international peace and security or to the defence of Western interests, which was often assumed to be the same goal. That was part of the justification used by Canada for its support of the Colombo Plan and, with modifications over time, it has remained a commonly employed aid rationale ever since.[19] On the other hand, Canada has striven to avoid having its aid become entangled in the internal politics of recipient countries and especially in conflict situations. In this regard, the Canadian approach stands in sharp contrast to that of the United States, which has long devoted large amounts of overseas assistance to military support of allies in the South and has otherwise involved itself directly in third world conflicts.

When one considers the record of superpower interventions, Canada's approach seems a very attractive one. It rarely adds fuel to the fire, although it may be asked whether Canada has done everything it might to help put out the flames. The answer to that question has been supplied over the years by Canadian support for and active participation in the international peacekeeping activities of the United Nations. It is this instrument rather than aid as such to which Canadian policy makers have looked as a means for Canada to help resolve international conflicts, although aid has been recognized as a means to keep the door open for peacekeeping. In defending the government's policy of providing aid to all Central American countries despite pressure to cut off countries with bad human rights records, former Secretary of State for External Affairs Joe Clark has said: "We have been urged to cut off links, to walk away. Some European countries have done just that. But when it came time to prepare for peace in Central America, it was not to those countries that the region turned. It was to Canada. For we maintained relations with the whole region, kept doors and borders open, to be in a position to assist when assistance was required."[20]

Despite its aversion to taking sides, Canada has been accused of just that on occasion and has often found its aid programs entangled in conflicts in the South. Canadian experience in Central America, Haiti, Ethiopia, Southern Africa, Sri Lanka and the Philippines, to cite only some examples, has demonstrated the potential of these apparently remote third world conflicts to generate controversy in Canada. Government aid programs have not been the only ones under fire. Canadian NGOs have placed their volunteers in situations which were sometimes highly dangerous and have had to confront questions concerning the role they can and should play in conflict situations.

The papers in this collection are intended to explore these issues from various vantage points. We stress the word "explore" because it will be evident by now that the thesis of aid as peacemaker consists of territory requiring exploration rather than precisely defined propositions calling for proof or disproof. As contributors to this study, we have chosen experts with a broad interest in policy and with the ability to communicate beyond the narrow circle of specialists. While the papers are particularly concerned with Canadian policy, we hope and expect they will be of interest to all those concerned with the issues of aid as peacemaker.

The papers can be grouped into three sets: the first consists of four papers which focus on different countries or regions in the world, namely Central America, Southern Africa, Sri Lanka, and the Philippines. The aim in this case is to permit comparisons of the Canadian aid experience in different parts of the third world and thereby test regional or country-specific lessons against one another. Next there is a set of three papers that discuss different "channels" or instruments of Canadian aid, namely the Canadian International Development Agency (CIDA), NGOs (specifically CUSO) and the United Nations. Here we want to get at the question of whether different aid instruments are more or less suited to coping with conflict situations and to playing a role as peacemaker. Finally, there is a set of four papers that discuss comparatively new initiatives for addressing the problem of third world conflict, namely the Canadian Centre for Human Rights and Democratic Development, the Food for Guns initiative of CARE, the project Immunization Cease Fires and the Horn of Africa Project.

Notes

1. House of Commons Special Committee on the Peace Process in Central America, *Supporting the Five: Canada and the Central American Peace Process* (Ottawa, July 1988), p. 22.

2. Lincoln P. Bloomfield, "Coping with conflict in the late twentieth century," *International Journal* (Autumn 1989): 776.

3. United Nations Inter Agency Task Force, Africa Recovery Programme/ Economic Commission for Africa, *South African Destabilization: The Economic Cost of Frontline Resistance to Apartheid* (United Nations, New York: October 1989), pp. 4–5.

4. See "Health in El Salvador: Casualty of War, Condition of Peace." (Washington, D.C.: *Physicians for Human Rights*, June 1990), p. 5.

5. Bernard Wood, "Peace in our Time? A Canadian Agenda into the 1990s" (Ottawa: Canadian Institute for International Peace and Security, January, 1990), p. 17.

6. Arms Control and Foreign Policy Caucus of the United States Congress, "The Developing World: Danger Point for U.S. Security" (Washington, August 1, 1989), p. ii.

7. Bloomfield, "Coping with Conflict," p. 778.

8. Derrick Poon Young, "A rebellion? They wouldn't dare" in *Globe and Mail*. August 1 1990, p. A19.

9. The Commission on International Development, *Partners in Development* (New York, Praeger: 1969), p. 53.

10. Fen Osler Hampson, "Building a stable peace: opportunities and limits to security cooperation in Third World regional conflicts," *International Journal* (Spring 1990): 483.

11. UN Inter Agency Task Force *South African Destabilization*, pp. 7–8.

12. United Nations Development Programme, *Human Development Report 1990* (New York: Oxford University Press 1990), p. 1.

13. *Ibid.*, p. 76.

14. For a discussion of the impact of conflict on humanitarian assistance, see: Minear, Larry. American Council for Voluntary International Action. *Helping People in an Age of Conflict*. New York, 1988.

15. See the report on the conference: *Conflict and Development in the Horn of Africa* (Hull, Quebec: CCIC, April, 1988).

16. Fen Osler Hampson and Brian S. Mandell, "Managing International Conflict: Security Cooperation and Third Party Mediators," in *International Journal* (Spring 1990): 193.

17. International Alert/International Peace Research Institute, "International Programme on Internal Conflict in Uganda 1987–89." (Oslo, July 1989), p. 4.

18. The Commission in Integrated Long-term Security, *Discriminate Deterrence* (Washington: Government Printing Office, January 1988), p. 15.

19. For a critical examination of this rationale for Canadian aid, see Spicer, Keith *Canada: A Samaritan State?*. University of Toronto Press, Toronto: 1966. Especially pp. 14–22.

20. The Right Honourable Joe Clark, Notes for a Speech on Canadian Policy Towards Latin America, University of Calgary, 1 February 1990, p. 4.

Part I: Country/Regional Case Studies

Aid as Peacemaker: Central America

David Close
Memorial University of Newfoundland

Central America's crisis did not end when the UNO (National Oppositional Union) defeated the FSLN (Sandinista National Liberation Front) in Nicaragua's February 1990 elections. Violent conflict still rages in Guatemala, and the economic challenges faced by the other countries of the isthmus make a Canadian finance minister's worst nightmares seem like sweet dreams. Still, the change of government in Nicaragua[1] and the Salvadoran peace accord, should send unmistakable signals to Canadian foreign policy makers: only where the contending parties are politically committed to securing peace and reconciliation (perhaps even at the risk of losing power) will it be possible to terminate persistent conflicts. I hope to be able to suggest how our development aid and diplomatic support might best be used in countries suffering chronic political violence by examining the cases of Nicaragua and El Salvador.

Central America occupied an important place in Canadian foreign policy in the 1980s; the crises in Nicaragua and El Salvador can fairly be said to have led to official Canada's discovery of Central America. In Nicaragua, the revolutionary regime of the Sandinista National Liberation Front faced U.S. financed and equipped counterrevolutionary insurgents throughout most of its ten and a half year existence. Despite this, both Liberal and Conservative governments maintained aid and trade ties with the revolutionary government from the time it ousted the Somoza family dictatorship in 1979 until its defeat at the polls in February 1990.

The situation in El Salvador has been different. A coup by reformist officers in October 1979 momentarily opened a path away from the oligarchic despotism that had dominated the country since 1932. By January 1980, however, the reactionary wing of the military had regained control and the country again fell under a pall of terror. By November 1980, the situation had deteriorated so badly that the government of Canada suspended bilateral aid because it feared for the safety of aid workers.

Four years later, however, Ottawa restored official assistance, arguing that improved conditions for human rights justified the change. Though this decision provoked heated debate, it raised important questions about the purpose and utility of aid sent to countries torn by war. I do not intend to evaluate this program, though I shall refer to it below. Rather, I shall look at three questions that necessarily arise whenever government must decide to commit official development assistance (ODA) to areas where there is persistent violent conflict.

The first simply asks what constitutes a case of persistent conflict and how such conflict affects development, regardless of how development is defined. My second question is more theoretical. It asks if there is a relationship between conflict, a country's development model and the aid that country receives. Put simply, we want to know if Canadian ODA can be expected to reduce conflict, intensify it, or affect it at all. In the cases of Nicaragua and El Salvador, this means raising the issues that inspired this collection:

- Why is there violent conflict in these countries?
- Should Canada be involved in these conflicts, even to the extent of sending aid?
- Can our ODA help bring peace?

Finally, I want to ask if our experience in El Salvador and Nicaragua in the 1980s teaches us any lessons. What, that is, are the technical and political limitations we can expect to face if we opt to establish a bilateral aid program in a country where there is an internal war?

Protracted conflict, aid, and development

Development, no matter how defined (a question I take up below), will be delayed and distorted where there is protracted conflict. Under such circumstances national security will be government's top priority, and social and economic programs will be judged according to how they affect the security problem. Moreover, such conditions make planning uncertain and hamper the delivery of projects and programs.

What should we call prolonged or protracted conflict? Indigenous internal warfare, as seen in El Salvador since 1979 and Guatemala since 1960, clearly qualifies, as does the externally supported insurgency Washington has aimed at Nicaragua. Both types of conflict produced death, destruction, and the disruption of national life on a massive scale over many years.

There are also other types of protracted conflict. Repressive regimes that rely on coercion to retain power, as did the Somoza dynasty, also belong here. By failing to develop civil conflict resolution mechanisms, such systems ensure that official violence is part of the everyday political order; the official violence frequently provokes a violent response. Further, even though the levels of social disruption are usually not as high as where there is open warfare, the endemic violence characterizing these regimes makes social progress difficult. In both cases we see high levels of violence diverting energy from other economic, political, and social problems. If we agree that development should aid the poorest, diversify a country's economy, generate more wealth, and guarantee individual personal security, prolonged conflict plainly obstructs development. To make matters worse, governments facing ongoing conflicts will be tempted to mobilize all their revenue, including ODA funds, to meet security needs.

We might argue that third world countries facing protracted conflicts are those which most need the assistance of the international community: without money and goods from abroad, even greater numbers will suffer. Attractive as this may be, it does not alter the fact that the aims normally espoused by Canada's public and private development agencies are not going to be met where there is endemic violence. Thus, if aid agencies are going to work in these regions, they will have to adjust their policies to fit existing conditions.

Though we usually think of development in terms of general social advancement and rising living standards, it is not a costless process. Modernizing a country's agriculture, for example, implies greater capitalization and rationalization of production. While this doubtlessly increases output, it also makes farm labourers redundant and pushes small holders off the land and into the city. As well, such changes may prompt producers to plant more profitable export products, like flowers, instead of foodstuffs for the local market. The result hardly looks like development, unless development is supposed to mean festering slums and costly imported food.

But how does this happen, and what does it have to do with protracted conflict? There are three broad developmental models available to countries: capitalist modernization, socialist transformation, and basic needs or growth-with-equity. Each defines development differently and marks out different paths to development. While we cannot consider these in depth, brief descriptions of each will inform later discussion.

Capitalist modernization holds that development occurs by using the private sector as an economic centre that generates the wealth needed to create jobs and pay for the social services needed to give the majority a decent life. The socialist model rejects this approach with the argument that only a planned economy where the state controls at least the "commanding heights" can eradicate poverty and create the conditions for a dignified existence for all. Finally, the basic needs or growth-with-equity approach can use either the market or a mixed economy as its engine of growth, but it features a conscious redistributive scheme to produce more equality than the market does.

In common with the rest of Latin America, except Cuba, El Salvador follows the capitalist model of development.[2] In a relatively wealthy country like Venezuela, the model works well enough to spur growth and spin off benefits that spell increased social mobility and higher living standards for at least some. But El Salvador is poor, and the wealth generated by capitalist development there (be it coffee, cotton, or goods assembled for export) is not great. Compounding the country's problems is a political system that sees the rich, in league with the military, control the state, thus ensuring that the state does not redistribute the benefits of growth to the poor. If anything, the state acts to shift wealth the other way, leaving in its wake an increasingly unequal society riven by class conflict.

An example will show how the system works. Cotton was El Salvador's boom crop of the 1950s and 1960s. To cash in on the boom, though, required not just good land, but also money for fertilizers, pesticides, and labour to pick the crop. These conditions gave an immediate advantage to the wealthy large landholders. It also greatly expanded the rural proletariat—the landless or land poor who survive as best they can as seasonal labourers—by driving peasants from their property, either through raised land rents or the eviction of workers made redundant by capital intensive farming techniques.[3]

This pattern of rule and wealth is not new in El Salvador. Since 1932 the elite and the army have joined forces to ensure that economic growth does not lead to social change which could produce democracy. Whenever potentially disruptive forces, even military reformers, have emerged, the reaction has been swift, sure, and usually violent. A political economy of violence has developed in El Salvador which produces profits, but not stability, equity, or democracy.

While El Salvador has known endemic conflict for over half a century, it is only since 1979 that this has taken the form of death squads and internal war. This was not a predictable outcome of its development scheme; yet the fact that modernization led by export agriculture could not keep chronic violence from becoming acute hardly enhances the stature of the model traditionally favoured by Western aid agencies. Obviously, the Salvadoran conflict is specific to that country, and we must be careful about the lessons we draw from it. Yet we must ask if a development model which seems to heighten social and economic disparities and to be preservable only by using force should not be reexamined. Such a reexamination, though, would require a total reorientation of the values and priorities of aid agencies, something not likely to be achieved in the absence of new directions from politicians.

Sandinista Nicaragua's preferred development path was strikingly different. It combined aspects of the socialist and basic needs approaches by making the state the centre of accumulation in a mixed economy. Its avowed aim, sought in accordance with "the logic of the majority," brought a literacy program, agrarian reform, and improved public health and education. To what extent was this path responsible for the violence that shook the country in the 1980s?

Whatever parallels may exist between the Nicaraguan and Salvadoran cases, one crucial difference remains: the violence in El Salvador is the result of an indigenous revolution; that in Nicaragua came primarily from an externally organized, financed, and armed counterrevolution. This counterrevolution sought to destroy the Sandinista state and its development model, which stressed radical social change.

Revolutions leave both losers and winners, and the losers are usually a dispossessed elite. This is certainly true of Nicaragua, where the dispossessed were the clique that surrounded the Somozas and some of the country's small class of big capitalists. Some losers, like Chiang Kai-shek or the shah of Iran, can only go off into exile nursing their hatred and dreaming of their eventual restoration. Others are able to fight more effectively because they can enlist the immediate support of an outside power. Nicaragua's counterrevolutionaries were in this position, enjoying the patronage of the United States.

The government of the United States, especially during the Reagan presidency, worked to bring down the revolutionary regime in Nicaragua. To this end, Washington turned to low intensity conflict (LIC), the currently favoured form of counterrevolution. LIC is a total war of attrition directed against governments. It concentrates as much on disrupting normal economic life and forcing resources to be shifted from civilian to military ends as on military victory.[4] In Nicaragua, LIC's chosen instruments were an assortment of ex-Somocistas, disgruntled peasants, rightist politicians who tired of civic opposition and their U.S. military and intelligence trainers and handlers. Taken together they formed the Contras, the major source of violence in Nicaragua in the 1980s.

Because the Contras were an instrument of U.S. foreign policy, there was relatively little the Sandinistas could do unilaterally to end the violence wracking the country. But where armed opponents of the regime followed their own agenda, as with the Miskito rebels of eastern Nicaragua, the government was able to reach a political settlement that ended the fighting and allowed reconciliation and reconstruction to begin. The Sandinistas showed the willingness and, when permitted, the capacity to end the violence in Nicaragua.

Can we say that either development model actually contributes to the creation or continuance of protracted conflict? El Salvador's version of capitalist modernization generates gross social inequalities. Massive inequalities spurred the lower classes to try to overcome them; this action by the lower classes prompted the ruling classes to turn to violence to keep the masses at bay. It is, then, possible to argue that ODA sustaining the reigning model of development in El Salvador also sustains endemic conflict in the country.

Nicaragua's transforming development model redistributed both wealth and political power to the advantage of the country's poor majority. Such a model is inimical to the interests of capital, both foreign and domestic. We must not, however, jump to the facile conclusion that Washington launched its low intensity war against the Sandinistas solely to protect Nicaraguan capitalists or U.S. investments; indeed, an examination of the Sandinistas' record shows that foreign investment was generally well treated and that local businesses received numerous incentives and benefits. Violence came to Nicaragua because the U.S. government refused to accept that a small country in its geographic sphere of influence might turn against it. Development aid to Nicaragua helped the Sandinista government cope with the costs of war, but it could not address these root causes of the violence.

Canadian aid and involvement

Faced with protracted conflicts which restrict development, the government of Canada must choose between pulling back, even pulling out and going swimming in a pool filled with sharks, as El Salvador's Guillermo Ungo termed it. Whichever course it chooses, Ottawa has to recognize that having more than minimal relations with states involved in long-term civil conflicts makes it impossible for us to remain above the struggle or to pretend our assistance is "apolitical." A look at our ties with El Salvador will highlight the arguments for both disengagement and engagement in cases of protracted conflict.

By deciding to restore bilateral aid relations with San Salvador in 1984, Ottawa clearly placed its money on Jose Napoleon Duarte's Christian Democratic government. While it was reasonable at the time to believe that a right of centre government (judged by Costa Rican standards, which are good benchmarks of the Latin American political centre) could bring the army and the conservative elites to back a constitutional civilian regime, these hopes were misplaced. This experience produced calls to distance ourselves from the Salvadoran government.

The argument for disengagement—for withdrawing assistance and perhaps even diplomatic representation—is premised on two related assumptions. The first is that ODA going to areas of conflict is likely to be wasted: prevailing conditions mean it cannot be put to good use. A variation on this theme was employed when Canada suspended its bilateral aid program in El Salvador in 1981, with the argument that the host government could not guarantee the safety of Canadians working there: no aid workers, no aid.

Development agencies and foreign ministries may see arguments of this sort as technical and politically costless. Cutting off aid to a regime fighting a protracted war, however, is far more easily seen as a hostile gesture toward that government. So even ostensibly neutral and technical reasons for pulling back from areas of conflict will be seen by some as disguised partisan motives.

A second, unambiguously political, case for disengagement is made on moral grounds. Some governments simply do not deserve aid. In fact, it may be better to deny the assistance in order to hasten their reform or replacement. This argument takes the following form with regard to El Salvador.

The Canadian government recognizes that the real sources of conflict and underdevelopment in El Salvador lie in that country's internal political, social and economic structures. Accordingly, it follows that our development assistance should support changing those structures. Yet the Salvadoran state (as it is now governed and as it is will be governed in the absence of radical reforms) resists change. It eviscerates a relatively mild land reform, winks at death squads, and crushes any and all indigenous efforts to relieve poverty or give political power to the poor. It is clear that there is no will to channel resources toward correcting the causes of conflict, poverty, and general underdevelopment. Consequently, development aid and perhaps even other forms of assistance should stop flowing.

Arguments for continuing full relations with El Salvador, or any other country involved in an ongoing conflict, also take two forms. One can argue that realpolitik demand that the broadest possible contacts be maintained with all states in the community of nations. Questions regarding the delivery of ODA, like those touching the recognition of governments, should be resolved according to strictly technical criteria. One must remember that Canada does not exist alone in the international system; we have allies whose opinions we must consider and whose interests we must take into account. The case, put briefly, is that we need to admit that morality has little place in international affairs and that we are often compelled to do business with distasteful partners.

Applying these principles to the Salvadoran case, we arrive at the following conclusion. Since the government has maintained diplomatic and aid relations with Sandinista Nicaragua, it has to balance these with ties to a rightist government aligned with the United States. This appeases the more conservative elements of cabinet, caucus, and the government's constituency, while it indicates to Washington that we have not abandoned the Western alliance. In essence, we trade Nicaragua for El Salvador; it is just a normal cost of pursuing an independent foreign policy. Moreover, policy makers would assert that good relations are needed with all countries in this troubled region if Canada is to play a constructive role in restoring peace: an honest broker must be trusted by all sides.

Continued engagement is also justified by the "double jeopardy" argument. People in war-torn countries suffer enough without being made to bear the extra burden of the removal of external assistance. This is an appealing proposition which subtly shifts the grounds of the argument. We are no longer talking about development (e.g., export agriculture-led capitalist modernization and its attendant social consequences) but about helping the helpless (i.e., humanitarian assistance). This relief may be our most valuable contribution in such circumstances.

Double jeopardy means taking sides, rather more than does blunt realpolitik, Unless this humanitarian aid is delivered through nongovernmental channels, it can be seen as consciously assisting the regime. Yet if it is sent through nongovernmental organizations (NGOs), assistance may lose it political impact, leaving the donor unable to influence the recipient. This seems to have been a dilemma the government confronted in deciding to restore aid ties with El Salvador.

The act of restoration itself was a clumsy affair, because the public rationale for our reengagement was El Salvador's supposedly improved human rights record. This move did get Canada more visibly involved in El Salvador; it showed the White House our Central American policy could be more even handed; it may have demonstrated Ottawa's *bona fides* to the region's three right wing governments. Someone probably saw this as a real coup, a marvelously dextrous political balancing act.

But we could have reopened aid links with San Salvador by announcing that aid workers could once again carry out their jobs. This would have aroused less controversy at home, because it would have kept us an arm's length from Washington's policy. Only if the government of Brian Mulroney intended to establish performance on human rights issues as a condition for receiving ODA would this have been adept politics. And even then, the government could have chosen a much stronger and more plausible test case. Thus, what may have been a useful aid program was overshadowed by the political context in which it was implemented.

But what about our involvement in Nicaragua? I referred earlier to the argument that Canada retains active aid programs with El Salvador—and Guatemala and Honduras, Central America's other rightist regimes—in order to justify maintaining a higher than expected profile in Nicaragua. Some sense of the height of this profile can be gained by noting that between 1981–87 Nicaragua received about 12 percent more Canadian assistance than did Honduras, which was designated a priority country by the Canadian International Development Agency (CIDA).[5] So Canada plainly chose to back in a tangible way the Sandinista view of development. How does this decision stand up in light of the arguments for engagement or disengagement set out earlier?

We can begin with the pragmatic argument for disengagement, namely that ODA to areas of conflict cannot really aid development. While I am not able to present an auditor's assessment of the effectiveness Canadian aid in Nicaragua, I will note that two-thirds of the country's population live in the Pacific region, which has been free of armed conflict. Further, though the efficiency of Nicaragua's government probably declined during the war years, it is worth remembering that Sandinista administration of development projects was lauded by the World Bank in the early 1980s. Therefore, technical arguments for suspending aid carried substantially less weight here than in the Salvadoran case, leaving only blatantly partisan (and Reaganesque) rationales open to those wishing to distance Ottawa from the Sandinistas.

This is not the place to ask why the governments of Prime Ministers Clark, Trudeau and Mulroney decided to pursue an independent path in the isthmus.[6] It does, though, seem reasonable to suggest that a Canadian government of whatever partisan or ideological stripe might wish to manifest its freedom from U.S. influence in the realm of foreign affairs, if only because there is so little chance to escape our great neighbour's economic dominance. To the extent that this or any other argument for an autonomous Canadian policy in the hemisphere is tenable, it would keep Ottawa from forwarding a moral argument for disengagement from Nicaragua which copied Washington's claim that the Sandinistas are moral pariahs. Thus realpolitik can explain our Nicaraguan policy.

What this line of reasoning implies is that the continuance or interruption of any ODA program in areas of protracted conflict rests on a bedrock of realpolitik. Yet this is an unreliable guide to action because it is made up of many factors, ranging in the cases here from the physical ability to deliver a program to a desire to be seen as an independent hemispheric actor. The realpolitik standard thus is subject to situational constraints. It might well be worth adding some subjective normative elements to the mix when searching for the most productive way to secure our national interest in aiding countries facing violent civil conflicts. The most vital of these elements has to be the linkage that exists between aid and peace.

Aid and peace

Can Canadian aid help bring peace to Central America? It is obvious that any answer has to be hedged with caveats and references to the dynamics of concrete conflicts. It is also obvious that Canada has to determine what constitutes peace in each country, which means choosing among the versions promoted by the parties to each conflict. We shall begin with this last issue, focusing as before on El Salvador and Nicaragua.

For the Salvadoran military, peace means exterminating the guerrillas. From this perspective, repeating General Martinez's *matanza* of 1932 can be a reasonable path to peace. And either LIC or conventional large unit warfare is acceptable, if it defeats the FMLN (Faribundo Marti National Liberation Front). Peace means victory.

Alfredo Cristiani's ARENA (National Republican Alliance) government was expected to favour the army's line or, at its most moderate, to continue upholding the position taken by his Christian Democratic predecessor. That stance, endorsed by the U.S. State Department and probably by Canada, defines peace as what follows after the guerrillas have surrendered and accepted the rules of the game set by the state. This resolution would keep the FMLN far from power, sustain a development model which official Western agencies find congenial despite its defects, and give liberal constitutional government another chance in El Salvador. Since this outcome has the backing of the U.S. government, El Salvador's major source of economic and military aid, it will be very hard for any government there to move very far from this line. To the extent that such a definition of peace implies, if not requires, the military defeat of the guerrillas, it is probably a recipe for continued violence.

Still Cristiani surprised observers in September 1989 by beginning direct talks with the FMLN. We should not, however, be surprised that those talks failed. Though it appears that elements of Salvadoran big business supported Cristiani's initiative, it was evident that the country's defence forces and most capitalists were opposed, and the position of the United States was not clear. As well, we should remember that official repression of labour, peasant, and student organizations never ceased, nor did army counterinsurgency actions or guerrilla operations. We can even question the government's intentions, for the talks ended with it insisting that a cease-fire precede any reform: the old story of making the guerrillas accept the government's notion of peace.

Thus, a path to peace minimizing structural change still has important support in El Salvador. This means continuing the agro-export capitalist modernization economic model and maintaining a political system which draws its governors and influentials from the same strata as before. At best, this keeps in place a status quo that produced ten years of violence; at worst, a victory for the established order could be a signal to the oligarchy that the time was ripe to extirpate and exterminate all reformist elements. Indeed, the most recalcitrant elements of the Salvadoran military and political elite may take the Sandinistas' electoral loss as the signal that the FMLN is now isolated and thus fair game for elimination.

What about other definitions of peace? The FMLN has altered its objectives and now seeks a more limited social transformation than it did in the past.[7] Yet it continues to demand that a process of democratization, i.e., some kind of structural change, be in place before the guerrillas lay down arms: the FMLN will join only a reformed political process.

Despite the outcome of the 1989 negotiations between the Cristiani government and the FMLN, the talks did register one signal achievement. Never before had the Salvadoran elites and their U.S. counsellors admitted the FMLN as a full partner in political discussions. That corner has been turned, and it is at least conceivable that diplomatic pressure could get the parties back to the table. There is precedent for this in

Nicaragua, so Canada's efforts might profitably be directed toward ensuring the 1989 opening does not close permanently. Nevertheless, we must realize that the FMLN loss of its ally in Managua may make negotiations more difficult in the short run, unless Washington sends a clear message to the contrary.

Looking at El Salvador, it is easy to conclude that ODA brings neither development nor peace without significant prior political change. One can even argue that aid given in the absence of major structural reforms can have the unwanted consequence of prolonging conflict, because the recipient may interpret our largesse as a vote of confidence. Even if the conflict there did not have deep structural roots, it is unlikely that *development aid* would have its desired impact (e.g., alleviating poverty and enhancing the participation of the marginalized) while even a low intensity war rages. Humanitarian assistance to help individual victims of violence, among whom must be included victims of official violence, is probably far more appropriate.

The bilateral aid deal struck between Canada and El Salvador in 1984 illustrates both the possibilities and limitations of ODA in countries engaged in protracted conflict. Canada's controversial project in El Salvador was a counterpart fund which saw about $8 million worth of Canadian fertilizer donated to El Salvador, to be sold through the Banco Hipotecario de El Salvador. The proceeds of these sales, about $5 million according to CIDA estimates, finance aid projects. On-site administration fell to the Canadian Hunger Foundation, which had funded sixty-six projects by early 1989. Most of these projects were quite small and were usually proposed by ad hoc community organizations.[8] Discussions with representatives of CIDA and the team which evaluated the project revealed that: (1) special care was taken to avoid charges of politicization in setting up the projects; (2) small scale, low profile projects with either a humanitarian or a community bent worked best; (3) the accountability mechanisms, or checks and controls, employed for this project were substantially stronger than usual; and (4) at least partially as a result of all of these measures, the program worked well.[9]

I am convinced that the care used to put this program into place and monitor it, as well as its tilt toward noncontroversial projects, are necessary components of any program of assistance in an area of persistent conflict. These steps allow Ottawa to avoid a too close identification with a government that, as in the case of El Salvador, has an atrocious human rights record and is notorious for its corruption. Emphasizing small projects increases the possibility that they will remain free from political interference and not be too closely linked with either the government or the opposition. In other words, a program like that used in El Salvador may make it easier for the donor government to maintain a presence in conflict ridden countries.

Whether it is an appropriate mechanism remains contentious. This much is clear, however. The El Salvador project has little to do with development, something to do with humanitarian assistance, and a lot to do with the perceived political need to be seen supporting, however indirectly, the government of El Salvador. It is a well-crafted technical solution to a ticklish political problem.

One has to wonder if these aims could not have been more easily secured by other means. Perhaps it would have been easier to show political support by adopting the recommendation of the House of Commons Special Committee on the Peace Process in Central America and posting a chargé d'affaires in San Salvador. As to the question of humanitarian assistance, Canadian NGOs have made a strong case that they, not the government, should distribute such aid. And, as the El Salvador program demonstrates, the projects themselves will have to be small and have a strong humanitarian assistance bias, because development is effectively impossible where there is significant conflict. Still an aid project is easier to wind up that a diplomatic mission. An NGO-run program brings fewer political benefits than a government-to-government one, and any bilateral ODA deal is more visible than none.

There are, then, going to be cases where Ottawa will want to have direct aid relations with governments involved prolonged conflicts. The bilateral aid program in El Salvador shows the constraints that Ottawa may have to accept to have an official ODA presence in such countries.[10] In that sense, it is a valuable lesson for Canadian foreign affairs officials.

Turning to Nicaragua, we must ask whether Canadian assistance to the Sandinista government during its decade in power retarded or advanced the cause of peace. This is especially pertinent in light of the FSLN's electoral defeat: did aiding the Sandinista system prolong a needless conflict? A good way to address this issue is to ask what the FSLN government gave Nicaragua and what their counterrevolutionary protagonists promised the country.

First, the matter of peace. Where the government was able to deal with independent forces (i.e., with the Miskitos, but not with the main body of the Contras) it was able to end the armed conflict. Moreover, in the period following the Esquipulas II treaty of 1987, Managua made substantial strides toward national reconciliation. In terms of both negotiating with the armed opposition and conciliating their civic opponents, the Sandinistas did much more than did the government in San Salvador.

Further, one should consider the behaviour of the Nicaraguan government during its tenure. Changes in the organization of government machinery made the polity more open and gave more weight to elections and representative institutions. As a result, conservative forces increased their scope of action within the machinery of government. The Sandinistas' promotion of significant structural changes contrasts with the El Salvador situation.

The political project of the counterrevolution, even though it was never a prominent part of the Contras' raison d'être and is now a dead letter, also stands in contrast to Sandinista actions. In calling for the break-up of cooperatively held land, the Contras effectively demanded that Nicaragua's agrarian reform be rolled back, thus recreating the conditions which brought the revolution in the first place. They also wished to return the private sector to its prerevolutionary dominance, another recipe for confrontation and conflict. Though this condition was not explicitly stated, a counterrevolutionary government could never give the Sandinistas a chance to regain power by constitutional means, an informal ban which would ensure continuing civil strife.

Considering these facts, it is easy to argue that maintaining aid ties with the Sandinistas was a logical consequence of a policy favouring democratic development in Central America. Yet have we been giving *development aid* to Nicaragua, or is this another instance of humanitarian assistance? And has our aid to the revolutionary Sandinista government been as much a political statement as our assistance to the conservative governments of El Salvador?

Regarding the first question, though little that could be called development has occurred in Nicaragua since perhaps 1984, there is reason to believe that by mid-1989 the country was on the brink of an era of dynamic reconstruction. Thus, investments in dairy operations or geothermal energy projects which paid no dividends while the war raged might begin contributing to the welfare of Nicaraguans as the fighting de-escalated. Viewed in this light, our ODA to Nicaragua did promote development.

Our political support for the Sandinistas was even more important to them than our economic help. Solidly in the anticommunist camp and generally counted among the world's conservative forces, Canada's continuing trade, aid, and political ties afforded the revolutionary regime a cachet of respectability. Combining ODA with obvious political support contributed to the survival of the Sandinista system and thus to the potential development of Nicaragua.

Toward a conclusion

By looking at how Canadian ODA might alleviate the effects of protracted violence in Central America, indeed at how Canadian aid might have any effect in a country racked by war, we may have taken the wrong route to understanding the relationship between aid and peace. We might, that is, have done better if we had conceived of development assistance as one tool used to *preserve* peace and *preclude* violent conflict. Favouring countries with good human rights records, and being aware that human rights have economic and social dimensions as well as political aspects, are two ways to do this. Similarly, we can emphasize projects to aid the marginalized in countries where government is already attentive to the demands of the marginalized.

If the above hints at "conditional" aid, my next suggestion is unabashedly political. Conflict is less likely to become violent where a political system is "permeable" and a wide range of interests can be articulated and accommodated. Though dealing with numerous conflicting claims can strain the resources of a poor country, the experience of liberal regimes like Costa Rica's and radical systems like Nicaragua shows it is not impossible. Implementing an aid policy built around such "soft" criteria as a state's pluralism and responsiveness to varied interests in society could even lead to acknowledgement that some development models are more likely than others to lead to political violence.

The problem with political criteria for aid decisions is that they are very subjective and hard to quantify. They cannot be applied easily by aid managers in Ottawa who spend little time on the ground in the recipient country. To use such standards effectively demands an in-country diplomatic and official ODA presence to provide politicians and civil servants in Canada the informed, seasoned judgements they need to assess the merits of policy alternatives. Unfortunately, we do not have this presence in Central America. Try as they might, our embassy staff in San José, Costa Rica, cannot develop the same feel for a country from even regular visits which they would from prolonged residence there. Accordingly, our policy must perforce be based on less than the very best possible intelligence.

Easier to achieve would be clear criteria spelling out when humanitarian assistance instead of ODA ought to be sent to areas of conflict. These standards might help avoid some thorny problems by allowing government to take some decisions out of the political realm. Several parliamentary committee reports have suggested guidelines which could be adopted; technical considerations, including the safety of aid workers, should also be among our standards.

Because we want our ODA to make greater contributions to promotion of peaceful, democratic development, we shall have to bring political considerations into the design and delivery of Canadian foreign aid. This is especially true where there is protracted conflict, because endemic violence can be resolved only through political action. Political action to bring peace will come only if the parties to the conflict have the political will to move from the battlefield to the negotiating table. If Canadian policymakers, elected and appointed, are unable to tell if this political will exists, our material assistance may actually prolong conflict.

Postscript: spring 1992

On New Year's Eve 1991 the Cristiani government and the FMLN signed an accord that ended El Salvador's twelve years of internal warfare. A combination of general war weariness, both sides' recognition of the military stalemate and the intervention of UN Secretary-General Javier Pérez de Cuéllar lay behind the settlement. Peace was the product of internal political will. Though Canadian aid had little to do with securing the cessation of hostilities, it is possible that our ODA can help preserve peace and preclude a resumption of fighting.

If aid from Canada and other donors helps put Salvadorans to work by hastening the country's economic reactivation, it will strengthen the peace. Moreover, if our assistance is channelled in ways which undermine the structures that created the original conflict, it can bring El Salvador the improved living standards and greater personal opportunities we normally associate with development. It is particularly important that we and other like-minded nations do all we can to facilitate agrarian reform, because the land problem gave rise to the country's protracted war.

Yet will we do anything? Now that the war is over and El Salvador out of the headlines will we see any need to help? Will new problems in eastern Europe catch our eye? Will Canada's own financial woes mean further cuts to the ODA budget? I trust that Ottawa will not turn its back on a decade of unprecedented involvement in strife torn Central America, now that its aid really has a chance to promote peace, equality, and development.

Notes

1. As this is written in March 1990 representatives of the UNO and the FSLN are engaged in creating a "democratic pact" which will (a) permit the newly elected government to take power while (b) ensuring the safety and institutional integrity of the Sandinistas and their supporters. Though this may seem faintly undemocratic to Canadians, such negotiations, which require both sides to demonstrate they have the political will to compromise, have formed the foundation of competitive democracies in Costa Rica and Venezuela.

2. Costa Rica was once clearly in the growth-with-equity camp, but has moved more securely into the capitalist group since 1978.

3. Descriptions of this process are found in Williams, Robert. *Export Agriculture and the Crisis in Central America*. Chapel Hill, NC: University of North Carolina Press, 1986; and Russell, Philip. *El Salvador in Crisis*. Austin, TX: Colorado River Press, 1984.

4. On LIC see *Low Intensity Warfare*. Edited by M. Klare and P. Kornbluth. N.Y.: Pantheon, 1988, and Saul, J. "Destabilization in Mozambique." *Studies in Political Economy* 23 (1987).

5. Data calculated from CIDA, *Annual Report* (Ottawa: Supply and Services Canada, 1982–3, 1985–6, 1987–8).

6. Surveys of Canada's recent Central American policy, which perforce include how this policy affected relations with the U.S., are found in Huard V.. "Quiet Diplomacy or Quiet Acquiescence?" *Canadian Journal of Latin American and Caribbean Studies* 13:2 (1988); and Rochlin, J.. "Aspects of Canadian foreign policy toward Central America, 1979–1986." *Journal of Canadian Studies* 22:4 (1987–88).

7. This program is set out in Villalobos, J.. "A Democratic Revolution for El Salvador." *Foreign Policy* 74 (Spring 1989), 103–122.

8. Interview with Tony Iezzi, El Salvador project evaluation team member, Ottawa, 31 January 1989.

9. Discussions held in Ottawa, 31 January 1989.

10. Part of the problem in El Salvador is that Canada does not have an embassy or consulate there to show the flag in the most literal sense. A mission there could also distribute the mission administered funds now handled from San José, Costa Rica. The cost of maintaining a mission could easily be offset by better intelligence and by being able to avoid the complications, political and administrative, which accompanied the restoration of bilateral aid in 1984.

Canada, Aid, and Peacemaking in Southern Africa

Dr. Linda Freeman
Carleton University

Before peace finally comes to Southern Africa, the settlement which will have to be forged will involve a profound transformation in South Africa—the transfer of power from a tiny, immensely privileged white minority to a black population which has endured immiserating poverty, gross inequality, and serious abuses of human rights. While the dismantling of formal legislated apartheid was well under way in the early 1990s, agreement on a new constitution to give the substance of power to the majority was much more difficult. By mid-1992, the white government in power was still unwilling to give up proposals which amounted to a white veto over a non apartheid government. In the social and economic spheres, redistribution of wealth and services in the most unequal society on earth seemed even more remote.

The end of white rule in South Africa is also essential for the region which has suffered greatly from the South African policy of de-stabilization estimated to have cost neighbouring countries $60 billion and over 1.5 million lives.[1] Although changes in the early 1990s offered some prospect of peace in Angola, de-stabilization continued in Mozambique with South African support. While the interregnum in South Africa has revived hopes for economic growth in the region, the legacy of the past is grim. As David Martin and Phyllis Johnson note,

> The impact of apartheid on the region, in economic, human and ecological terms, represents a holocaust that few outside the region, and many within it, neither know about nor can comprehend. The economic costs probably exceed the foreign debt of the SADCC region by three times. The mental and physical scars are deep. The human cost is on a staggering scale in some countries, for a generation that has known nothing but war, a cost to be carried forward for decades. And for the region's ecology, apartheid has exacted from it a price from which it can never recover.[2]

Within South Africa the cost in terms of destroyed lives and lost opportunities is impossible to calculate.

Yet in the 1990s, South Africa is clearly in a process of profound transition. The Pretoria regime has embarked on a negotiating process through CODESA,[3] a conference which has brought together nineteen political parties, including the African National Congress (ANC) and the South African Communist Party. The central issues to be determined are the form of interim government which will take over from the apartheid regime and the nature of a new constitution.

The immediate factor in initiating these changes was a shift in power at the top of white politics in 1989. While the replacement of P.W. Botha by F.W. de Klerk as state president made change possible, larger internal and international pressures made change necessary. Wars in the region—notably South Africa's participation in UNITA's struggle in Angola and military defeat at Cuito Cuanavale—had become too costly both in terms of white lives and South African resources. Namibia, too, had become an expensive legacy and irritant for international opinion, and so South Africa relinquished control there as well. Inside South Africa, the state's attempts alternately to win the hearts and minds of the black inhabitants of the townships or to clamp down through repression had made the economic burden intolerable.

At the same time, the international campaign for sanctions made new capital in the form of either loans or investment extremely difficult to obtain and escalated the price and complexity of international trade. Sanctions are estimated to have cost the South African economy about $27 billion, and produced such a negative climate for business that the private sector in South Africa exported a sizeable portion of its capital, thus accentuating the crisis.[4] By late 1988, South Africa actually had smaller foreign reserves than its tiny neighbour, Botswana.

Moreover, despite all conjecture to the contrary, polls showed that a significant proportion of the white community became more rather than less willing to compromise as the going got tougher.[5] With no end in sight to black protest and mass struggle, the reasons for change had become overwhelming. A referendum for white voters in March 1992 finally committed the white community to a process of reform.

Yet, given the history of white determination to hang on to privilege and power, the conjuncture is unusual and fraught with danger. The tortured nature of negotiations has borne witness to the efforts of the current regime in South Africa to keep control in the transition period, especially in the drafting of a new constitution. Its hope is to retain a white veto through various constitutional devices, including a powerful and unrepresentative upper house which would override a democratically elected lower house. Of particular interest in the constitutional discussions has been the protection of property rights, which would freeze the status quo and ensure that whites would retain their position by class if no longer by race. Other measures of privatization, de-regulation, and devolution of power to local government have had this same objective.

At the same time, state security force involvement in promoting and supporting violence in black townships in the early 1990s added a dangerous undertow to constitutional proceedings. Not only did it breed distrust, but also the conviction that the state's strategy was to weaken the ANC's political constituency. In the process, the social fabric of South Africa was ripped apart.

Not surprisingly, black leaders wanted the West to maintain economic sanctions until clear, irreversible progress was made in securing genuine majority rule. They have been particularly concerned with the decision of Britain, the United States, Japan, and a number of European countries to reward Pretoria's gestures of reform even though the substance of power remained in white hands. In their view, the readiness of the West to welcome the de Klerk government back into the international arena has compromised international support for a genuine transformation in South Africa.

From this perspective, assistance to peacemaking in Southern Africa involved far more than supporting the process of negotiation in the short term or even promoting the long-term development of South Africa's human and natural resources. The stark reality of Southern Africa is that neither peace nor development is possible for the region as long as the white minority holds on to power in South Africa.

What, then, has the role of the Canadian state been in the context of these dramatic, even revolutionary changes in Southern Africa? Canada, no less than any other Western country, has been faced with hard and soft options in its approach to Southern Africa and faced also with competing internal and international pressures. Like much of the West, its record is complex and contradictory.

It will be argued here that Canada's solidarity has been patchy, stronger on rhetoric than substance. At the same time, the record of the Brian Mulroney government has been significantly better than previous Canadian governments on this issue. Thus, one saw both a commitment in principle to economic and diplomatic sanctions and the introduction of the first economic sanctions ever adopted by a Canadian state. At the same time, the sanctions adopted were limited and the claims made for them excessive. Moreover, until the release of Nelson Mandela, the Canadian state offered no more than a lukewarm relationship with the African National Congress, the main black liberation movement, and chose instead easier forms of assistance.

The Canadian state and the struggle against apartheid

At home and abroad, it is claimed that the Mulroney government has taken a major leadership role in the fight against apartheid. At the 1989 Commonwealth meeting in Kuala Lumpur, Prime Minister Mulroney went so far as to claim that he had "staked out for my successors the high moral ground" of opposing apartheid unequivocally, that after becoming prime minister he had taken bold steps because he had "looked around and saw no one else" doing anything on the issue.[6] On his visit to Canada in June 1990, Nelson Mandela paid special tribute to Mulroney's efforts to combat apartheid in the Commonwealth, at the United Nations, and in a range of other international organizations.[7]

Certainly in the mid-1980s, Mulroney battled along with the Prime Ministers of India and Australia to develop a strong Commonwealth policy on sanctions and to see that Canada imposed a series of concrete economic measures restricting trade with South Africa. In particular at the Commonwealth mini-summit in London in August 1986, Mulroney personally confronted British Prime Minister Margaret Thatcher in a vigorous battle to secure a united sanctions policy against South Africa.

Following the release of Mandela from prison, Joe Clark, Canada's then Secretary of State for External Affairs, travelled to Lusaka to welcome Mandela on his first visit outside South Africa. In June 1990, The Canadian government warmly welcomed Mandela on a visit to Canada, treating him as a virtual head of state.

In addition, in the early 1990s Canadian leaders stood firm against the temptation to lift sanctions as a reward for de Klerk's first reforms, even though most other Western countries speedily dropped sanctions and moved quickly to renew economic ties with South Africa. Despite the dismay of some senior civil servants and the Canadian private sector, in particular the Canadian Exporters' Association, Canada honoured its role as chair of the Commonwealth Foreign Ministers' Committee on South Africa, the body which had specified terms for ending sanctions. Thus in 1991 Canada lifted only the soft "people" sanctions involving cultural and scientific ties. In early 1992, Canada also ended sanctions on the export of a range of high technology goods to South Africa but kept the rest.

The Canadian position was to wait until irreversible progress had been made in the dismantling of apartheid. Specifically this was defined in September 1991 as "transitional mechanisms ... which would enable all the parties to participate fully and effectively in negotiations." Indeed, Canada's Secretary of State for External Affairs Barbara McDougall had hoped to lift trade and investment restrictions while visiting South Africa in April 1992, but insufficient progress at the CODESA negotiations precluded this option. Though state and municipal authorities in the United States kept sanctions, and loans from foreign banks and international financial institutions awaited a settlement, Canada's position had become increasingly lonely by mid-1992.

In its decision to adopt and sustain sanctions and to welcome Mandela as leader of the ANC with such pomp and ceremony, the Mulroney government broke with a tradition established during the Trudeau period. For years, Canada had guided its South African policy according to the concept of "balance," an approach diametrically opposed to notions of solidarity with the struggle of the black majority. Thus while Canadian leaders had denounced apartheid loudly in international gatherings in the 1970s and early 1980s, they had opposed sanctions and supported unfettered economic relations with South Africa.

In 1970, a government white paper had openly supported Canadian capital in its bid to take advantage of "the better than normal opportunities" of trading and investing with the apartheid state as a "balance" to Canadian interests in social justice.[8] One minor gesture to reduce official promotion of Canada's economic relations with South Africa in the late 1970s in the aftermath of the Soweto riots had almost no impact on patterns of Canadian trade and investment. In addition, while Canada had adopted United Nations sanctions against military exports, enforcement of these rules was quite slack. A Canadian firm, Space Research Corporation, helped South Africa develop an artillery gun, the G-5, which has the capability to deliver tactical nuclear weapons and has become an important military export. Thus in the Trudeau years, Canadian policy on South Africa—with its flourishing economic relations, loopholes on military exports and full diplomatic relations with the white regime—left the Canadian state open to charges of insincerity if not hypocrisy in its claim to be supporting the struggle against apartheid.

While the Mulroney policy on South Africa was superior to that of its predecessors, it, too, was less than officials claimed. Mulroney's promise in October 1985 at the United Nations General Assembly that Canada would adopt full economic and diplomatic sanctions against South Africa, except if there were evidence of irreversible progress in ending apartheid, became an embarrassment for Canadian officials for the rest of the decade. Serious consideration was never given to the option of reducing Canada's diplomatic relations and economic sanctions were neither comprehensive nor mandatory.

In response to pressure from interests within the private sector and the Conservative Party in Canada, trade sanctions were never increased and financial sanctions remained voluntary and, at times, ignored. Thus in 1989 it was discovered that the Bank of Nova Scotia loaned $600 million to MINORCO, a subsidiary of the giant South African transnational, Anglo American Corporation.[9] At the start, trade sanctions affected only about one-quarter of Canada's total trade with South Africa, and, by 1989, Canadian imports from South Africa had climbed back almost to the presanctions level.[10]

With declining great power support for change in Southern Africa after 1987, Mulroney also seemed to have lost interest, except on the occasion of Commonwealth heads of government meetings or forays at the United Nations. Joe Clark talked constantly of "sanctions fatigue," and played a major role in the Commonwealth Committee on Southern Africa in trying to stall initiatives promoting additional trade sanctions. The reversion in 1990 to the stronger policy of the mid-1980s represented a hasty climb back on the bandwagon.

The Canadian state and the African National Congress

Canada's approach towards the African National Congress has also gone through a series of twists and turns. Until the mid-1980s, the ANC was permitted contact with only the most junior Canadian diplomats. However, following the uprising in South Africa in the mid-1980s and the advent of the Mulroney government, ANC officials were given much greater access. Indeed, Clark remarked that he has met more regularly with Thabo Mbeki, the ANC official responsible for international affairs, than with many Western foreign secretaries.

Yet, at times and at their worst, Canadian officials adopted a patronizing tone towards the ANC, and lectured the organization on the need to be "moderate." In a letter in December 1989, Clark stated that

> ...the Canadian government has been pleased by the moderation in the attitude of the ANC. That moderation has been encouraged by Canada. The ANC now stresses the desirability of and increased prospects for peaceful, negotiated change rather than of violent revolution. It also recognizes that there are other legitimate voices of opposition in South Africa, and that discussion and co-operation with them are possibilities worthy of pursuit.That moderation is also reflected in the ANC's document on negotiations.[11]

This attitude was particularly noticeable in the official reception for ANC President Oliver Tambo in August 1987. Although Tambo came to Canada by official invitation, external affairs officials attempted to suggest he had come at his own initiative. Both Mulroney and Clark lectured Tambo publicly on the ANC's adoption of the armed struggle and the Communist affiliation of many of its leading members. By contrast, a short three years later, Mandela was asked to address a joint session of Canada's House of Commons and Senate.

In terms of material assistance to the ANC, the Canadian state has also reversed itself several times. Following the Ottawa Commonwealth conference in 1973, the Trudeau government recognized, in the communiqué's final words, "the legitimacy" of the struggle of liberation movements in Southern Africa "to win full human rights and self determination." It also promised humanitarian assistance through matching grants to Canadian and international non-governmental organizations (NGOs). Until 1979, Canadian NGOs received matching grants of about $110,000 for multiyear programs for an agricultural training centre, an ANC school, a research and information centre, clinics, and day-care centres. Then in the brief period of the Clark Conservative government, a new policy ruled out assistance to the ANC. Throughout the 1980s, both the final Trudeau government and the Mulroney administration continued to oppose any except token assistance to the ANC, and many officials insisted that the government had never provided any in the past. Thus, in the late 1980s, while Sweden provided $10 million and Norway $6 million[12] annually to help the ANC develop the political and economic structures to prepare them to govern, the Canadian International Development Agency (CIDA) turned down almost all requests for funding. Up to Mandela's release, Canada's only direct aid to the ANC in the 1980s was support for a day-care centre through a tiny $65,000 grant each year for three years. In this period, direct material assistance from Canada to the ANC was almost entirely a contribution of Canadian society, not the state, primarily through private donations to Canadian churches and NGOs.

With the release of Mandela from prison, official attitudes changed again. During Mandela's visit to Canada in June 1990, the government promised about $6 million to assist in the repatriation of South African exiles and refugees—still not an open commitment to assist the ANC, but tangible assistance nonetheless. In 1992, CIDA, Canada's official aid agency, together with the International Development Research Centre, focused a large part of its aid strategy inside South Africa on enriching the skills of future South African leaders within the ANC in the sectors of economic analysis and urban planning.

The reasons for Canada's changing approach towards the ANC have gone through an evolution. Originally, the decision in 1979 to halt assistance to the ANC was a product of Cold War perceptions and opposition to the ANC's use of violence against a government with which Canada maintained full diplomatic relations. In 1981, Secretary of State for External Affairs Mark MacGuigan developed a second argument—that Canada's membership in the Contact Group, a five nation Western effort to secure independence for Namibia, precluded support for any antiapartheid work as it would harm Canada's "neutrality" with South Africa.[13] To these arguments about the ANC's "violence" and the need for Canadian neutrality, officials added a third argument in the late 1980s: that Canada was not able to provide direct material support to the ANC because an all party agreement precluded aid to foreign political parties.

Thus, at a time when the ANC desperately needed major Western assistance to enable it to confront the established, sophisticated, and well-financed institutions of the South African state and to reestablish its own organization inside South Africa, Canada provided only indirect, minimal resources, far short of the $20 million which Mandela had sought from Canada.

In the early 1990s the Canadian state changed direction again with the assumption that, ultimately, an ANC-led government will take power and that its cadres need training. This assistance will include training for other leaders in civil society with the inauguration of a new research institute on economic policy.

Canadian assistance inside South Africa

Indeed well before the watershed changes in South Africa in 1990, the Canadian state had chosen a softer option, sidestepping the ANC as the channel and focusing instead on direct assistance to black South Africans inside South Africa. This assistance was supplemented by high profile diplomatic support for antiapartheid activities. Thus, Canadian officials based in Pretoria attended trials, funerals, and demonstrations, thus providing both a witness and testimony to the outside world's interest and, to some extent, a protection for South Africans participating in them.

Prior to the 1980s, the Canadian government had contributed generously to a series of multilateral programs—the United Nations Educational and Training Program for South Africa, the Inter-University Exchange Fund and the United Nations Trust Fund for South Africa. In the 1970s, CIDA also began to offer matching grants to Canadian NGOs operating inside South Africa for work with black trade unions, community development projects, assistance to small scale agriculture, and basic services such as water supplies and health care. In addition, a small bilateral program was offered through the embassy's mission administered funds.

During the 1980s, Canadian assistance for individuals and groups inside South Africa evolved from grants for general development through international agencies and Canadian NGOs to a program focused on education and to, a lesser extent, on funding for a range of overtly antiapartheid activities. As interest in South Africa escalated after the Vaal uprising in the mid-1980s, the Canadian assistance program dramatically increased. From the period when it took office (1984–85) until 1989–90, the Conservative government spent an annual average of about $7 million/year on assistance to South Africa, about seven times more than the previous Liberal government.[14]

Much of the program was focused on assistance to black education, building on a $1.5 million five year scholarship program operated by World University Service of Canada (WUSC) from 1983 on. In 1988, the South Africa Education Trust Fund was established to provide a variety of training programs in Canada— for black South Africans in universities; in short-term placements with Canadian NGOs; in technical and professional work programs with industry, services, and public administration. In the first three years, the Trust Fund spent about $2.55 million, educating about fifty South Africans in 1990 and 100 in 1991. In January 1990, Clark announced that Canada would provide another $15 million for an expanded second phase of the Canadian Education Program.

In a second important way, the Mulroney administration has broken with earlier precedents. While earlier governments had challenged the concept of legal and humanitarian assistance for political prisoners, detainees, and their families as being too political, from the mid-1980s until 1991, the Mulroney government provided over $2 million annually for these purposes, with a large portion being channelled through the Canadian branch of IDAFSA (the International Defence and Aid Fund for South Africa.)[15]

The most unusual aspect of the government's approach to assistance in South Africa was the launching of a program to fund overtly antiapartheid activities, in some cases by South Africans inside South Africa. These consisted of a $1 million fund to counter South African propaganda and censorship and a fund to support dialogue and negotiations among South Africans which amounted to $5.7 million by 1991–92.[16]

To some extent, the fund to counter South African propaganda and censorship was another soft option, offered at the 1987 Commonwealth Heads of Government meeting as a way of diluting the reaction to Canada's unwillingness to toughen trade sanctions. As Zimbabwe's Minister of Foreign Affairs Nathan Shamuyarira pointed out, this contribution to fighting apartheid was "peanuts," equivalent to what Zimbabwe spent in a day in countering South African de-stabilization. The second fund to support dialogue and negotiations, however, constituted an imaginative attempt to support a range of social institutions under attack by the South African state, in particular the alternative press. In addition, grants have promoted research, conferences, professional institutes, youth organizations, and cultural groups which are involved in the transition process of building a nonapartheid future.

This direct assistance, though constrained by the small size of many of the projects, provided strategic support to a wide range of groups in South Africa. They earned Canada a high profile on the ground and were the basis on which anti-apartheid activists argued in the 1980s for a continued Canadian diplomatic presence.

How then to evaluate Canada's aid to peacemaking in South Africa? On the official side, senior members of the Canadian staff of the Pretoria embassy have argued that Canadian policy "has hit it just about right." In its assistance to organizations fighting apartheid and then to those involved in the negotiating process, the Canadian state has clearly supported those who have battled against overwhelming odds for a genuinely democratic future in South Africa. In the struggle to develop a strong Commonwealth policy against the determined opposition of Margaret Thatcher, Mulroney, along with Prime Minister Bob Hawke of Australia and the late Prime Minister Rajiv Gandhi of India, deserved the title of leader.

Yet on the diplomatic front, there was more than just the dramatic encounter of Commonwealth meetings. The Mulroney Government started strongly and then went into a hiatus in 1987 when the "step by step approach" became marching on the spot. Ironically, in somewhat unhappily honouring its position in the Commonwealth by holding on to sanctions, Canada resumed its leadership position on South Africa in 1992.

Weighed against this fairly strong record of Canadian aid and diplomacy in South Africa has been the refusal of the Canadian state to impede trade and investment with South Africa in more than a token way. Thus in company with other Western countries, Canada's economic relations with South Africa continued to flourish in the last years of old style apartheid, buttressing the activities of the South African state.

Despite the imposition of some sanctions, Canada's two way trade with South Africa reached $4 billion in the 1980s, double the level in the 1970s. Compare this level of trade with the approximately $50 million given through the much vaunted program of Canadian assistance to South Africa in the 1980s. Sanctions for the financial sector were always voluntary, as exemplified by the Bank of Nova Scotia's refusal to honour them. Thus, on closer inspection, Canada's actual contribution to peace-making in South Africa was much more mixed than official pronouncements suggest.

Aid and peacemaking in Southern Africa

Just as Canadian assistance inside South Africa has had to be assessed in terms of its general support for "getting rid of the system," so, too, must Canada's involvement in the region to the north. As we have seen, in the last two decades, all the other countries of Southern Africa have been freed of white minority rule only to fall victim to South Africa's ruinous policy of de-stabilization. The chaos in the region has added an extra dimension to the environment in which Canadian assistance has operated and an extra urgency to the struggle against white control in South Africa.

In company with most other Western countries, the Canadian state started postindependence relations in Southern Africa in a suboptimal position. During the wars of liberation, the Canadian state's approach towards FRELIMO in Mozambique, MPLA in Angola, ZANU in Zimbabwe and SWAPO in Namibia was not unlike the stance adopted towards the ANC. It argued against the violence of the armed struggle, counselled moderation, and provided minimal support. In all cases, this policy ignored the historical reality of mass support for these movements which, without exception, brought these organizations to power. In some cases, Canada's position was in alliance with the colonial power— as in the case of Portugal (a fellow member of NATO) during the period of its colonial wars in Southern Africa—or intended to soften black African reactions to the colonial power—as in the case of Britain in Rhodesia.

To remedy this history and to counter the effect of Canada's continuing economic and political relations with South Africa, Canada established a number of diplomatic missions in independent black Southern

Africa—in Lusaka in 1973, in Harare in 1980 and in Windhoek in 1990—
and launched a major program of development assistance in the region.
Before 1970, Canada's ODA in Africa had been concentrated in anglophone
West Africa and East Africa.[17] However, during the 1970s, Canada's
ODA to Southern Africa expanded from under $1 million in 1969–70 to
about $45 million in 1978–79 and then more than tripled to about $150
million in 1988–89.[18] During the 1980s, CIDA provided an annual average of about $70 million to the region.

Despite the impressive growth of Canada's aid program to Southern
Africa, its relationship to either peace or development is complex. The
dilemma was how to support long-term development in the context of
South Africa's deliberate promotion of instability.[19] The escalation of
regional wars came into particularly sharp focus in two cases in which
Canada was involved—in Canadian assistance to Mozambique and in its
assistance during the transition period in Namibia following South
Africa's military defeat in southern Angola.

In other areas, Canada's programs of bilateral assistance and its
growing support of the regional organization SADCC (the Southern
African Regional Development Co-ordinating Conference) attempted to
strengthen the autonomy and interconnection of the region. Yet even
there, Canadian assistance operated within constraints implicit in South
Africa's domination of the region.

Security assistance and Mozambique

The contradiction of Canadian assistance to long-term development in a
region de-stabilized by South Africa was posed in a particularly sharp
form in Mozambique. Beyond food aid and assistance through Canadian
NGOs, the main form of Canadian assistance to Mozambique in the 1980s
was help through the SADCC program to refurbish the Nacala and
Limpopo railway lines—two of Mozambique's main transportation
routes. In this case, the projects were threatened by the activities of
Renamo, an antigovernment guerrilla group trained, supplied, and
supported by South African security forces. It made little sense to help
the Mozambican government rebuild railway tracks one day, only to
have them blown up the next. Even Canadian NGO assistance organized
through a consortium, COCAMO, was hobbled by Renamo activities
which kept volunteers city bound and projects limited to a tiny area
adjacent to the city of Nampula.

In recognition of the severity of Mozambique's plight, the Canadian
government eventually offered a small program of security assistance to
the front line states and, in particular, Mozambique. Countries like
Britain had already established a precedent and embarked on major
training programs for Mozambican army personnel in the area. Canada's

program involved military training, logistical support for defence forces (clothes, fuel, food, spare parts and communications equipment,) and balance of payments support to help meet security costs. Assistance to Mozambique under this program amounted to about $4 million, and much of it was used to clear brush along the Limpopo railway line to forestall rebel attacks.

There is no question that Canada's program of security assistance to Mozambique provided important help in the defence of Canada's aid projects. Still it was a very limited response to a very desperate situation, even with a follow-up expansion of the military training component.[20] The Canadian government's fear of a strong public reaction to this form of assistance precluded much more. Mulroney announced the program as "assistance to preserve development initiatives," scarcely a ringing statement of solidarity against South African de-stabilization.

Peacekeeping in Namibia

A second case where Canadian involvement in the region has been affected profoundly by the South African connection has been in the assistance provided to bring South Africa's war in Namibia to an end and to secure Namibian independence. In the late 1970s, Canada joined the Contact Group, a body of five Western nations which attempted unsuccessfully to negotiate with South Africa to end its trusteeship of Namibia. Canada also participated actively in UNTAG, the United Nations Transition Advisory Group which helped co-ordinate the process of registration and elections which preceded Namibian independence in March 1990.[21]

Although Canadian assistance played a small role in this international effort, its involvement came at a price. In the early 1980s, Canadian officials insisted that negotiations by the Contact Group meant that Canada must abandon antiapartheid activities and adopt a state of neutrality towards South Africa. In fact, Canada's principal representative to the Contact Group, William Barton, suggested that membership in the group was used by all five Western countries "as a stalking horse to conceal their unwillingness to act against South Africa under any circumstances."[22] Again in 1989, an External Affairs official stated that Canada had interrupted its struggle against white rule in South Africa because it did not wish to upset the final stages of independence in Namibia. "It's not an ideal time to disturb the weaning mother," he said.[23]

In addition, the Canadian government halted direct assistance to Namibia's principal liberation movement SWAPO at a time when help was most desperately needed. Therefore, while the opposition DTA party received massive funding from South African and West German sources for its election campaign, SWAPO was cut off from its principal sources of funding and fought the independence election at a severe disadvantage. As had been the case with South Africa, Canada chose instead to offer assistance to programs inside Namibia through Canadian and international NGOs and a bilateral program of scholarships for Namibian students.[24] In the transition process, Canada also offered $2 million to help repatriate Namibian refugees.

Canada's approach to Namibia, then, was cautious and safe, certainly not one to sustain the legends of leadership. Through its participation in larger international initiatives, its deference to South Africa when negotiations were in train and in its arm's length dealings with SWAPO, its emphasis has been on neutrality rather than solidarity. Partly, this stance was related to Canada's desire to stay in step with the rest of the West and to be part of an international peacekeeping effort.

There is no question either that this international effort brought Namibia to peace and independence in the early 1990s, after a brutal war against South African occupation. Yet after independence, Namibia quickly lost the attention and interest of a donor community responding to changes in eastern Europe and the disintegration of the Soviet Union. With a stagnant aid budget, CIDA, too, offered a mere $5 million to Namibia in the first two years of independence. As a result, the Namibian government has not had adequate resources to tackle the severe legacy of South African domination and the dramatic inequalities between black and white citizens.

Moreover, as long as the current regime survives in South Africa, Namibia's security and economic well-being and, in particular, control over its only deep water port at Walvis Bay remain hostage to Pretoria. Therefore Canada's contribution to peacemaking in Namibia is to some extent directly related to its record on South Africa itself.

Development assistance to the region

These same considerations also apply in an assessment of much of Canada's official development assistance program in Southern Africa. In the first instance, these programs were initiated in an attempt to ameliorate the effect of Canada's continuing economic relations with South Africa. Thus in 1970 the government white paper talked of development assistance in Southern Africa as a way of expressing Canada's social justice values, to balance the desire to have economic growth through continued trade and investment with South Africa.[25]

As a result, in the 1970s CIDA inaugurated major bilateral programs—usually technical assistance to ministries in capital cities and large infrastructural programs—primarily to Malawi, Zambia, Botswana, and Lesotho. With the advent of South African de-stabilization in the 1980s, CIDA's program was transformed by the addition of a major regional section to support SADCC, an organization of nine Southern

African states[26] formed in 1980 with the explicit goal of decreasing the region's dependence on South Africa. Since 1983–84, Canada has provided about $195 million to SADCC, with about 80 percent of its funding going to the organization's priority areas of regional transportation, energy, and communications.

Especially noteworthy is CIDA's assistance to the restoration of the Nacala and Limpopo railway lines through Mozambique and the planning of a regional railway workshop to help service the region's locomotives and rolling stock. Such projects have helped other African countries lessen their dependence on South African ports for their trade. CIDA projects have also improved regional energy supplies by connecting the power grids of Zambia, Zimbabwe, and Botswana. Of particular help in developing regional autonomy has been a CIDA project to supply telecommunications equipment to make Zambia rather than South Africa the regional telecommunications transit centre. In the 1980s, CIDA also attempted to stop purchasing goods and services for its projects from South Africa and shipping them through South African ports.[27]

There is no question that these projects provided major assistance to the region's bid to become free of dependence on South Africa and to build stronger communications, energy, and transport routes. As the 1970s white paper had intended, the projects provided testimony of Canada's good faith to the independent governments in Southern Africa. Yet to some extent, the programs were also chosen as a soft option, an easier alternative in the short term than confronting the white regime in South Africa itself. Few of the projects had to face the direct danger posed by Renamo attacks on the Nacala and Limpopo railways, but all were affected by the cost of the devastation wreaked by South African policies. Not surprisingly, African leaders expressed a strong preference for more forceful action by the West against white rule in South Africa rather than increased programs of development assistance in the region. Substitution of development assistance for sanctions, as one former African president in the region put it, constituted "fattening us for the slaughter."[28]

Conclusion

Central to any assessment of Canada's recent contribution to peacemaking in Southern Africa is its general position on South Africa. What must be weighed is the level of support which Canada implicitly afforded to the white regime through continued economic relations versus the backing it gave the black majority and its major organizations in their struggle against apartheid. In this context, Canadian policies have at times operated in contradictory ways, ways that sought soft options in difficult and dangerous situations.

While Canada moved steadily away from an earlier cordiality with the white regime in Pretoria, its shift to warmer relations with black South African leaders was tardy and, until Mandela's release, quite tepid. Sanctions against South Africa were limited and late, support for the ANC minimal and even later. Throughout the last few decades, except for a brief period in the mid-1980s, Canadian trade with the apartheid regime flourished. When an opportunity to bolster Canada's international peacekeeping reputation arose in Namibia, Canadian officials seemed willing to ease up on pressure against South Africa. Even the impressive programs of development assistance in the region were initiated in 1970 as a way of avoiding the tougher alternative of interfering with Canadian trade and investment with South Africa.

Against this record, one has small but imaginative programs of assistance inside South Africa which helped South Africans struggle against the awesome force of the apartheid state, a mixed but fairly strong record on the diplomatic front, and a refusal, with other Western countries, to abandon sanctions in the early 1990s. In the region, there is no question that many of the projects assisted by Canada, especially those in transportation and communications, contributed to lessening the region's dependence on South Africa in a period when autonomy from South African was an important goal.

Despite its modest contribution to change in Southern Africa, the state has been skillful in maximizing Canada's reputation for leadership on the issue. Time and again, it has reaped the reward of its initial actions, pointing to other Western countries whose record has been so much worse. African leaders have praised Canada immoderately, hoping thus to keep the policy on track. A sober examination of the record, though, reveals a policy with many shortcomings, a contribution to peacemaking which was limited and equivocal—if the end of white domination, peace in Southern Africa, and development for the region were, in fact, the primary goals.

Notes

1. United Nations, Economic Commission for Africa, *South African Destabilization— the Economic Cost of Frontline Resistance to Apartheid* (October 1989), pp. 4–5.

2. David Martin and Phyllis Johnson, "South Africa and Its Neighbours," Draft Study for the Commonwealth Committee of Foreign Ministers on Southern Africa, CFMSA (89) 2, Harare, February 1989, 12.

3. Conference for a Democratic South Africa.

4. A study by the Washington based Investor Responsibility Research Centre cited in "Half of whites ready to compromise under impact of sanctions, says US study," *Southscan* (18 May 1990): 134.

5. *Ibid.*

6. Cited by Ross Howard, "Mulroney takes credit for antiapartheid push," *The Globe and Mail*, 21 October 1989, p. A4.

7. Canada, House of Commons, *Debates*, 18 June 1990, p. 12923.

8. Canada, Department of External Affairs, "United Nations," *Foreign Policy for Canadians* (Ottawa,1970), pp. 18–20.

9. MINORCO, a subsidiary of South Africa's giant transnational, Anglo American, was involved in an unsuccessful bid to take over a British mining company, Consolidated Gold Fields.

10. In 1985, the year preceding adoption of sanctions, Canadian imports from South Africa were about $228 million. After some fluctuation, by 1989, Canadian imports were almost back to normal at $206 million. Canada, Trade of Canada, *Imports by Countries*, 1985–1989. Ironically, sanctions have hurt Canadian exporters more than South African since exports are still down by about one-third.

11. Letter to CUSO Executive Director, Chris Bryant, 18 December 1989, p. 2.

12. Nicholas Woodsworth, "How the West Assists Southern Africa's Revolutionaries," *Financial Times*, 15 March 1989, p. 4.

13. Communication to the Canadian branch of IDAFSA.

14. Calculations from CIDA *Annual Reports* and interviews with CIDA officials.

15. The international body of International Defence and Aid (IDAF) decided to end its operations and in 1991 the Canadian wing ended its activities.

16. Communication from an External Affairs official.

17. Only about $5 million of ODA went to Southern Africa in the 1960s.

18. Unless otherwise noted, statistics on ODA come from CIDA *Annual Reports*.

19. See Joseph Hanlon, *Beggar Your Neighbours*. Bloomington, Indiana: Indiana University Press, 1986 and *Frontline Southern Africa—Destructive Engagement*. Edited by Phyllis Johnson and David Martin. New York: Four Walls Eight Windows, 1988.

20. The expansion of Canada's Military Training Assistance Program (MTAP) from $550,000 in 1988 to $1.8 million in 1990 was designed to allow Canada to increase substantially its security assistance to countries in Southern Africa facing de-stabilization. Government of Canada, "Funding Increase to Assist Southern African States," *News Release*, #176, 26 July 1989.

21. The Department of National Defence sent 250 people to provide military logistical support; the RCMP sent 100 to act as police observers, and the government sent about fifty civilians to help UNTAG observe the elections. Canada also offered two Hercules aircraft for internal airlifts and provided 400 highly visible ballot boxes.

22. Cited in John Walker, "Canada Can't Afford Namibia Plan Stalemate," *Ottawa Citizen*, 16 September 1981, p. 3.

23. Paul Koring, "Muting of policy on S. Africa due to Namibia, officials say," *Globe and Mail*, 23 September 1989, p. A5.

24. Canada has provided just under $6 million in assistance to Namibia in the past and has offered $4 million for the first year of independence.

25. Canada, Department of External Affairs, "United Nations," *Foreign Policy for Canadians* (Ottawa, 1970), p. 20.

26. These were Angola, Botswana, Lesotho, Malawi, Mozambique, Swaziland, Tanzania, Zambia, and Zimbabwe.

27. Thus, from 1986 to 1989, the value of goods and services procured outside South African and shipped via SADCC ports for the SADCC aid program increased by 372 percent.

28. Oakland Ross and Michael Valpy, "Front-line aid no substitute for sanctions, Mugabe says," *Globe and Mail*, 19 September 1987, p. A1.

Principled Intervention: Canadian Aid, Human Rights and the Sri Lankan Conflict

David Gillies
McGill University

Introduction

Once a focus of international interest for its stable policy and progressive welfare system, Sri Lanka today is a grim exemplar of the global resurgence of communal violence. Indiscriminate "revenge" killings, disappearances, torture, incommunicado detention, the erosion of civil liberties, and the abuse of emergency powers are routine features of the political landscape. Closer now to Lebanon than Costa Rica, Sri Lanka's democratic stability has been shaken by a cycle of ethnic violence that will shape its political course for several generations.[1]

Human rights are said to be a "fundamental and integral part of Canadian foreign policy."[2] In practice, however, there remains an "inescapable tension between human rights and foreign policy."[3] An adequate response to abuses beyond national borders may require interference in the internal affairs of another state, a practice which is at odds with respect for the equally fundamental norm of state sovereignty.

During the 1980s, donors such as Canada, the Netherlands, and the Nordic states have explored the prospects for conditioning development on human rights criteria.[4] Two key concerns are: (a) the use of aid as a punitive lever against rights-repressive regimes; and (b) the potential of "political aid" as a catalyst to build democratic institutions and maximize the participation of target groups. A third concern, as yet scarcely considered by aid donors, is the human rights impact of individual projects. It is this issue which is a central focus here.

This case study examines Canada's aid program in Sri Lanka, but pays special attention to the Maduru Oya project, a dam and irrigation scheme, which was the focus of a dispute about ethnic resettlement ratios. The dispute threatened to reproduce the national conflict within CIDA's lead project in Sri Lanka.[5] The study underlines the conundrums faced by policy makers when an ethical concern for human rights confronts traditional international norms of nonintervention and sovereign jurisdiction over domestic affairs. Before examining Canada's record, however, we must briefly consider the roots of the conflict and the extent of human rights abuses.

Paradise lost: from model democracy to political cannibalism

The intractability of Sri Lanka's ethnic conflict is politically focused on the substance and scope for power devolution, and on the failure to find a formula for devolution acceptable to all parties. Democratic governance has given way to political decay, ethnic violence, and civil war. Some welfare programs have been cut back as defence spending has increased; by 60 percent in 1986 and by another 50 percent in 1987, when 35 percent of the government budget was spent on security.[6] The World Bank estimated the economic costs of the conflict at U.S. $1.8 billion by 1987.[7] Sri Lanka now joins a growing list of third world protracted social conflicts, resistant to durable solution and susceptible to periodic phases of violent confrontation.[8] What went wrong?

Alleged discrimination against the Tamil minority by Sinhala-dominated governments is a key element in the conflict. The impetus for state-sponsored discrimination was a combustible mix of Sinhala chauvinism, competition for jobs, and population pressures.[9] It took six main forms: discrimination in language, education, economic development, employment, land and, for some Tamils, citizenship.

Human rights abuses are the most visible expression of conflict.[10] All armed actors, state, nonstate and external (India), have committed atrocities in a spiral of terror and counterterror perhaps unequalled anywhere.[11] The toll of political violence may have reached 12,500 deaths between 1983 and 1988.[12] The barbarity has, if anything, become more acute, leading one observer to speak of Sri Lanka's descent into "political cannibalism."[13] In 1989, an estimated 30,000 people were killed in political violence.[14]

Human rights lawyers have also been victimized, and since at least 1987, local aid projects and development workers have been sporadically targeted. These developments add to the climate of insecurity surrounding donor aid projects in the country.

Numerous human rights missions and the weight of the principal UN human rights bodies point, at a minimum, to government complicity or toleration of rights abuses by security forces.[15] This assessment, however, must be tempered by the recognition that Sri Lanka faces a national emergency threatening the survival of a democratic state, and that radical Tamil and Sinhalese groups have used terror and violence with impunity.

Canada and Sri Lanka: a basis for policy coherence

Canada's first foray in international development began with its aid to the Commonwealth sponsored Colombo Plan in 1950. Initially, Canada endorsed Cold War thinking and saw the Colombo Plan as a way to stave off Communism in South Asia by a timely injection of Western aid. Over time, geo-strategic concerns were superseded by more benign thinking. Sri Lanka's image as a model third world democracy with a commitment to social justice, the imprimatur of the World Bank-led aid consortium, and the potential for commercial advantage were the main reasons for subsequently building a large aid program. By the early 1980s, Sri Lanka was the largest Canadian aid recipient in Asia on a per capita basis.

Canada now has few competing interests to muddy a consistent and principled human rights policy towards Sri Lanka. A possible exception is the Commonwealth link, which may have raised the stakes against a punitive or assertive statecraft. Economic interests were not a stumbling block when Canada had to rethink its aid relationship with Sri Lanka. Canadian bilateral ODA of $27.99 million in 1985–86 almost matched Canadian exports of $28.89 million that same year. Canadian imports from Sri Lanka in 1985–86 stood at $35.81 million, giving Canada a small bilateral trade deficit. Hence, Canada's minimal trade interests did not clash with human rights imperatives.

In other respects, Canada's domestic politics added a potentially helpful role in the resolution of the ethnic conflict. Canada's federal experience, multicultural image, and periodic crises of culture, language, and power sharing between the two dominant groups, amount to a "political self-interest in the survival of binational states."[16] This potential remained underdeveloped in the early stages of the Sri Lankan conflict and is only now, in the 1990s, being built into Canadian policy toward Sri Lanka.

Ethnicity, land and discrimination in the Maduru Oya scheme

A key element of the Sri Lankan government's (GOSL) economic restructuring was a plan to dam, divert, and harness the waters of the Mahaweli Ganga, the country's major river system. The river had been exploited for irrigation and agriculture nearly two thousand years ago by a sophisticated hydraulic civilization. The new plan was to build fifteen reservoirs: four on the Mahaweli, ten on its tributaries and one, to be built by Canadians, on the Maduru Oya. These dams would then generate up to 550 megawatts of hydro-electric energy and feed a complex and extensive system of canals and dykes to irrigate 360,000 hectares of scrubland.

Several sound development goals came together in the Mahaweli scheme.[17] Building the dam and irrigation systems would create local employment and transfer technology. The harnessed energy and water would irrigate scrubland in the infertile dry zone of the island's North and East. Irrigation, in turn, would make possible the resettlement of up to 750,000 landless peasants on small scale farms on once barren land.

The GOSL saw the scheme as a safety valve to relieve population pressures in the island's overcrowded, Sinhala-dominated South and Southwest. This was a megaproject with something for everyone: capital intensive infrastructure, with rich pickings for Western engineering and construction firms, a poverty alleviation component consistent with a Sri Lankan commitment to equity, increased agricultural productivity, and the harnessing of infertile land. Inspired by the engineering feats of an ancient kingdom and hailed as the world's largest foreign aid project, the Mahaweli scheme was to be a symbol of progress and national identity. None of these hopes materialized, however.

Instead, the scheme became another irritant adding to the already explosive communal tensions. Tamil critics of the plan claimed that Mahaweli continued the historical agenda of Sinhala-dominated governments to use resettlement to undercut Tamil claims on the eastern province.

Whatever the motives, events conspired against the government. Armed conflict and a dispute over resettlement ratios killed the project. By the late 1980s, the Mahaweli scheme was more a white elephant than a proud symbol of progress. Reservoirs lay dormant; the irrigation systems were still not built; the surrounding land remained barren and unused. In March 1990, the World Bank finally pulled out, sounding the death knell for the scheme. Canada and several other donors are now on the point of following suit, no longer prepared to operate in a climate of fear or to allocate funds to a project that is going nowhere.

(a) The Maduru Oya project: an aid planners nightmare

The Sri Lankan government established a Ministry for Mahaweli Development to oversee the project and commissioned aid donors to construct the dam and irrigation systems. The main donors were West Germany, Sweden, the United Kingdom, the United States, Saudi Arabia, Canada, and the World Bank. Canada has been associated with the scheme since 1980. A consortium of Canadian firms, including Acres of Ontario, built a large rock-fill dam and tunnel project to divert the waters of the Maduru Oya. This was the first phase in a plan to irrigate over 39,400 hectares of land.[18] CIDA provided $100 million in funding.

Canada's problems with the Maduru Oya complex began at the point when work was to start on the next phase: an irrigation and canal system to convert the scrubland into productive, small holder farms. Canada had allocated $60 million to Phase IV of the Mahaweli project in the form of equipment, training, and technical assistance. Yet politics quickly got in the way, and just $12 million has been disbursed on engineering studies, not construction.

The World Bank allocated U.S. $42 million for the Maduru Oya complex. Saudi Arabia was to build the canal system but pulled out in 1984 before starting work, as a retaliation for Sri Lanka's growing links with Israel. The European Community took over from the Saudis but never started because security concerns made work impossible in the Maduru Oya catchment area.

Interviews with CIDA and External Affairs officials suggest that at the planning stage virtually no attention was given to the project's impact on the fragile ethnic balance of Batticaloa district in which resettlement would occur.[19] There is no evidence of sensitivity to human rights matters such as participation and nondiscrimination by, for example, canvassing the opinions of local Tamil politicians or ensuring that an equitable ethnic balance was inscribed into the memorandum of understanding between the two governments. CIDA seems to have uncritically accepted the government's proposed resettlement formula. Canada's unwillingness to examine the political implications of the aid project was to prove costly.[20]

The outbreak of armed conflict in the eastern province in 1983, and its escalation in 1984, compelled Canada to consider whether the project would add to the communal tensions between Tamils and Sinhalese. Ottawa concluded that the GOSL's resettlement ratios for the right bank of the Oya river compromised Canada's equidistant and relatively passive position on human rights and threatened to plunge Canada into a political controversy at home and abroad. At all costs, Ottawa wished to avoid any perception that it was taking sides in the conflict, or that it was associated with actions which discriminated against the Tamil community.

The heart of the matter was this: should resettlement proceed on the basis of national or district ethnic ratios? The GOSL had devised a resettlement formula that mirrored the national ethnic balance—that is, 74 percent Sinhalese, 12 percent Sri Lankan Tamils, 6 percent plantation Tamils, 6 percent Muslim and 2 percent other. By this formula, the Sri Lankan Tamils would make up just 12 percent of the 750,000 people settled in the Mahaweli Scheme.

This seemingly fair provision was politically explosive because a number of the irrigation projects were in Tamil majority districts, and the resettlement formula threatened to weaken that majority. From a Tamil perspective, the national formula masked a hidden United National Party (UNP) agenda. Resettlement on the right bank of the Maduru Oya meant a rapid influx of Sinhalese to Batticaloa district, where the Tamils comprised more than two-thirds of the population.[21] Following the national formula would have altered the district demographic balance and undermined the precarious Tamil claim on the eastern province as a whole. Their slim majority in the province was the basis of the Tamil claim for district development councils and substantial provincial autonomy.

A second formula—favoured by the Tamils and eventually by Canada—was that resettlement should proceed according to a district ethnic formula. In effect, this meant that the right bank of the Oya river would be settled predominantly by Tamil farmers. The formula would preserve, rather than erode, the Tamil majority in the Batticaloa district.

The Sri Lankan government had always contested the concept of a Tamil "traditional homeland" in the eastern province. It reasoned that the fruits of the Mahaweli project should be available to all ethnic groups and denied that it made a deliberate attempt to alter the ethnic balance.

Canada became concerned about Maduru Oya because President Jayawardene's "national ethnic formula" was announced just before an All-Party Conference looking for a consensus on the resolution of the Tamil national question. At that time, the government and TULF, a Tamil political party, had proposals for district development councils (DDCs). In 1984, these DDCs were still seen as a viable way to devolve power locally and enhance Tamil autonomy without fracturing the Sri Lankan state. Jayawardene's timing of the resettlement formula could not have been more ill considered, and his announcement of it put in question the government's commitment to find a workable solution, or to grant meaningful local autonomy to the eastern province Tamils. A senior diplomat described the national ethnic formula as "a type of gerrymandering." The formula "heightened the sensitivity of the Oya project well beyond the local impact." Jayawardene's formula put Canada "in a difficult position because as an aid donor you can't go around telling a recipient how it's going to conduct its internal affairs, particularly over sensitive issues, such as land resettlement. A principle of domestic jurisdiction [over internal affairs] has been our tradition. On the other hand, we weren't very happy about our money going into something that was going to cause more dissension, and, in fact, to a scheme you could argue simply wasn't fair."[22]

Canada was careful not to adopt an overtly punitive approach and tried, instead, to set its concerns in the context of the All-Party Conference and as an opportunity for ethnic reconciliation. In a carefully modulated dialogue, Canada made clear its preference for a district ethnic formula favouring the Tamils, though "formally we resisted dictating our own formulas and ratios." As a senior official recalled: "The line I took was not 'you will settle this or this percentage of a particular ethnic group or we will not pay the money' but 'this aid program...is a gesture of Canada's good will. We don't want to get caught in a political issue so why don't you sort out a solution with all the communities to ensure that it does not become an issue....' Surely if you're looking for reconciliation a [district formula] is a golden opportunity to prove that the government is concerned with their future."[23] The bottom line, however, was unequivocal. Canada might have to reconsider its funding of the Oya project if the Sri Lankan government remained intransigent. Canada's overture led to a lengthy and ultimately fruitless dialogue between the two governments. "This little minuet" went on for almost two years, between 1984 and 1986, but the Canadians never got a clear answer. The implicit attitude of the Sri Lankans was "you sign the cheques fella, let us deliver the goods."[24]

Canada recognized its potential leverage as an important player in the Mahaweli Scheme. Aid was now vital to an economy unsettled by the conflict and as a substitute for risk capital that has all but dried up. There was also a potential signal effect. As one official explained, the Sri Lankans "didn't want a major donor like Canada to be seen as lagging behind in delivering aid because it might worry other donors."[25] The two-year diplomatic tussle ended as a stand-off. The Sri Lankans never said "yes—we accept the district formula," but Canada never said "we are pulling out."

(b)   Policy Options: the big stick or business as usual?

Canada did, however, canvass a number of options, including aid suspension. A closer look at the policy process is revealing. The narrative, as recounted by some of the key participants, uncovers the institutional differences between External Affairs and CIDA, the role played by individual policy makers, and the shrewd assessments of the opportunities and limitations of Canadian influence.

With the escalation of the conflict during 1985, and with growing protests about human rights abuses by Tamil groups in Canada, External Affairs undertook a protracted review of its relationship with Sri Lanka. There were two broad focuses of concern. First and foremost was the status of the aid program. The conflict was by now so bad that it was clear the entire program, and not just Maduru Oya, would have to be re-thought and adapted to the new realities.

A second, more muted, discussion centered on a potential role for Canada as a bridge builder, moving the warring parties toward reconciliation. Secretary of State for External Affairs (SSEA) Joe Clark took a personal interest in this option and in exploring greater UN involvement. Meanwhile, Sir Shridath Ramphal, the Commonwealth secretary general, wrote to Joe Clark to canvass support for a South Africa-style eminent persons group. This idea was dropped when the Indian foreign ministry in Delhi sent Ramphal a clear message to "back off."[26] Clark was also informed by the Indian foreign minister that a resolution of the conflict was India's responsibility. "Told clearly `that is the way it is,' Clark finally believed it" and dropped the good offices idea. In 1986, it made sense to regard India, the regional power, as the only country able to carry the big stick, but in light of its violent and ineffectual record in Sri Lanka, one can only lament that Canada and the Commonwealth did not promote a bridge-building role more aggressively.

The adaptation of the aid program revealed a distinctively Canadian form of bureaucratic politics: initially wide institutional differences

which are partially muted by a genuine effort at consensus building.[27]
There were at least three competing constituencies, each with its own
diagnosis and preferred remedy.[28] The Asia-Pacific branch of External
Affairs was pessimistic about Sri Lanka's future. It preferred a gradual
withdrawal of aid with a retargeting of unused funds to less troubled
recipients—in Southeast Asia, for example.[29] External argued that the
premises for Canada's presence in the country had radically altered. The
large aid program had "emerged historically, but had never been matched
by any objective assessment of the nature of Canadian interests in the
country." The rationale for aid to a model developing country was now
"obviously undercut." Moreover, though still confined to the North and
East, External saw that the conflict was likely to worsen: "The trend line
was down and it was going to stay down."[30] There were vague sound-
ings about closing down the high commission in Colombo, but they
were never seriously mooted. Basically, "our inclination was to scale
down our presence and hunker down for the long haul."[31] This first
constituency saw "no purpose in clinging to the assumption that the next
round of talks would produce a solution so that we could all get back to
business as usual."[32]

CIDA was a second constituency. The agency combined a "peculiar
mix" of idealism, organizational imperatives and hard-nosed pragmatism in arguing that Canada should maintain its current aid volume and
proceed with the next phase of Maduru Oya. The idealism was a natural
expression of CIDA's institutional mandate to help the poorest groups
and countries. CIDA saw no reason to undermine its developmental
objectives to make a political point and argued strongly that Mahaweli
combined sound development goals, such as poverty alleviation, relief of
population pressures, and enhancement of the carrying capacity of the
most infertile parts of the island.

CIDA's organizational imperatives centered on worries about continuity and on disbursement pressures. Unused funds would be allowed
to lapse and with it the program would simply wither away. According
to one External official, CIDA has a "desperate concern about the lack of
continuity" if the program were allowed to phase down or particular
projects were abandoned. There was also visible resentment at CIDA
about the intrusion of political issues into the technical problems of aid
delivery. CIDA's pragmatic antipathy against using aid as a political
lever had less to do with defending a development profile in Sri Lanka
and rather more to do with its relationship with some high profile
Canadian companies contracted to work on Mahaweli.

CIDA officials "spoke with disarming frankness" of the commercial
contracts already negotiated with three of Canada's largest engineering
firms. They had, in any case, already sunk $100 million into building the
Maduru dam. CIDA saw no way for Canada "to quietly phase down"

after it had spent $100 million. With $60 million still allocated to the project and with prestigious companies "with bags of political influence" hinting at litigation if the project stalled, CIDA wanted to proceed "without being reckless, in order to realize the developmental potential and commercial benefits."[33]

As one diplomat read CIDA's position, the agency "was more concerned about the direct access of these companies to their own Minister...and was quite unmoved by the fuss going on about human rights violations."[34] For CIDA, human rights were "a political problem for the Sri Lankans to sort out. For some time CIDA did not want to read the telexes the way we [at External Affairs] did."[35] Once CIDA agreed that the situation in Sri Lanka was "disturbed," its fall back position was that pulling out was uncalled for because there was a political dialogue under way.[36]

The final constituency, at the opposite pole to CIDA, canvassed the potential of using aid as a political lever. It was projected by a single influential individual, Marcel Massé, then top civil servant at External Affairs. As a former CIDA president Massé was then, and still is, very interested in the concept of aid conditionality.[37] Massé's "fascination" with aid as a foreign policy lever, rather than "any particular affinity" for Sri Lanka, prompted him to get his bureaucrats to "tell him whether he could or could not exercise leverage."[38] He knew that conditionality—a threat to suspend aid unless the Sri Lankans improved their human rights record and moved towards reconciliation—was not something that Canada could apply unilaterally. It could only work in concert with other donors.

After canvassing other donors, it became clear that conditionality was not a viable option. The Americans were opposed and the Europeans were not interested because of commercial interests or diplomatic ties. No other donor faced a human rights issue at the project level as Canada did. Acting alone Canada "would not have much clout when weighed against the total emotional involvement of national survival. [The Sri Lankan] government was never going to trade-off even a valuable aid project against the issue of national sovereignty. So the scenario simply played itself out."[39]

The upshot of this debate was a memorandum to the SSEA. The minister was presented with two options: Option A—to cancel the project, as External favoured, and Option B—to keep the project alive at a slow disbursement rate, as CIDA preferred. The minister chose Option B, which kept the project alive and enabled the Canadian firms to carry on the engineering studies at a cost of just $5 million over eighteen months. In effect, the decision was "a matter of buying time politically. [The project] wasn't frozen in an explicit sense; it simply wasn't going anywhere."[40] After protracted discussions, CIDA managed to persuade the Sri Lankans to sign a new memorandum of understanding which formalized the snail's pace disbursement rate.

Canada's principled action may have had a modest payoff. One of the first breakthroughs in the discussions between Sri Lanka and India which led to the peace accord was an agreement that the right bank of the Maduru Oya would be mostly Tamil. As one senior official observed, "I like to think our initiative had some influence. Had we agreed with the [national ethnic formula] this breakthrough may never have been possible."[41]

The internal policy review also led to three new operating principles applicable to the entire aid program, not simply Maduru Oya. First, Canada would not take any action likely to worsen the communal conflict. Second, Canada would take into account the communal dimension of any work it did. Third, where feasible, Canada would actively promote projects that fostered ethnic harmony and understanding. In practice, the second and third principles were very difficult to realize. While some modest mission administered funds were directed to women's groups and Tamil groups in the North, and more use was made of NGOs, the escalating conflict made it difficult to identify projects "to foster ethnic harmony."[42] Thus, with few projects in Tamil areas, Canadian aid to Sri Lanka was declining by 1985–86. And as one official noted, "the aid program became even more commodity centered and formula driven."[43]

Multilateralism: the Sri Lanka aid group

Another arena in which Canada began to take a more critical position on Sri Lanka was the annual aid group meetings. But whereas human rights are a legitimate focus of attention at the UN, it is rare for donors to raise such political issues in multilateral aid forums. At the 1988 Paris meeting of the Sri Lanka aid group, the comments of the Canadian delegate were only obliquely critical, noting, for example, that "defence continues to demand a high level of expenditures, one of the many direct links between the economy and the civil conflict."[44] The statement also voiced Canada's concern "as a long-standing partner with Sri Lanka, about the severity of [its] problems and...the need for early policy decisions and action to end the downward spiral in which Sri Lanka has been now caught for many years."

At the 1989 aid group meeting, Canada took a tougher line. The Canadian delegate stressed that:

> it is not purely economic considerations which concern us.... Mr. Chairman [we] would be remiss not to bring to the group's attention our concerns about the difficulties now being faced in implementing development programs.... First, there is an increasing problem in retaining personnel—the very heart of long-term and effective development in rural areas in particular. Second, there are increasing problems in obtaining reliable transportation.... Third, there appears to be a decreasing availability of local funding.... Fourth, there are increasing risks to development personnel as well as threats to innocent civilians.[45]

In a break with tradition, Canada noted that "a number of delegates have raised the issue of human rights in Sri Lanka. Canada has not traditionally raised this issue in consultative forums.... We do, however, share many of the concerns mentioned by [other] delegates and have raised these bilaterally with the government of Sri Lanka."[46]

Summary

By 1989 Canada seemed to have finally abandoned its agnostic position. One Canadian official argued that "a special responsibility lies with the [Sri Lankan] government for human rights because it is responsible for the administration of law."[47] The official also noted the growing presence of private militias, some responsible to senior government ministers, and death squad activity linked both to the militias and the security forces.[48] A measure of its resolve on human rights was that Canada was now prepared to raise the issue at the aid group meeting.

There is a certain irony in this turn of events. Canada was less critical in the early stages of the conflict, when the circumstances were comparatively clear: fighting was geographically confined to the North and portions of the East, and the principal cleavage pitted government forces against Tamil guerrillas. By 1989, human rights abuses were being committed by at least five armed groups, and the conflict was not so much within, as between, the two main communities. This complexity must cloud any clear assessment of government responsibility. One can surmise that sheer numbers of killings may have tilted Canada to a more critical position on Sri Lanka. As we shall see, understandable security concerns also played a part.

Preparing for the worst? In search of a new Canadian development role

We saw earlier that the decision to put the Maduru Oya scheme "on hold" and the inability to find enough small scale projects in Tamil areas meant: (a) that Canadian aid to Sri Lanka became largely commodity based, and (b) that overall bilateral ODA began to fall off. The extent of this decline in ODA disbursement is shown in Table 1, which records a drop from a peak of $46.02 million in fiscal year 1982–83 to $24.50 million in fiscal year 1987–88. Especially revealing is the rising disbursement trend line prior to 1983, when armed conflict emerged in earnest, and its rapid decline thereafter. Prior to 1983–84, Canada was thus fully committed to the Sri Lankan government and to national development. Growing evidence of discrimination and ethnic tension was not reflected in Canadian ODA. As the table indicates, ODA disbursements actually rose during the early 1980s.

Table 1

Canadian Bilateral ODA to Sri Lanka 1980–1988

Year	$ Millions
1980–81	37.69
1981–82	42.24
1982–83	46.02
1983–84	35.41
1984–85	24.43
1985–86	18.72
1986–87	17.87
1987–88	24.50

Source: Canadian International Development Agency, *Annual Report* (various years) and *Country Profile: Sri Lanka* (Hull: CIDA, 1989).

In 1990, Canada sought to recast its relationship with Sri Lanka. The country program review (CPR), a five year exercise, which sets the funding levels and parameters of the aid program, was the formal reason for the policy review. Yet the exigencies of aid delivery made the reassessment imperative. The CPR was set in the context of the worst year of violence in the last decade, a growing "aid fatigue" among the donor community, fears for the security of aid personnel, and a new "get tough" attitude which has led some donors to threaten aid suspension if the government of Sri Lanka does not improve its human rights record. The brief opportunity to end hostilities and build a more durable peace after the departure of the Indian army proved ephemeral.

The policy review brought together the principal departmental players involved with Sri Lanka. External Affairs and CIDA were the lead agencies, but Immigration and Finance (responsible for multilateral lending) played a subsidiary role. The recommendations are premised on a recognition that economic growth and development cannot proceed without political and communal stability. Hence, "Canada's long-term policy in Sri Lanka is to promote political stability and economic growth." The specific recommendations are as follows:

(a) to seek a resolution [of the conflict] based on compromise and devolution of power to the provinces,
(b) aid to be premised on equitability of the fruits of development to all Sri Lankans regardless of ethnic background,
(c) to acquaint Sri Lankan leaders with the Canadian experience in bilingualism and multiculturalism,
(d) to raise more intensively our concerns with Sri Lankan authorities on human rights,
(e) to cancel projects which cannot be implemented under present circumstances,

(f) to refocus development assistance programs on the root causes of the current conflict, such as ethnic animosity, by job creation and youth education,

(g) to support key institutions which can play a role in economic reform and in promoting human rights and democratic development,

(h) to promote community level economic activity especially among disaffected youth...whose unfulfilled aspirations have fuelled the conflict,

(i) to assist multi cultural organizations in the delivery of basic social services and, when conditions are ripe, to assist in reconstruction and rehabilitation.[49]

Discussion

The policy options are a curious mix of pessimism and optimism and mirror the uncertainty about Sri Lanka's future. Pessimism is evident in the decision to close down the Maduru Oya scheme and twenty smaller projects. They can no longer be implemented because of a climate of growing danger for project personnel and because the Sri Lankans cannot meet the local financing costs.[50] The security dimension is all too real. CIDA has not so far lost any of its personnel, but it has recalled some local staff from the field NGOs supported by South Asia Partnership, CIDA's main conduit for grassroots work, has had two of their local staff killed, allegedly by the People's Liberation Front (JVP).[51] An External Affairs official saw the security issue as currently more pressing than human rights conditionality: "The linkage of human rights and aid is not being drawn extensively by Canada...."[52]

The optimistic recommendations try to promote human rights and ethnic reconciliation. Canada's new International Centre for Human Rights and Democratic Development could play an important role in this regard, although the details have yet to be settled.[53] There is scope for funding human rights and legal aid groups, although in the light of recent U.K. experience (considered below) care will have to be taken not to alienate the Sri Lankan government or to endanger the recipients of funding. There is a creative proposal to acquaint Sri Lankan leaders with the Canadian experience of bilingualism and multiculturalism. One may be excused for thinking this suggestion naive or simply too little, too late. The recent constitutional crisis pitching Quebec against some sections of English Canada, and the federal and provincial governments' questionable handling of the Oka dispute, may put in doubt Canada's ability to "teach others."[54] It is, nevertheless, encouraging to see Canada search for a role in building a less violent Sri Lanka. Finally, also welcome is the addition of a human rights dimension to ensure that future projects pay attention to equity issues.

The policy review calls for a tougher stance on the Sri Lankan Government's human rights performance. Although Canada's views will be communicated in private meetings with the UNP government and in concert with other donors, there is growing Canadian impatience with the government's intransigence on human rights. As one official complained: "We do not see any evidence that [the government] will rescind the emergency measures which we feel legitimize human rights abuses.... What we haven't seen is a stated recognition by the government that they have a human rights problem... [or] that they have a human rights policy that they intend to push through.... We would like to see an acknowledgement that the government has been as culpable as the other [armed] groups. Their insistence that there is no government involvement is pure nonsense."[55]

Still Canada's "get tough" attitude does not mean suspending government-to-government aid. One reason is that cutting aid would "damage" the groups Canada is trying to help. More revealing, however, was an acknowledgement that aid suspension runs the "risk of establishing precedents [and strengthens] the voice of the more aggressive NGOs" demanding an automatic aid penalty against repressive regimes.[56] The recommendations give Canada's aid program the flexibility to make a contribution to Sri Lanka's still very uncertain future.

The leverage of aid

As the ethnic conflict has deepened, there is growing evidence of "aid fatigue" among the donor community and signs of a new willingness to use aid as a political lever. The most visible sign of fatigue is the World Bank's decision to pull out of the Mahaweli scheme. On 31 March 1990, the date by which the scheme was originally scheduled for completion, the World Bank informed the Sri Lankans of its decision to abandon Mahaweli. As a bank official explained: "we were no longer able to justify to our management funds that had been unused for the better part of a decade."[57] The decision was a simple recognition that the project "was just not going to fly" and had become "an embarrassment" to the donors and the Sri Lankans alike. The timing, coinciding with the departure of the Indian army, could not have been worse and appeared to send an ambiguous signal. Acknowledging that the pull out effectively killed the project, the official stressed that the bank had not "abandoned" Sir Lanka, but was shifting from project aid to a greater emphasis on macroeconomic planning and fast disbursing program aid.[58]

Whatever the motives for lapsing funds, the bank's action, as chair of the aid consortium and ultimate guarantor of Sri Lanka's external funding, underlines the growing frustration among the donor community. Its impact will be deeply felt by the government, since the bank was a prime architect of the original scheme.

Aid fatigue is not confined to the bank. In a striking departure from earlier thinking, the Dutch, in mid-January 1990, warned the Sri Lankans that unless there was an improvement in their human rights record by June, the Netherlands would cut the size of its aid program.[59] Even the U.K., linked to Sri Lanka by history and the Commonwealth, lost patience with the Sri Lankan government when the latter cited Britain's funding of a Tamil Law Society as support for a terrorist organization.

In an interesting example of donor co-ordination, the Dutch have taken a leadership role in canvassing support from Norway, Canada, Germany and Sweden and plan to use the quiet diplomacy technique of a joint political *démarche* to focus the concerns and strengthen the leverage of like-minded donors.[60] Canada has agreed to join this initiative, but prefers not to publicly censure the Sri Lankan government.[61] As late as October 1989, the Dutch, while critical of Sri Lanka in the aid group, and with several projects in abeyance, saw no immediate need to threaten aid suspension. Since then, however, they have concluded that development work is impossible until the security situation and human rights improve.

Several aid donors are now prepared to use aid as a lever to press for an improved human rights record and several, including Canada, are willing to work together. This is a measure of the perceived severity of the human rights abuses and the resolve of the donor community to press for change. Yet there is also a certain irony in this development, given Norway's almost lone voice and actions to protest government abuses in the mid-1980s and Canada's punctured trial balloon on "concertation." Evidently, sheer weight of numbers (an estimated thirty thousand killings in 1989) and a growing inability to deliver aid in conditions of palpable fear have finally galvanized the donor community into action.

The donors are in a commanding position to pressure the Sri Lankans. Foreign aid has become a vital prop for an economy sagging under the weight of rising spending on internal security and a 1988 debt profile of U.S. $5,189 million, or 75 percent of Gross National Product (GNP).[62] The World Bank estimated that Sri Lanka would require U.S. $2.4 billion between 1990 and 1992. Despite growing misgivings, the aid group pledged U.S. $787 million to Sri Lanka for 1990.[63] Meanwhile, the government can no longer finance the rupee expenditures for aid projects and has asked for more donor local cost financing.[64] These facts give the aid group a lever to press for change. There are, however, limits to the assertiveness of donors such as Canada, the Netherlands, and Norway. Each accepts a degree of information sharing but prefers a largely bilateral approach to aid leverage. A sufficiently strong signal can be communicated by simply threatening suspension. No one has so far raised the prospect of applying sanctions through the World Bank by conditioning new loan approvals on human rights criteria.

The timing of donor *démarches* and aid leverage seems calculated to press the Sri Lankan government to seek a permanent end to hostilities, a lifting of emergency regulations, and a rapid improvement in human rights. Yet in the light of the carnage which has unfolded since 1987 and the abysmal record of the Indian peacekeepers, one wonders if a more assertive and principled use of leverage prior to 1987 may have contributed to a speedier end to the conflict. The potential leverage of aid was as visible between 1984 and 1987 as it is now. Why did the donor community take so long to act?

Conclusion

Human rights are the first casualties of ethnic violence. One lesson from Sri Lanka is that discrimination and the denial of group rights, particularly Tamil self-determination, fed the conflict which endangered the fundamental rights of all citizens.

Canada's response to the Sri Lankan conflict was initially agnostic, carefully avoiding any punitive signals, such as suspending the aid program on human rights grounds or freezing commodity aid and balance of payments support. CIDA faced a complex political and human rights issue at the project level. The issue demanded and produced a clear-headed and principled response. Since 1989, however, Canada has grown more critical of the Sri Lankan government's human rights record and less willing to maintain a large aid program. This mirrors a trend among all the major donors in Sri Lanka. One outcome of the deepening violence is that several donors have tried to co-ordinate their efforts to apply pressure on the Sri Lankan government. Separate initiatives along these lines by Norway and Canada some years earlier did not succeed.

Several conclusions emerge from this case study. First, human rights issues, such as access to land, are embedded in the design and implementation of ODA projects. Donors ignore them at their peril. Conditionality is usually seen as a general policy issue with implications for the sum total of a donor's activity in a recipient country. Canada's experience with the Maduru Oya project suggests that donors who fail to consider the human rights implications of individual projects may be unwitting accomplices to human rights abuses.

Second, Canada was caught unprepared by the 1983 riots and the ensuing conflict. It appeared to have no human rights policy initially but was compelled by circumstances to develop one. Third, contrary to the fears of some practitioners, concern for human rights need not unduly damage the aid relationship. Despite some turbulence, there has been no serious deterioration in bilateral relations. Fourth, a more interventionist and punitive form of aid leverage was briefly considered by Canada but found to be impractical without active donor concertation.

Fifth, a mild form of bureaucratic politics accompanied the policy process. However, these centrifugal pressures were contained by a culture of consensus building. CIDA held strong reservations about the intrusion of politics in aid planning and the loss of program continuity and commercial opportunities. It successfully resisted the withdrawal of commodity aid and balance of payments support as a punitive human rights lever. Sixth, the resettlement issue was a principled Canadian human rights intervention, worked out before the domestic discussion on the linkage of human rights and development aid.[65] However, the Mahaweli experience has not, so far, led to any CIDA policy to put proposed megaprojects routinely through a "human rights filter."[66]

The current aid policy in Sri Lanka is driven as much by pragmatism—development is stalled by the conflict—as by any overriding concern for human rights. Safety issues are, of course, vitally important. Nonetheless, there is something hollow about considering withdrawal only when development work is on hold. That was the motive for Canada's departure from Uganda, and in part, from El Salvador and Guatemala. CIDA's willingness to continue commodity support also needs to be scrutinized. Commercial considerations seem to underpin the agency's reluctance to acknowledge that commodity and import support help prop up a repressive regime.

The motives for aid "conditionality" include retribution, coercion to alter behaviour, and avoidance of complicity with a repressive regime. Canada has been reluctant to condition aid to Sri Lanka on human rights performance. It was used in a principled way to register concern about resettlement ratios and avoid complicity with unjust policies. On the other hand, there is no clear evidence that wielding the big stick, either alone, or in concert with other donors, will force the GOSL to take negotiations or its human rights record seriously.

Given the renewed violence after the departure of the Indian army in March 1990, it would be sanguine to suppose that development aid can play much of a role as a peacemaker. Nevertheless, Canada has belatedly recognized that greater support for civil society, despite the uncongenial setting, is a necessary, albeit insufficient, condition for peace. Peace, distant though it may seem, is still the best guarantor of human rights.

Notes

1. Good accounts include *Sri Lanka in Crisis and Change*. Edited by James Manor. New York: St. Martin's Press, 1984; and Tambiah, S.J. *Sri Lanka: Ethnic Fratricide and the Dismantling of a Democracy*. Chicago: University of Chicago Press, 1985.

2. Response of the Government of Canada to the Report of the Special Joint Committee of the Senate and the House of Commons, *Canada's International Relations*. (Ottawa: Minister of Supply and Services, 1986), p. 71.

3. R.J. Vincent, *Human Rights and International Relations* (Cambridge: Cambridge University Press, 1986), p. 129.

4. See generally, *Human Rights, Development and Foreign Policy*. Edited by Irving Brecher. Halifax: Institute for Research on Public Policy, 1990; and Tomasevski, Katarina. *Development Aid and Human Rights*. London: Pinter Publishers, 1989.

5. I am grateful to Professors Baldev Raj Nayar, Lakshman Marasinghe and T.A. Keenleyside for comments on an earlier draft and to Canadian officials for policy insights. The views developed here should not be attributed to officials or institutions mentioned in the text. A comparative version of this study is to be published by the Norwegian Ministry of Development Cooperation as "Principled Intervention: Norway, Canada and the Sri Lankan Conflict."

6. *Lanka Guardian*, 15 March 1987.

7. *Far Eastern Economic Review*, 3 December 1987.

8. Edward A. Azar, "Protracted Social Conflicts: Ten Propositions," in *International Conflict Resolution: Theory and Practice*, eds. E. Azar and J. Burton (Sussex: Wheatsheaf Books, 1986).

9. See Kingsley M. De Silva, "Discrimination in Sri Lanka," in *Case Studies on Human Rights and Fundamental Freedoms: A World Survey*, ed. V. Verhoven, vol. 3. (The Hague: Martinus Nijhoff, 1976), pp. 73–119.

10. See, for example, *Cycles of Violence* (Washington, D.C.: Asia Watch, 1987); *Political Killings in Southern Sri Lanka* (London: International Alert, 1989); and *Human Rights in Developing Countries, 1989* eds. Manfred Nowak and Theresa Swinehart (Kehl & Strasbourg: N.P. Engel Publisher, 1989).

11. In 1989, the main protagonists included the Sri Lankan army, Indian Peace-Keeping Force (IPKF), Tamil Tigers, EPRLF, PLOTE, and the DJP/JVP. There were also private militias organized by prominent politicians—e.g. the Green Tigers.

12. John Bray, "Sri Lanka: Things Fall Apart?" *The World Today* (August/September 1989), 156.

13. *Far Eastern Economic Review*, 27 July 1989. Indiscriminate "revenge killings" are almost routine.

14. David Housego, "Death toll in Sri Lanka may be as high as 30,000," *Financial Times* (London), 17 January 1990.

15. At the 1987 UN Human Rights Commission, Canada, Norway, and Argentina successfully sponsored a resolution critical of the Sri Lankan government's human rights record.

16. Sheldon Gordon, "A test for Sri Lanka," *Globe and Mail*, 7 April 1886.

17. Telephone interview with Mr. A. Tsui, World Bank official, 5 April 1990.

18. *Country Profile: Sri Lanka* (Hull: Canadian International Development Agency, 1989).

19. Interviews in Ottawa, January and April 1990. Regrettably, a request made under the Access to Information Act to examine confidential files was denied by CIDA.

20. The narrative here draws from interviews with Canadian diplomats based in Sri Lanka between 1982 and 1987. The interviews took place in Ottawa in February and March 1990.

21. In 1981, the ethnic distribution in Batticaloa was Sinhalese, 3.2 percent; Sri Lankan Tamils, 70.9 percent; Moors (Muslims), 32.9 percent; others 1.9 percent. Department of Census and Statistics and Ministry of Plan Implementation (Colombo, 1982), p.32.

22. Interview in Ottawa, 17 February 1991.

23. *Ibid.*

24. *Ibid.*

25. *Ibid.*

26. Interview with Canadian diplomats, Ottawa, 17 February 1990.

27. The differences between the endemic bureaucratic conflicts in the U.S. system and the more muted Canadian version are explored by Kim Richard Nossal in "Allison Through the (Ottawa) Looking Glass: Bureaucratic Politics and Foreign Policy in a Parliamentary System," *Canadian Public Administration* vol. 22, no. 4 (Winter 1979).

28. Interview in Ottawa, 26 March 1990.

29. One External Affairs official bluntly asked: "Why the hell were we emptying $125 million a year down a rathole like Sri Lanka?" Interview in Ottawa, 26 March 1990.

30. *Ibid.*

31. *Ibid.*

32. Interview with External Affairs officials in Ottawa, 17 February 1990.

33. Interview with a CIDA official, 9 January 1990.

34. Interview at the Department of External Affairs, 29 March 1990.

35. *Ibid.*

36. *Ibid.*

37. As CIDA's current president, Massé is energetically exploring greater aid conditionality in the context of structural adjustment.

38. Interview with a Canadian government official, Ottawa, 26 March 1990.

39. *Ibid.*

40. Interview with a government official, Ottawa, 17 February 1990.

41. Interview at the Department of External Affairs, Ottawa, 17 February 1990.

42. Interview with a senior Canadian official, Ottawa, 17 February 1990. CIDA began to work with Sarvodaya—a Gandhian grassroots organization and one of the largest NGOs in the third world—and South Asia Partnership, an umbrella group of Canadian NGOs active in Sri Lanka.

43. *Ibid.* Commodity aid subsidized Canadian potash producers and helped CIDA approach, if not entirely meet, its annual disbursement quotas. While an argument can be made that potash and food aid have developmental benefits, they are not, strictly speaking, poverty alleviation mechanisms. In fact, by the sale of these Canadian commodities on the local market the Sri Lankan government is given foreign exchange which can be used for nondevelopmental, and possible repressive, purposes. This possibility seems not to have concerned CIDA.

44. Statement by Canada at the Sri Lanka Aid Group Meeting, Mimeo, Paris, 30 June 1988.

45. *Ibid.*

46. *Ibid.*

47. Interview with an External Affairs official, Ottawa, March 1990.

48. *Ibid.*

49. This list is reproduced from Government of Canada files. Interview with an External Affairs official, Ottawa, 29 March 1990.

50. An internal telex from the Canadian High Commission to Ottawa headquarters noted that the Sri Lankans have accepted the pull out. "We were not left feeling we were seen by the Sri Lankans as [project] killers," the telex observed. Telex on Subject of Mahaweli, dated 2 January 1990.

51. Interview with Richard Harmston, executive director of South Asia Partnership, Ottawa, 14 February 1990. The victims were Mr. M.I.M. Cassim and Mrs. W.L. Fernanda. Cassim reportedly contacted SAP headquarters fearing a threat on his life just days before his murder. Fernanda was thought to have been killed for her local political work and membership of the UNP.

52. Interview in Ottawa, 29 March 1990.

53. Interview with an External Affairs official, 27 March 1990.

54. See also the highly critical Canadian Human Rights Commission assessments of state treatment of Canada's first people's. Canadian Human Rights Commission *Annual Report 198.* (Ottawa: Minister of Supply and Services, 1988).

55. Interview in Ottawa, 27 March 1990.

56. Interview with an External Affairs official, 10 March 1990.

57. Telephone interview with a World Bank official, 2 April 1990. The bank had allocated U.S. $24 million to the fund from the International Development Association (IDA)—its soft loan window.

58. *Ibid.*

59. David Housego, "Death Toll in Sri Lanka may be as high as 30,000," *Financial Times* (London), 17 January 1990.

60. Interview with a Dutch official, The Hague, June 1990.

61. Interview with an External Affairs official, Ottawa, 29 March 1990.

62. Economist Intelligence Unit, *Country Report: Sri Lanka.* Report No. 1 (London, 1990), p. 21. The debt burden is partially lightened because 65 percent of it is on concessional terms.

63. *Ibid.*

64. Housego, "Death toll."

65. The principal statements are *For Whose Benefit?* Report of the Standing Committee on External Affairs and International Trade on Canada's Official Development Assistance Policies and Programs. Ottawa: Queen's Printer, 1987; *Canadian International Development Assistance: To Benefit a Better World.* Response of the Government of Canada to the Report by the Standing Committee on External Affairs and International Trade. Ottawa: Minister of Supply and Services, 1987; and *Sharing Our Future.* Hull: Canadian International Development Agency, 1988.

66. This issue is examined by James C.N. Paul, "International Development Agencies, Human Rights and Humane Development Projects," in *Human Rights, Development,* ed. I. Brecher, pp. 275–328.

Canadian Aid, Social Change and Political Conflict in the Philippines—Prospects for Conflict Resolution

David Wurfel

University of Windsor

Out of poorly informed political judgement, bold innovation, and controversy, has come a CIDA program for assistance to NGOs which, despite its errors—and even contrary impact in Negros—may eventually be said to have made a small contribution to the resolution of the deep ongoing conflict in Philippine society. Though it may be too early to make a conclusive assessment, this tentative finding comes from numerous conversations with NGO representatives and government officials in both Canada and the Philippines, 1988–90 and from two visits to Negros.

To understand the impetus behind CIDA initiatives, one must first understand the politico-economic context in the Philippines in the mid-1980s. By early 1985 the economy was in rapid decline. Over 30 percent of the labour force was estimated to be unemployed; inflation was around 50 percent; political dissent, both violent and nonviolent, was at an all time high. The president's health was precarious. Spurred by the prospects of succession, the moderate opposition was beginning to pull together, so that by November, when President Ferdinand Marcos announced an early election, it was possible to bring unity around Corazon Aquino, widow of the slain senator. But the unity did not include the Communist Party of the Philippines, which announced a boycott of the elections—even though some leftist groups did support Aquino.

When the election was held in February, fraud was rampant. Yet the independent count by the National Movement for Free Elections (NAMFREL), the reports of hundreds of foreign observers, and the escalation of nonviolent action by Aquino supporters, made it difficult for Marcos to sell either to the Filipino people or people abroad his supposed "reelection." Thus when a segment of the military mutinied against Marcos, it had wide popular support. The inauguration of Aquino as president was confirmed by the departure of Marcos a few days later. The world had watched while peaceful demonstrators stopped pro-Marcos tanks. The euphoria was contagious; Cory took office on a wave of popularity. TV coverage made Canadians much more aware of the Philippines than ever before, and in February 1986 their impressions were very favourable.

In the last years of the decaying Marcos regime, the Canadian government had wisely kept its distance, in part by not approving new government-to-government economic assistance. In February 1986, however, there was popular backing—as well as advice from allies and economic self-interest—for moves to support the new democratic regime. Clearly President Aquino needed all the help she could get. She was confronted by near economic collapse, an overwhelming foreign debt, a thoroughly corrupt bureaucracy, and widespread insurgency in the countryside. The restoration of democratic institutions, which she accomplished in 1986–87, was only a small part of the task she faced.

Negros was one of those provinces most devastated by the rapacity of Marcos cronies, as well as declining world prices. The Philippine sugar industry, centred in that province, had suffered both from a fifteen year low in prices and also from the extractions of the Marcos backed sugar monopoly. Sugar planters were protesting vociferously—some of the larger ones may have had to sell an extra Mercedes. Hundreds of thousands of workers were jobless, their families on the verge of starvation. The Communists made the most of this crisis.

Fear of the strength of the revolutionary movement among sugar planters was probably at its peak just before the 1986 elections. The majority recognized that a legitimately elected president would make it easier to "restore order" and thus backed Aquino. Some, like Daniel Lacson, even proposed projects that would help feed their penniless workers, showing a sense of the patron's responsibility toward his clientele. (This included very limited temporary "land reform," such as in the PLOW Land Sharing project administered by the Chito Foundation and supported by Howard Dee's Assisi Development Foundation.) The more short-sighted planters showed no such responsibility, but expanded hacienda security forces.

In 1986, just as Canada was launching new aid initiatives, the situation in Negros began to change. The revolutionary movement itself lost ground in the middle class because of its failure to back Cory Aquino. Conflict also grew within the movement over that question. Aquino was popular and appointed as acting governor the moderate reformer Daniel Lacson. (He was elected governor nearly two years later.) With an upward turn in sugar prices, however, most planters, with new hopes of profit, didn't even want to listen to proposals for moderate reform. Instead many expanded their commitment to private armies or helped finance the Philippine Constabulary Forward Command (PCFC,) a PC auxiliary under control of the provincial PC commander.

By 1987, when the president issued her executive order declaring in principle that all croplands would be subject to reform, sugar prices had jumped by one-third over 1986. So reform was even more unpopular. Some of the most conservative planters formed the secret Negros

Independence Movement, vowing to fight for secession if necessary to retain their land. In the other camp, disagreements within the Communist Party over the decision not to extend the cease-fire, but to escalate the fighting, led to some important defections, including the provincial party chair himself. With reduced incentives for reform, hardliners came to the fore both among the planters and the insurgents.[1]

The PC commander, Lieutenant-Colonel Coronel, in order to assert tactical control over numerous private armies springing up and to increase the funds available, proposed the creation of the Sugar Development Foundation, the primary purpose of which would be to levy a uniform lien on all sugar planters to finance the centralized para-military force, which was already abducting, shooting, and killing church workers, union organizers and other peaceful civilians, as well as fighting the New People's Army (NPA). Such a lien was ordered by the Sugar Regulatory Administration in the following year and was expected to generate P 40–50 million per year. This served to institutionalize the polarization between left and right. By 1989 the bishop of Bacolod, Antonio Fortich, who had often served as the only communication link between government and radical opposition, was retired by the Vatican. His replacement began to reverse some of the policies of Bishop Fortich, who was a strong proponent of land reform and a tireless defender of human rights—so much so that his residence was twice bombed by landlord-backed vigilantes.

In the capital the president, threatened by coups and semicoups, gave larger and larger concessions to the military in order to win them over.[2] Any leadership for the enforcement of human rights was abandoned, while in Congress Aquino's brother, Representative Jose Cojuangco, led the landlord bloc in emasculating land reform legislation, so that by the time it was enacted it was almost impossible to implement. Thus a regime which had taken power on a wave of "people power" had moved so far to the right as to make some of its policies indistinguishable from those of its predecessor. It was in that national context that Governor Lacson also moved to the right. While he may have been a "moderate reformer" out of power in 1985, by 1988 he was embracing the military and finding it difficult to push through his earlier ideas on partial land reform. He was a member of the landed elite and could not veer too far from its consensus.

Canadian aid

In 1986 Canada made two innovative initiatives, one at the national level and the other for Negros, both relying on Philippine NGOs to carry forward local projects. The national scheme, which came to be known as the Philippine Development Assistance Program (PDAP), was the fruit of a proposal made in 1985 by a group of "centrist" foundations at CIDA's invitation: the Association of Foundations, the Philippine Partnership for the Development of Human Resources in Rural Areas (PHILDHRRA), the Asian NGO Coalition, Philippine Business for Social Progress, and the Assisi Development Foundation. These foundations, accustomed to drawing on the business sector for funding, were quite frank in admitting that the economic crisis was "drying up" their sources[3]—thus the timeliness of the arrival of CIDA on the scene.

In describing the kind of projects which would be funded, these foundations listed "permanent social change" as one of the "desirable project criteria,"[4] but what was more noticeable was that their proposal continued to talk of the poor as "clients," the terminology of traditional social work. Nor was mention of "permanent social change" convincing in light of the proposal that, for management training PDAP should call on Sycip, Gorres, Velayo and Co. (SGV) the largest accounting firm in the Philippines which served most of the major corporations. In fact, it was also proposed that SGV, along with the Asian Institute of Management (AIM) would have associate members on the PDAP program committee which would approve all projects.

In June 1986, CIDA announced funding of $4.88 million for PDAP for four years. Howard Dee of the Assisi Development Foundation became chair of the Philippine committee. A prominent Christian Democrat and philanthropist, he had substantial investments in Canada. Maria Hulme of HOPE International Development Agency of Vancouver headed the Canadian committee.

Under PDAP the project cycle begins with an idea by a Philippine NGO proposed to the committee in Manila. If approved, it is forwarded to the PDAP secretariat in Ottawa, which seeks a Canadian NGO sponsor through which CIDA funds would be channelled. Among the thirteen Canadian NGOs who were invited to participate in PDAP, some of the largest decided not to participate. There were those who criticized the rather narrow spectrum of Philippine NGOs with whom CIDA initiated dialogue. While PDAP may have been an efficient mechanism for the delivery of funds to certain types of worthwhile projects, it could not be considered to have played any kind of reconciling, bridge-building role among NGOs or PDOs (Peoples' Development Organizations) of different political orientations.

It was clearly in Negros that the need for bridge building was greatest. The widespread malnutrition and near starvation of some residents made Negros the centre of international media attention in 1986. It was natural for the Canadian embassy in Manila to direct a delegation headed by Tory MP James Edwards to the island in April. Edwards, like many other foreign visitors, was particularly impressed with Acting Governor Lacson, his vision, his articulate delivery, and his apparent commitment to reform and development. In June, External Affairs Minister Joe Clark also met Lacson and announced that an innovative program for Negros would be the centrepiece of a new $100 million five year CIDA commitment to the Philippines.

In September 1986, the two governments signed a memorandum of understanding for an $11 million Negros Rehabilitation and Development Fund (NRDF.) "In the short term," said CIDA, "the NRDF can provide immediate relief to the people most seriously affected by the collapse of the sugar-based economy, especially the sugar workers in the area. Over the longer term, an objective of the NRDF is to help foster self-sufficiency and enhance the decision-making capacity of the rural and urban poor of Negros by providing them with access to land, technology, agricultural inputs, education and other key productive resources."[5] The NRDF also set as a goal to "play a major role in the socio-economic transformation of one of the most distressed provinces in the Philippines," indeed an ambitious aim.[6]

The central role of acting Governor Lacson is seen in the fact that he chose "six individuals…with strong track records in NGO development work" to sit on the NRDF program committee authorized to approve projects. The only two additional members were representatives of the Philippine government and of CIDA. CIDA funds were channelled through this committee and a "CIDA monitor" held office in Bacolod to help keep tab on projects approved. (From 1987 to 1990 it was Greg Forbes, a young Canadian with considerable experience in co-operative work in the Philippines who, with the help of his Filipino wife, has a good understanding of Philippine society.)

It is not surprising that Lacson's nominees were members of the Negros economic elite. In fact, most of the Lacson nominees were also board members of elite foundations which quickly became beneficiaries of NRDF funds, e.g., the Chito Foundation, the Negros Economic Development Foundation, First Farmers Human Development Foundation, the J.F. Ledesma Foundation, and In-Hand Negros. Buasdamlag Inc., the largest beneficiary (with an approved amount of nearly P 9 million) was also landlord controlled. Granting began in January 1987; all of the above had grants approved in the first six months.

Some of the consequences of this somewhat incestuous relationship did not improve the reputation of the NRDF. For instance, In-Hand Negros, which included the governor's wife on its board, hired piece workers for an average of $1.50 per day to manufacture toys for export. The wage, shocking as it was, was not unusual for Negros; what was more surprising was that board members of this "nonprofit" organization received $700 a month in stipends or more than half the annual salary of a school teacher.[7] Buasdamlag Inc. contracted out the administration of some of its projects to Kabalaka Development Foundation, another creation of the planters. According to local priests, Kabalaka field workers sometimes charged farm workers who failed to sign up for Kabalaka projects with being members of the NPA—which provided military and para-military forces with a license to kill. Kabalaka agents were also accused of "educating against land reform," and one of Kabalaka's leading figures was reported to be a founder of a planter-backed vigilante group. In fact, NRDF's own investigation of Buasdamlag projects discovered enough disquieting aspects to warrant cancellation.

Numerous complaints about NRDF's elitist orientation filtered back to Canada through Canadian NGOs with partners or friends in the Philippines. The leftist National Federation of Sugar Workers (NFSW,) headquartered in Bacolod, was especially upset with a program that it believed was merely propping up a "feudal" system. Even though invited by CIDA to do so, NFSW refused to make a project proposal to NRDF, probably fearing rejection, given the make-up of the program committee, or board.

By June 1987 negative reports on NRDF were of sufficient weight that the Canadian Council on International Cooperation (CCIC) organized a small meeting with CIDA representatives. Finally CIDA itself decided that the wave of criticism, about PDAP as well as NRDF, was so serious that it organized a series of major consultations across the country (Montreal, Toronto, Ottawa, and Vancouver) in January and February 1988. CCIC helped in the preparation for these sessions, which constituted an unprecedented consultative effort by CIDA on behalf of a particular country program.

After lengthy introductions about the aims and structure of the entire CIDA undertaking in the Philippines, discussion at these consultations turned to the controversial aspects. On the whole this observer found CIDA representatives remarkably open and accepting of criticism. The main thrust of criticism of PDAP was that it excluded progressive NGOs and PDOs in the Philippines and thus discouraged the participation of some Canadian NGOs. CIDA insisted that there was an openness to meeting with all organizations in the Philippines, except the NPA, but conceded that "there was perhaps not enough communication with the [Canadian NGO] community when PDAP was in its formative stage and that its focus may be too narrow."[8] In fact, in March the PDAP Philippine committee decided to expand its membership and revise project selection criteria to include more community organizing activities.

The discussions on NRDF were perhaps even more "spirited." All sessions addressed the failure of NRDF to give sufficient attention to land reform, the very core of "social transformation." There were suggestions made, some specific and some not, that NRDF grants may have been given to groups and individuals in some way associated with the vigilantes, prime suspects in many human rights violations.

Subsequently CIDA did prevail on the NRDF board to cancel the Buasdamlag project, and even before the consultations, CIDA attempted to expand the character of the board with the appointment of Sister Michele Gamboa, a person respected by progressive elements within the church. Later in 1988 CIDA began to insist that any new project must contain some permanent land reform, at least as one element, with the transfer of titles to farmers or farmers' co-operatives.

Fortunately by 1988 CIDA had abandoned the position of a previous Canadian official in Manila that "the opposition of Canadian NGO's to direct funding [of Philippine NGOs] is one of the most regressive anti-developmental stances which has ever been adopted by anybody involved in development work." What was earlier perceived in CIDA as blanket opposition by some Canadian NGOs to "direct funding" was primarily a displeasure with a lack of voice in determining the range of Philippine NGOs to be funded.

Significantly changing the range of groups to be served by existing funding institutions is not an easy task, however. Even a new direction by the CIDA representative appointed to the NRDF board in 1988 faced opposition. Some of the more conservative sugar planters on the board were actually required to resign after they had tried to block CIDA-favoured reforms. Replacements included an ineffectual "small farmers' representative," Gaston Ortigas of Asian Institute of Management (AIM) in Manila, who is firmly committed to land reform despite his elite background, and Monsignor Victor Rivas, vicar-general of the diocese of Bacolod, an articulate speaker for progressive elements within the church. Acceptance of Rivas was particularly difficult for Lacson. At one NRDF board meeting in early 1988, CIDA pressure succeeded in securing the adoption of a policy that planters' groups were not to be recipients of NRDF funds—but at the subsequent meeting the decision was rescinded. Acceptance of the principle that all new projects should include an element of permanent land reform came only after a threat of complete withdrawal of CIDA funds. Thus, inevitably, the attempt to reform NRDF to bring it into line with policies more consistent with CIDA's general objectives shattered the earlier image of NRDF as a body controlled by Filipino decision makers.

One can see in the nature of the projects approved in 1988 and 1989 a greater emphasis on church groups and co-operatives. However, the increased tension in the board slowed down the rate of grant decisions. (30 decisions in 1987 and 18 in 1988.) While $2.7 million was disbursed by May 1987, by 1 July 1989 there had only been an additional $2.8 million in disbursements. Even with a renewed commitment to reform by CIDA and an attempt to restructure the board, it seemed hard to alter old patterns.

The ODISCO Farm Systems Development Foundation project was approved in March 1988. An independent study by the Institute of Philippine Culture gives an insight into ODISCO operations through the eyes of the military and of the small farmers.[9] In one *barangay* a teacher was afraid to let ODISCO use a school building for an "Economic and Social Awareness Seminar" because "the military is very suspicious and does not trust anybody." So the vice-president of ODISCO wrote a letter to the Philippine Constabulary provincial commander informing him about the seminar and inviting him to attend. The Commander replied that there was no need for him to attend since "ODISCO is for the good of the people."

The ODISCO project consisted of the provision of *carabaos (water buffaloes)*, ploughs, and farm inputs to farmers and also included educational and training programs. The eleven *barangay* residents who had received *carabaos* reported that they had to repay ODISCO, plus 10 percent of the recipient's net harvest per crop to cover the expenses of the ODISCO personnel supervising the project. When asked to characterize ODISCO's presence in the community, one resident said that it "would free the farmers from poverty through the use of technology." Others saw ODISCO simply as a source of *carabao*. Still other informants said that "ODISCO teachings were based on the holy Bible and stressed the eradication of such vices as smoking, drinking, gambling, and dancing. But since both instructors and attendants in ODISCO seminars didn't follow some of these teachings, the seminars fell short of their goals." A friendly relationship with the military and a fundamentalist religious orientation were typical of conservative NGOs in Negros.

Apparently CIDA decided that any attempt to fundamentally alter the structure of PDAP would be difficult. (After all, Dee had good Canadian connections.) Some members of PDAP identified with the Aquino government and deeply resented criticism of it. Thus, they were not disposed to cooperate with NGOs or PDOs whose criticism of the regime was quite fundamental.

By late 1989, however, there was clearly an awareness in some sectors of PDAP that there was a need to shift emphasis. In the November 1989 issue of its monthly magazine, *Partnerships*, prominent attention was given to the activities of the Coalition for Peace, which involved some people also working in PDAP-connected NGOs. The same issue of *Partnerships* also examined project organization and emphasized the need for democratic participation, noting that the continued use of the term "beneficiary" implied a patron-client relationship rather than a fully democratic process. A later issue (January/February 1990) high-lighted human rights problems in an article by a staff member of Taskforce Detainees. PDAP may have had some potential to be a bridge builder across lines of conflict.

CIDA's most innovative and constructive response to criticism of its Philippine program was, in any case, the formulation of an entirely new structure, after lengthy consultation. The consultation process itself was

unprecedented and indirectly promoted peace. The flexibility and innovation of Jim Carruthers, counsellor (development) in the Canadian
embassy was key to the success of the wide ranging consultation. It now
also seems apparent, however, that External Affairs was subtly shifting
its view of the Aquino administration from the earlier total embrace to a
more "critical collaboration." This shift made it easier, perhaps even
imperative, to consult with a wider range of Filipino groups, including
those in principled opposition.

The format proposed for a large "NGO consultation" was as part of
the country program review (CPR) which CIDA is supposed to initiate
every five years. After preliminary conversations both with representatives of PDAP and CCIC, and a special CIDA attempt to dialogue with the
National Council for Peoples' Development (NCPD,) including the
Sugar Workers' Federation, there was general agreement that a consultation should be held in June 1988, with responsibilities for the secretariat
shouldered by the Philippine Partnership (PHILDHRRA) and CCIC
representatives on the steering committee. At the meeting in Tagaytay,
a pleasant hill station less than two hours from Manila, there were over
fifty persons in attendance, almost all representing NGOs and mostly
Filipinos. Guest speakers, including some of the country's most outstanding intellectuals, addressed the general political, economic, and
social situation, as well as particulars of the CIDA program or the role of
NGOs. The workshops produced a rather progressive consensus on a
number of issues, especially considering that some NGOs present had
close links with the business sector. As the preamble to the subsequent
report put it, "Development...cannot be divorced from the process of
democratization."[10] Thus militarization and human rights violations
were identified as major obstacles to NGO development work. Jim
Carruthers, speaking for CIDA, confirmed that "Social change [in the
Philippines] is essential and urgent. The NGO community is, and should
be, a major player in social change."[11] Plenary sessions sometimes addressed what were for CIDA very sensitive issues; one concluded, clearly
referring to NRDF, that "funds should not go to landlord-initiated
NGOs." Another session summed up the discussion: "In response to
threats [of militarization], NGOs see the need for coalition-building and
advocacy on social and human rights issues." Overall these consultations
were described by one participant as realistic in the face of grave threats
and yet somehow optimistic about what could be accomplished.

CCIC had made it clear that their representatives came to Tagaytay
merely to make a critique of CIDA's programs, hoping to have an impact
on CIDA's thinking, but without any commitment for a future role.
Nevertheless a Canada-Philippines NGO Steering Committee came
out of the June consultation. The original mandate was only to build on
the considerable consensus among NGOs that emerged in Tagaytay,

facilitate ongoing dialogue with CIDA, and monitor the preparation of the country program review to try to ensure that NGO concerns were given proper consideration. Yet after three meetings the steering committee actually produced a proposal for a new structure and new program to be called PCHRD (Philippine Canadian Human Resources Development.) Consensus building had been jeopardized in January 1989 by the withdrawal of the National Council for People's Development (NCPD) representative from the steering committee, apparently as the result of a development in Negros, but in a few months he returned. This was especially important since the NCPD was the farthest left of the groups involved and its absence would have undermined the attempt to build a broad coalition.

PCHRD is unique, both in Philippine experience with foreign aid donors and in the history of CIDA. It goes farther to build bridges over conflict than anything else CIDA has yet done. The ten Philippine NGOs represented on the Philippine Coordinating Committee range all the way from Philippine Business for Social Progress (and thus an overlap with PDAP) to the NCPD. (PDAP, without alteration, has had its funding extended.) A Canadian Coordinating Committee of wide membership was also formed. The two coordinating committees together formed a joint committee which is the governing body of PCHRD, authorized to allocate funds to projects proposed unless a single grant exceeds $200,000, in which case CIDA must also concur. CIDA will make available to PCHRD $15 million over five years. There is no other structure funded by CIDA anywhere in the world where NGOs are given such a sweeping role in making project decisions with CIDA funds, and especially where local NGOs are given an equal voice with Canadian organizations. In fact, many people in the Philippines were surprised that Ottawa gave its approval.

At the same time that PCHRD was phased in, NRDF was phased out. All of the original $11 million was committed to projects and CIDA allowed the program to come to an end when its originally contemplated four-year life span was reached in 1990, though some disbursements were made even later. Canadian participants at the Tagaytay consultation believed that the consensus there against NRDF had a large part to play in the CIDA decision. But difficulties of trying to implement NRDF's intended goals in cooperation with Governor Lacson, more and more representing the interests of the Negros landed elite, as well as budgetary pressures, were surely sufficient grounds for the phase out.

The impact on conflict

Having described the recent history of CIDA funding for NGO administered development projects, and the political and economic context in which this took place, the question arises whether any of this made a contribution to conflict resolution or the promotion of peace. Note that the question is being asked only about aid channelled through NGOs, not about government-to-government aid. If we should venture into the latter category we should face the awkward fact that the largest segment of Canadian aid to the Philippine government is in the form of commodity imports, the proceeds of which amount to budget supplements. In a situation where the military budget has risen rapidly in the last three years, can it not be said that Canadian aid helped make that possible? (To be sure, some commodity imports generated counterpart funds designated for public high schools.) Has peace flowed from this strength? It is difficult to make any such connection. Some other dimensions of Canadian aid, such as support to linkage projects between educational institutions, probably have a rather neutral impact on the peace promotion dimension. Let us, therefore, remain focused on aid through NGO channels.

But can we even assume that aid devoted to the purpose of development, if administered by NGOs, will help resolve conflict? A prior clarification of the nature of "development" and of "conflict" is in order. But before tackling the definitions we must recognize that whether it is $11 million for NRDF, $4.8 million initially for PDAP, or even $15 million for PCHRD, these are small sums in relation to an economy with an annual Gross Domestic Product (GDP) of over $40 billion. Canada is not a large actor on the Philippine scene, providing only about 1 percent of all ODA, and NGO administered funds are less than 15 percent of CIDA's Philippine budget—though a higher percentage than for any other donor to the Philippines. Yet "peace" or "conflict" are not social conditions or processes which can be measured quantitatively. Interventions which are quantitatively small can, if they are seen as morally right and based on an accurate assessment of the situation, have a significant impact on peace and conflict resolution. This is true, in part, because such interventions act as a catalyst to other groups and agencies, foreign and domestic. It may be a bit like acupuncture—if you hit the right nerve, you can do a lot with a single needle. Aid magnitude is not, therefore, by itself an important issue.

Except in Mindanao, conflict in the Philippines is not of ethnic origin, as it is in many parts of the third world, but is conflict among social classes—and perceived as such by the protagonists to an increasing degree. It occurs because at least a portion of the peasants and workers have become aware of the inequities heaped upon them by political and economic institutions and wish to change those institutions, or at least the policies they impose. Some are willing, if pressed, to use violence to achieve those ends, while others are not. Unfortunately the government often fails to make that distinction and thus by its actions drives the nonviolent into the arms of the violent—as has happened with so many basic Christian communities in Negros.

Because this is the nature of the conflict, it is clear that it cannot end without the widespread infusion of justice into social relations. It may be suppressed for a time, but then reappear, as it did in 1969. The appearance of peace may result from the exhaustion of the antagonists, but if the cause of the conflict is not removed, this appearance will be temporary. Under these circumstances, as Gerald Schmitz has noted, real peacemaking is "a call to nonviolent action to transform social structures."[12]

If peace requires justice, how is justice to be established? Does "development" insure social justice? If by development we mean simply economic growth, then the answer is clearly "no." All economists now agree that rapid growth inevitably increases social inequity, they only disagree on how much and for how long—and why. Fortunately, the concept of development which wraps greater equity into the required definition has had increasing use around the world in the last decade. It is largely a question of perspective: if you are a national economic planner it may be possible to equate Gross National Product (GNP) growth with "development," but, if you are poor peasant, "development" that makes the rich richer and leaves the poor behind is hardly to be desired. Let us define development, therefore, as growth with justice—and with empowerment of the powerless. For if the poor do not acquire the power to make effective demands for social justice, they will not get justice; it does not come automatically, even with a development strategy which sets out to allocate larger shares to the poor.

This was the problem in Negros. The rhetoric was right. The NRDF was to fund projects "benefiting the poor." The "guidelines" even announced that "NRDF seeks to foster the self-sufficiency and enhance the decision-making capacity of its target beneficiaries." Despite the guidelines, in the first year the funds were channelled through landlord foundations. NRDF bankrolled the preservation of existing patron-client relationships—far from the intended "transformation of existing social structures." This is not surprising, really. Foreign aid, or any other external intervention, cannot be neutral; it either reduces social justice or enhances it. The result is determined by the channel chosen. Since foreigners most often deal with political and economic elites, their assistance usually reinforces inequality.

In Negros in the 1980s there were important mass-based NGOs which, if they had been willing to implement projects for community organization and agricultural improvement, could probably have made a small contribution to the enhancement of social and political equity, and thus, potentially, to the resolution of conflict. Yet there were two reasons why that was unlikely. First, there was an ideological chasm in Negros in the 1980s between genuinely mass-based organizations, on the one hand, and the government and economic elite on the other. CIDA, whose personnel inevitably moved primarily in government and elite circles, found it very difficult to bridge the gap. Secondly, so did the mass-based organizations. They were deeply imbued with a "them-us" dichotomy, and CIDA officers seemed to be among "them," especially after the establishment of the NRDF board. To be sure, the Sugar Workers' Federation would probably have been happy to become the sole channel of CIDA funds in Negros, especially if they had been given entirely without strings or any kind of project supervision. For the Federation (NFSW) had priorities which sometimes conflicted with CIDA's ideas of full transfer of project funds to stated beneficiaries. (So also did landlord foundations; CIDA was not able to police their improper diversions of funds either.) In sum, polarization in Negros made it impossible for CIDA to deal even-handedly with oppressors and oppressed. There was a war going on and each side had marshalled its forces. Monsignor Rivas, standing in the midst of the battle, put it very gently; said he, "NRDF is a drop in the bucket toward real social change in Negros."

What happened to the Candoni postharvest facility in early 1989 helps to clarify the nature of the situation. The Candoni project allocated nearly P 3 million in July 1987 to the Negros Economic Development Foundation (NEDF,) originally founded by Governor Lacson, to buy a rice mill, threshers, and dryers. It was operational by 1988 and in March 1989 it was attacked and destroyed by the NPA—the first NRDF project to suffer in this way. Those attempting to explain, or even justify, the attack point to the tie with Governor Lacson and his increasing unpopularity in Communist circles. Some also suggest that the Samahang Nayon, or village co-operative, which was operating the rice mill, was controlled by the military—it did happen elsewhere—and was denying use of the mill to any farmers suspected of being communist. The Canadian Christian Anti-Communist Crusade, on the other hand, gloats that this action proves that Marxist revolutionaries really do not have the interest of farmers at heart but believe that the masses must suffer more in order to increase their commitment to armed struggle.[13] While such an idea can be extracted from Marxist literature, it is unlikely to guide local NPA commanders. Their followers were being denied the use of a needed facility, if it was controlled by the military, and thus NPA leaders acted within their framework of justice to destroy what was seen as primarily benefiting the "exploiters." Access to the mill was also consolidating a clientele which was being used against the left—a problem for the NFSW in most NRDF projects.

While it is thus probably inevitable that NRDF would itself become engulfed in the conflict in Negros, the way in which it was set up hastened the process. There was not a sufficiently careful prior study of the political situation and no evidence of "consultation" beyond the circle of Lacson's friends. Some of these same sorts of mistakes seemed to have been present in the formation of PDAP. NGO officers most eager to meet CIDA were those first contacted; out of this a program plan emerged. Serious consideration did not seem to be given to alternatives. Thus projects were funded which, even if they did not strengthen traditional patrons, as in Negros, were not exactly effective in mobilizing the poor in the struggle for justice. There is little evidence that initially PDAP contributed either to genuine development, including empowerment, or, therefore, to peacemaking, though later there was some desire to pursue these goals.

What is a source of hope is that CIDA seemed to have learned from earlier mistakes. The thoroughness and caution of the consultation leading up to the formation of PCHRD earned CIDA wide respect in the NGO community, thus forming the basis of trust for future co-operation. Furthermore, CIDA provided the venue for fruitful dialogue among Philippine NGOs that had never before met and may have previously viewed each other with suspicion. The dialogue and the opportunity to participate in a new NGO/development process strengthened the hand of the moderates on both left and right. Since NGOs across the spectrum have influential friends in both the government and opposition, if understanding is increased and hostility reduced among NGOs of different persuasion, it may rub off on other elites in conflict. PCHRD has also increased the chances for success of projects which include community organization and empowerment as well as welfare, and thus improve the prospects of a nonviolent struggle for justice.

The Philippine committee of PCHRD was, of course, not allowed to make political statements. Yet inevitably it was enmeshed in the political process. The felt need to respond to events around them brought a creative response from PCHRD affiliated NGOs—and some others—in the middle of 1990. Acting independently of the Canadian aid framework, they formed the Caucus of Development NGO Networks. The issue which spurred the creation of this new coalition was the discovery by President Aquino of the political uses of NGOs. She launched a national program, entitled Kabisig, to enlist local governments as well as NGOs in a network of government funded development projects. Hundreds of new "NGOs" were formed by local elites to be ready to avail themselves of the billions of pesos promised—shades of NRDF! Genuine NGOs were wary of this process, however, and most did not co-operate. The new caucus produced a statement in July explaining the rationale for this nonco-operation. It called Kabisig "a ploy for shifting resources for patronage away from traditional politicians in Congress to local governments." The statement continued: "Moreover, Philippine development NGOs, by nature, operate autonomous of government.

This being so, tapping development NGOs to become members of a government-initiated political movement, where they would become mere instruments in the implementation of government programs, would be tantamount to co-opting NGOs into government, violating the principle of NGO autonomy."

After the devastating earthquake in mid-July 1990 the caucus also called "upon the warring government and revolutionary forces to cease from hostilities and muster their energies toward assistance to the victims and their families during this period of emergency." Thus this caucus, claiming leadership of some 1,3000 NGOs, Peoples' Organizations, co-operative, church, and community groups, brought together largely because of participation in a Canadian-supported project, constituted perhaps the most direct linkage between aid and peacemaking. They had been able to bridge differences among their own constituencies to attempt a broader peace-promoting role.

Sober reflection, however, reminds us again that the role of CIDA and the NGOs in the total political and social system is still a minor one. So that the ability of PCHRD to contribute to peace promotion is heavily dependent on many other extraneous factors, most particularly on the attitudes of political and economic elites. Dark clouds have occasionally appeared in the sky. Congress debated a bill at one point to require a central government registry of all NGOs and PDOs, which would have demanded addresses of officers and lists of members—something that military intelligence had been wanting for a long time. But NGO lobbying helped head off congressional action. A similar threat was found, however, in the announcement by the Philippine military of a handsome price on the head of a top official of the National Council for People's Development (NCPD), an entirely legal organization.

These are hints that CIDA will be dragged into the fray on human rights violations if it is going to be able to preserve one of its most prestigious programs. In fact, if PCHRD members do become the targets of gross human rights violations and CIDA doesn't take a stand, the inaction could trigger so many withdrawals as to cause the program's collapse. A commitment to development with justice also requires, of necessity, a commitment to human rights. If external intervention is invited in one endeavour, it cannot be excluded from the other. The obstacles are many, as we have seen, but insofar as PCHRD can sustain dialogue across the political spectrum, and can promote development with justice, while protecting the human rights which must be exercised in that process, it will have made some contribution to conflict resolution and the promotion of peace in a land which has certainly enjoyed too little of it in recent years.

Notes

1. Gregg Jones, *Red Revolution: Inside the Philippine Guerrilla Movement*. (Boulder: Westview Press, 1989), p. 250.

2. See David Wurfel, "The Philippines' precarious democracy: Coping with foreign and domestic pressures under Aquino," *International Journal*, XLIV (Summer 1989): 676-697.

3. Association of Foundations, Philippine Partnership for the Development of Human Resources in Rural Areas (PHILDHRRA) the Asian NGO Coalition, Philippine Business for Social Progress (PBSP) and the Assisi Development Foundation, "Philippine Development Assistance Program: A Proposal," p. 9.

4. *Ibid.*, p. 19.

5. Canadian International Development Agency (CIDA). "CIDA in the Philippines: Operational Projects," (Hull: CIDA, 1988).

6. Negros Rehabilitation and Development Fund (NRDF). "Special Progress Report." (June 1987).

7. Peter Laurie, "Canada-Aid: Keeping the Peasants Down," *This Magazine* (1988): 23–29.

8. Canadian Council for International Co-operation (CCIC). "Report on Consultation Meetings between CIDA Philippines Bilateral Program and Canadian International Voluntary Development Organizations, Jan. & Feb. 1988." (Spring 1988), p. 6.

9. Romana de los Reyes et al, "Process Monitoring Report on the BARC in Barangay Sta. Rosa, Murcia, Negros Occidental," (Institute of Philippine Culture, Ateneo de Manila University, April 1989), p. 2,5, and pp. 7–8.

10. *Partnership: The Philippine-Canadian NGO Consultation for CIDA's Country Program Review*. (Tagaytay, Philippines, June 1988), xi.

11. *Ibid.*, p. 15.

12. Gerald Schmitz, "Aid and Peacemaking: Some Reflections," unpublished paper submitted to the second "Aid as Peacemaker" workshop (November 1989).

13. See "The CIDA Class War in Negros," *Canadian Digest* I:4 (October 1989).

Part II: Aid Channels

CIDA as Peacemaker:
Integration or Overload?

Gerald J. Schmitz
The North-South Institute*

> *We did an internal report which held up 10 objectives and showed that for each one of them there were objectives that went in entirely contrary directions, and yet all of them were endorsed objectives of the Canadian aid program.*

Margaret Catley-Carlson, President of CIDA, June 1985[1]

The basic notions underlying foreign aid are deceptively simple. We want to help less fortunate countries improve their standard of living and especially to alleviate the distress of millions of poor and hungry people. We give aid primarily for humanitarian reasons, but it is also seen to be a useful instrument of diplomacy and of mutual benefit in an increasingly interdependent global economy. At least that is what we tell ourselves. Over the years, as aid has been formalized into "official development assistance" (ODA), it has evolved into an enterprise much larger, more permanent and administratively complex than could have been envisaged when Canada began giving aid four decades ago. The Canadian International Development Agency (CIDA), established in 1968, has both benefited and suffered from this institutionalized expansion. CIDA has become another bureaucratic player in Ottawa's gray universe of acronyms, as vulnerable as any other to fiscal uncertainties and organizational and policy competition.

I do not know if "peace promotion" numbered among the ten contrary objectives mentioned by Catley-Carlson, CIDA's president from 1983 until 1989, but something similar and equally vague assuredly would have been included. Indeed the official "political" goal of the aid program describes it as "one means to increase stability and improve the chances for peace in the world." What this means concretely is another matter. Neither the nature of the concepts of "peace" and "development," nor the linkage between them, are self-evident. CIDA, moreover, is usually too preoccupied with juggling multiple priorities and managing its immediate bureaucratic environment to devote much attention to

* Currently Program Director for Human Rights and Democratic Government, on leave from the Library of Parliament Research Branch. This essay, written during 1989-90, has been slightly revised and updated. The views expressed remain those of the author alone.

such matters. One of the purposes of this essay, therefore, is to start the
process of thinking seriously about how CIDA might contribute to the
peaceful resolution of conflicts which are harming the development
prospects of many of its partners in the South.

This preliminary exploration will not shy from confronting the
peculiar difficulties of CIDA's situation: the external and internal bureaucratic constraints; the important controversies over using aid to
"export" Canadian values—even when these are seen to reflect universal
norms (e.g., human rights); the necessary rebalancing of priorities within
CIDA's decision "tree"; the myths and misunderstandings which clutter
much of the debate over so-called "motherhood" objectives; and, last but
not least, the practical problems associated with bringing new ideas to
bear on an agency which probably sees itself as already overloaded by
reformers' good intentions. Integrating a peace-building dimension into
the Canadian aid program seems nonetheless to be a worthy challenge,
even if it disturbs CIDA's peace along with that of more powerful
interests. That is an opening bias which I hope survives the test to which
it is put in the following pages.

The foreign policy environment and CIDA's choices

That CIDA is not the master of its own policy framework is perhaps to
state the obvious. It is, however, critical to understanding the responsive
capacity of the agency when new challenges are addressed to it. Unlike
the International Development Research Centre (at least until the 1992
federal budget), the Canadian Institute for International Peace and
Security (abolished by the 1992 budget), or the latest addition to the ODA
family, the International Centre for Human Rights and Democratic
Development, CIDA has never been an autonomous body with control
over its budget. It is an executive creation which operates as a "department" for the purposes of the Financial Administration Act, but has no
separate statutory existence. In 1987, the government rejected the recommendation in the Winegard report, *For Whose Benefit?*, that the aid
program administered by CIDA be given a specific legislative mandate.[2]
Moreover, the Minister of External Relations and International Development, responsible for CIDA's day-to-day activities, is only a junior
minister within the complex tripartite structure of External Affairs and
International Trade Canada (EAITC).[3] There is no assurance that CIDA's
concerns will be strongly represented at the cabinet table.

The history of the aid program shows that CIDA has scored few
victories in the games of interdepartmental bargaining and competition
for influence. The lack of result from the vaunted *Strategy for International
Development Cooperation 1975–1980* is a prime example of this relative
impotence and attendant policy dilemma. Bureaucratic politics are often

more decisive in determining what gets funded and what does not than the musings of politicians and vague assertions of goals put out for public consumption.[4] CIDA knows that, in general (there are exceptions), it is subject to strong domestic political and commercial pressures far more than it is able to bring to bear a third world development perspective on other aspects of Canada's foreign relations. That, combined with the effect of criticisms by successive auditors general, may help to explain why CIDA has tended to emphasize improved management of aid delivery over policy innovation—the "how" of what it already is doing over the "why not?" of what it could do if given the chance. Simply put, CIDA's job has been to carry out its assigned foreign policy tasks and to keep peace with as many constituencies as possible, while staying out of trouble and out of the way of more centrally placed bureaucratic actors.

CIDA's role within the foreign policy environment is primarily as an executing not a policy-making instrument. Nor should it be assumed that the foreign policy tasks referred to above fit into some rational and coherent overall design. Policy is much more driven by incrementalism, force of circumstances, or the changing preferences (and sensitivity to interest group and mass opinion) of elected officials and public servants. As McChesney and Berry observe: "In general, foreign policy-making in Canada is reactive, short term, ad hoc, and diffuse ... Broad or lofty principles have a rough time working their way through the bureaucracy to or from the minister."[5] In the case of CIDA and ODA, there are several ministers with whom to contend, and the principles are so loose and elastic as to give little actual guidance in deciding resource allocations. Of course choices have to be made. Some projects are approved; others not. Programs are expanded or cut. New ones are created. The process is seldom straightforward, transparent, or done with an eye to rigorous consistency.

The following description gives some reasons for the typical messiness of CIDA's environment.

> Foreign aid is a policy arena where a myriad of diverse interests converge and compete for favourable outcomes. Whatever rational objectives CIDA's ministers and managers may design for aid programs, they are constrained by a host of institutional actors, and, in turn, by their constituencies with their particular interests. In addition, CIDA's policy and program objectives have to be matched with the priorities of the recipient governments. If the policy-making process appears to be complex, its implementation occurs under even more trying circumstances.[6]

This picture may induce frustration on the part of CIDA's political and bureaucratic masters, but it can also be useful in fending off the "unrealistic" ideas of purists and idealists. Running a multibillion dollar aid program is no Sunday school exercise, they can be admonished.

As well, while humanitarian motives undergird public support for CIDA, it is important not to overlook the "realpolitik" which lies behind the origins and evolution of the Canadian aid program. During the formative years of the 1950s in particular, a key strategic-political justification for giving aid was to promote international peace and security— defined in Cold War terms to mean protecting Western security and economic interests against the spread of Communism. This rationale largely disappeared in subsequent decades, leaving only a lingering faith in global economic advancement as a means to peaceful coexistence. Meanwhile, conflicts in the South multiplied. Now, at the threshold of a post-Cold War era of common security arrangements, it may be opportune to renew the peace-promoting role of aid freed from the dead weight of superpower rivalries and ideological competition for spheres of influence. It is at least worth asking whether part of an anticipated, if so far elusive, East-West "peace dividend" can be captured for peaceful development purposes in the South.

Involving CIDA in conflict reduction and management, or more positively in "peace-building" activities, nonetheless represents an explicit repoliticization of the aid program which is not without considerable political risk. This is not a choice of direction which CIDA could make on its own, apart from funnelling an occasional small amount of money to nongovernmental organizations (NGOs) engaged in working for peaceful changes within conflict ridden societies. Strong commitment would have to come from the government, specifically the Secretary of State for External Affairs, with CIDA's peace efforts receiving full cabinet and departmental backing. Moreover, the political impetus would have to overcome the organizational and policy fatigue which the aid agency probably feels in the wake of recent reviews and the difficulties of implementing decentralization and the rest of the new *Sharing Our Future* strategy with fewer resources than expected. More attention to peace promotion within the CIDA program is not likely to succeed in this climate if it is seen simply to add to the burden on the aid agency without first having been absorbed into the existing priorities, decision structures, and resource use patterns of ODA.

Problems of values promotion in the Canadian aid program

There are probably those within CIDA who would like to conceive of ODA as a technical resource transfer, nothing more. Aid helps poor countries to build roads, schools, hospitals, etc., and generally to boost living standards and national income. The volume of aid should roughly correspond to the extent of the "need" (which is seldom defined by the poor themselves); otherwise aid should have no normative, political, or—worse—ideological, agenda of its own. The problem with this one dimensional view of aid is that it is ahistorical and deceptive.

First, the Canadian aid program has always involved much more than supposedly altruistic technical assistance. The focus of the Colombo Plan on Commonwealth nations and the Communist threat in Asia was surely no accident. The high level of "tying"—the requirement that assistance take the form of Canadian goods and services—reflects a judgement, however flawed, about the interests of the Canadian state. Political and economic considerations have quite openly, and as a matter of course, influenced country eligibility and the size of aid allocations. Western notions of what constitutes good economic and development policy have been transferred along with the concessional loans and grants. In the 1980s, economic "conditionality" became very explicit as most developing countries were pressured into adopting "structural adjustment" programs. Acceptance of these donor prescriptions can be a strict condition of receiving any aid at all.

Second, as the aid program has grown and diversified, the governmental policy framework within which it is enmeshed has become more complex and exacting. The ethical issues surrounding ODA have similarly evolved beyond simple humanitarian impulses. Partly this is a reflection of changes in our own society and of increased questioning of the dominant development paradigm. If aid is working, why are there still so many poor and hungry people? Why are there so many human rights violations in the South? Why so few stable and functioning democracies? Why so much environmental destruction? With more awareness of the difficult, necessary political process for achieving sustainable human-centred development, these value laden concerns have been pressed with vigour on official Ottawa through parliamentary and other public channels.

There are at least four values, based on a "cosmopolitan" global ethics, which the Canadian aid program claims to promote: maximizing benefits to the poor, improving the condition of women, increasing observance of internationally recognized standards of human rights, and minimizing environmental damage from development. To this list has now been added democratic "participatory development" and "good governance," though these goals are more contentious and less defined. CIDA has adopted as its mission "sustainable development"—economic, social, environmental, cultural, and political.

Before adding "peace promotion" to the above lists, questions need to be raised about how well these officially proclaimed values and orientations have been in fact digested by CIDA and embraced by its policy-making masters. Cranford Pratt argues that government responses have lagged behind an apparent "humane internationalist" consensus within parliament and the political culture at large.[7] Indeed, he contends that during the past decade there has been an erosion of the ethical content of Canada's North-South policies. Analyzing three major foreign policy statements between 1978 and 1986 he finds:

> The references to ethical obligations towards the peoples of the third world in these official documents are limited and cramped. This is in significant contrast with earlier policy statements. *Foreign Policy for Canadians*, the 1970 white paper, listed the promotion of social justice as one of the six basic objectives of Canadian foreign policy. It commented that unless Canadian social values were conceded an influence on foreign policy they would be likely to atrophy at home. The CIDA strategy paper of 1975 acknowledged that changes to the international economic order were needed in the interest of equity. As well, Prime Minister Trudeau recurrently acknowledged the force of this argument. There is, in contrast, no recognition in the more recent documents of any Canadian interest in reforms to the international economic order in pursuit of equity, and no mention of the need for foreign policy to be ethically responsible or to reflect Canadian values.[8]

This assessment may be unduly pessimistic, but there is no doubt that government responses have been equivocal on the more contentions issues of attaching value based conditions to the aid program—the primary instrument of Canadian foreign policy in many developing countries. Despite the 1988 strategy paper's declaration that human rights criteria are to be a factor in determining aid eligibility, Canada has been slow to develop an integrated human rights oriented approach to development assistance. Decisions taken on human rights grounds are still quite rare and seldom unambiguous. Indeed, argues Pratt, "when a strong lead is given politically for a more forceful human rights policy, there is a recurrent tendency for the bureaucracy to minimize its significance rather than to capitalize upon it."[9] This has not changed much, notwithstanding the prime minister's bold statements to Commonwealth and Francophone summit meetings in the fall of 1991, linking human rights to aid. As well, there is no indication of more than a tiny fraction of the aid budget being devoted directly to human rights promotion.

In discussing an earlier draft of this paper, Julian Payne of CIDA vigorously defended official efforts to put Canadian ODA on a values based footing. Yet his challenge to Pratt's argument must be measured against his evident annoyance that CIDA's job has already been made too difficult without adding peace making activities to the list. I believe Payne's protests tend to confirm Pratt's thesis as stated. When it comes to the ethical content of foreign policy, the pressures to stand pat or do less cannot be ignored because they often outweigh the voices raised in support of an expanded internationalism.

Reinforcing internal impediments to policy change are fears that donors' value judgements might constitute undesirable "interference" in the sovereign affairs of other countries. Canadians are understandably sceptical of American style appeals to impose "Western values" on

weaker nations, especially given the sorry history of U.S. economic and
security assistance to governments with notorious human rights records.
Even in the new East-West climate created by Mikhail Gorbachev, some
Americans who supported President Reagan's "democracy crusade" of
the early 1980s believed that the U.S. must continue to wage the struggle
"militarily, economically, politically, and ideologically." Following "victory" in the Cold and Gulf wars, the pursuit of development, human
rights, and peace may still be assumed to be within the context of a *Pax
Americana* (updated as the New World Order), or at least a Western
capitalist ethos.[10]

Canada has generally eschewed such combative, interventionist
approaches in favour of quiet, preferably multilateral, diplomacy. Fortunately, with regard to bilateral actions as well, there are the positive
examples of international values promotion by highly respected Nordic
aid donors.[11] It is much easier to justify the normative context of an aid
program when its clear purpose is the developmental benefit of the
recipient, as distinct from considerations of strategic self-interest by the
donor state. Nonetheless, even when the values being promoted are
proclaimed to be "universal," great care and sensitivity need to be
exercised so that recipients are also involved in the decision-making
process. It is not enough for Canadians to agree among themselves
without listening to their ODA partners. As Martin Rudner cautions:

> The precedence given to domestic consultation over development dia-
> logue suggests there may indeed be elements of policy tension and even
> goal conflict between the two. In particular, the emphases placed on
> human rights, on women and on the environment enter into the new
> strategy as quasi-conditions of Canadian development assistance policy.
> This is tantamount to imposing normative forms of conditionality on
> Canadian ODA. It is certainly Canada's sovereign right to attach policy
> conditions and precepts to its aid contributions, especially when these
> represent the normative prescriptions of the Canadian public and Parlia-
> ment. And yet Canadians should be aware that developing countries as
> a group vehemently decry any and all policy conditionality as a matter of
> principle. The manifest preference of government and public for domestic
> consultations on aid policy implicitly subordinates the principle of devel-
> opment dialogue to the politics of policy conditionality in Canadian
> development assistance.[12]

The most difficult cases for CIDA and the government are likely to
be situations which are full of conflict and ideologically polarized.
Decision makers will be pressed by domestic constituencies and their
own guidelines to "do the right thing." At the same time, taking certain
normative actions such as denying aid on human rights grounds may
limit future influence and preclude Canada playing an effective peacemaking role. In other words, ethical foreign policy objectives which are
mutually reinforcing in theory can result in uneasy trade-offs in the field.

A primary task, therefore, should be to minimize these compromises. What is needed is a better way of integrating clear aid objectives within overall international policy and the elaboration of a judicious public policy framework on values based interventions which is coherent, consistent, and therefore credible. That means the process leading to decisions and their implementation must be substantial enough and transparent enough to been seen by Canadians as worth supporting.

Between maintaining the fiction that our aid is neutral or value free, and seeking to impose our values on others, there is ample ground to be explored. For Canada to enter into productive dialogue with aid recipients, clarity is essential about developmental objectives and purposes, and the ethical dimensions of these. As yet, however, the Canadian aid machinery often seems unprepared for that sort of engagement. One result of muddled policy on "conditionality" and values promotion is that the role of aid will remain too often poorly understood or subject to sharply conflicting interpretations. At a time when public support for a large ODA budget seems soft, this should be a prime source of concern to CIDA policy makers.

Inside CIDA's "Christmas tree": root and branch or ornament?

One interpretation advanced by CIDA insiders likens the aid agency to an overburdened "Christmas tree." Politicians and well-intentioned reformers keep adding attractive objectives and conditions to the ODA program tree without fully realizing the expenditure consequences in terms of scarce time and resources. CIDA as "peacemaker?" One can almost hear a chorus of sighs that CIDA is already too busy trying to show how it is being environmentally sensitive while promoting respect for human rights and the role of women. With due respect to Julian Payne, there is a mostly unspoken implication that these more recent goals interfere with, or are at least not central to, CIDA's main task, which is to distribute aid from Canada to places where it is needed, serving Canada's foreign policy interests in the process. From a "realist" perspective, the weight of new policy ideas and the corporate energy consumed in order to appear responsive to these ideas, is viewed sceptically as a drag on efficient aid delivery.

The more idealistically minded within CIDA would probably agree with its critics that such a perception is exaggerated and unhelpful. Yet they also observe that in the actual process of determining the aid program, the major pressures are usually fiscal and bureaucratic, not pressures created by a creative rethinking of development policy. Administrative realism remains the order of the day. Conversations with CIDA officials confirm the constant pressure to move money, contracts, and projects. When new ideas are accepted, often rather equivocally, at the policy level, it is far easier simply to repackage what CIDA is already doing (or planning to do) in light of these ideas than to begin redesigning the content of programs or devising new ways of delivering aid. In other words, the politicians' speeches and the public presentation may change, but, for most CIDA employees, it will be business as usual. The decentralization initiative combined with a loosening of tying rules might have been expected to shake things up and encourage ideas to percolate up from practitioners in the field; yet in the context of budgetary cutbacks, hard scrutiny of costs tends to overshadow the benefits to be realized from progressive innovation. In a defensive and apprehensive CIDA, performance may fall short of promise. For each step forward, there is a nervous reaction and subsequent retrenchment. It is too soon to tell whether a strategic management review of the organization during 1991–92 will allow CIDA to escape this corporate mold.

Risk-taking creativity has been more possible so far on a small scale in the "special" programs branch of the CIDA tree. It has not been a noted feature of the main program trunk which still relies heavily on tied food aid, lines of credit, and commodity transfers. In only one area (not counting environment and development) has values based programming really developed. The evolution of the Women in Development (WID) program is instructive in part because it is exceptional. The WID policy framework benefited from fortunate timing. It was put in place when women's equality rights has just been enshrined in the Canadian constitution. During WID's formative years, both the ministers responsible and the president of CIDA were women. WID's staff is small—six officers plus consultants in 1990—but it makes up a division with its own director in the professional services branch, having moved out from the policy branch into the main operational trunk of CIDA. Given sufficient political consensus and will, the WID policy had the chance to secure its place institutionally. Although new questions are being raised about the policy's effectiveness and adequacy, in decision-making terms, WID has arrived: it cannot be dismissed as a mere ornament on the ODA tree.[13]

Subsequent attempts to attach a comprehensive set of human rights policy conditions to CIDA programs stand in marked contrast. Although the 1987 Winegard report, *For Whose Benefit?* strongly urged the elaboration of an operational "human rights in development" policy framework, there is still resistance to moving forward in creating one. At the political level there is acceptance of the principle that human rights should be an important factor in development assistance decisions. Still government responses sometimes give the impression of being more cosmetic than concrete.[14] For example, CIDA's new "human rights unit" turned out to consist of a single individual. The annual report for 1987–88 contained nary a word on human rights, and occasional references to human rights in subsequent agency documents merely repeat statements of intent taken from the 1988 *Sharing Our Future* strategy document. Unlike the cases of WID or environmental assessment criteria, mention of a specific developing country's circumstances or Canadian actions is rare except when included for effect in ministers' speeches.

Recent years' budget cutting exercises have provided little evidence of the weight given to inclusion of human rights judgements in aid decisions. Following the budget of April 1989, cuts were determined without apparent reference to human rights concerns, although memoranda to cabinet do contain such information. The process itself is secretive and not designed for public enlightenment. The numbers tell a story, however. In addition to administrative decentralization and public affairs, the only area of funding growth that year was industrial cooperation, a program responsive to Canadian business which aims to boost private sector involvement in third world development. Also spared from the budget axe was a $60 million Canadian contribution to an International Monetary Fund (IMF) structural adjustment program for Guyana. While the money was to come from CIDA, the policy initiative in this case came from the Department of Finance. Indeed the linkage of bilateral ODA to market oriented economic prescriptions, enforced by the international financial institutions, has emerged as a central element of aid policy conditionality, a trend reinforced by the return of Marcel Massé to CIDA's presidency from his position as Canada's executive director at the IMF.[15]

So while support for structural adjustment has quickly become a root and branch aspect of CIDA programming in some debtor countries, human rights promotion might more aptly be compared to a tender new shoot with a few fluttering leaves. The government did approve, in December 1986 (even before the Winegard report), the idea of an institute for human rights and democratic development, and Parliament passed a statute creating an International Centre for that purpose in Montreal in 1988, but it took several more years for it to become operational. (Ed Broadbent was appointed its first president in early 1990). Beyond its work to create another specialized institution, CIDA supports a growing number of activities which promote human rights values. Examples include grants to various human rights bodies and advocacy groups, to NGOs such as Peace Brigades International, and the channeling of aid through innovative partnerships with grassroots organizations. Yet the whole is less than the sum of these ad hoc or arm's length parts. One still does not get the sense, as with the economic policy conditions, that a human rights approach is solidly rooted in CIDA's thinking, structures, and operations.

The place of values within Canadian aid programs therefore remains somewhat in limbo despite occasional acknowledgements of the interrelationship of development, human rights, peace, and social justice.

Values based objectives and conditions are clearly more than trouble-some ornaments on CIDA's Christmas tree, but they have not been consistently embraced either, or their implications fully understood. In the mid-1980s, Canada suspended aid to a major project in Sri Lanka on explicit human rights grounds. Funding was only resumed when Canada was satisfied that the climate had improved and benefits would be shared by the Tamil population. This was an example, however isolated at the time, of a human rights action with a potential peace-building effect. Despite the ongoing violence afflicting that troubled land, Canada has tried to exert a human rights presence.

The Guyanese case was different. Canadian involvement became an object of protest both in Guyana and among Canadian NGOs because of its support for an IMF adjustment program which increased societal tensions and conflict. Critics wanted aid and debt relief tied instead to human rights observance and democratic reform. In 1991, Canada was out front in efforts to restore democracy in Haiti after a violent coup. But the imposition of sanctions perversely cut off assistance to prodemocracy forces within the civil society even while it hurt the regime. This untidy picture raises doubts about making room for possible peace objectives on CIDA's unsteady decision tree.

Conceptualizing peace promotion as part of the Canadian aid "vocation"

It is not necessarily CIDA's fault that Canada's aid programs send out mixed signals. Aid is part of a foreign policy which serves multiple interests. To ask for a completely values based foreign policy is to ask the impossible. In addition, I share the concerns raised by Julian Payne that ODA loses focus and impact when it is asked to do too much in too many places, perhaps being pushed into roles that, although worthy, may not be appropriate. Yet it is legitimate to query whether CIDA possesses a coherent normative philosophy of human centred development or a clear eyed, critical vision of how to apply its stated principles to concrete situations. Without such an operative framework, real engagement in the risky business of peacemaking will not happen even if opportunities exist for such a role. Canada will accept well-earned plaudits for partici-pating in multilateral peacekeeping functions, but no more.

There are several conceptual obstacles to further engagement by CIDA which need to be addressed. The first is the comforting notion that CIDA is successful precisely because it avoids taking a stand, much less taking sides, in an actual conflict situation. Calling aid a "Canadian vocation," CIDA's former president wrote that: "Canadians are quite united in the view that there is no single way to do anything. Perhaps the struggle to survive—despite climate, domination, and competition—has fostered the attitudes, skills, and habits of consensus building, compromise, and negotiation. There is no 'Canadian way.' So we listen. Around the world, governments have made a point of praising not only Canada's involvement in projects, but its spirit of balance, flexibility, and willingness to incorporate others' values."[16] Whatever values we have, we do not impose them. In other words, we are acceptable because we choose not to make ourselves unacceptable?

A pose of virtuous moderation can be an asset in trying to maintain *bona fides* with many different regimes. Yet in making it appear as though Canada has no agenda of its own, it ignores the other interests of the Canadian state as well as the reality that aid is not a neutral instrument and never less so than today. In the case of Guyana cited earlier, Canadian aid was tied explicitly to adherence to IMF prescriptions which are far from "value free," with predictably controversial results. If Canada is prepared to take the heat in order to promote economic discipline in developing countries, what justification remains for not doing so in the similarly perilous pursuit of human rights and pacific goals in these countries? Instead of trying to close the barn door when the horses have already left, the real issues are which ones to ride and how.

The second obstacle to critical engagement is to assume that the relationship of peace to development, and by extension development assistance, can be passive and linear—that no special effort is required because aid supports economic development and therefore by definition helps bring about peace and prosperity. In fact, the very meanings of "peace" and "development" are the subjects of highly charged political and ideological debates. What if building peace means having to disturb the peace of those who benefit from a violent status quo? Perhaps peace with justice is even a revolutionary project.[17] Is not peace part of the realization of fundamental human rights?[18] And so on. At the polar opposite, peace can also be identified with counterrevolution: with "pacification" and security assistance to governments which violate human rights ostensibly to preserve stability and social order. The disputes over the appropriation of this "motherhood" goal have consequences beyond the semantic which cannot be escaped.

Linking foreign aid to peace in more than a symbolic way means entering the real world of political-ideological struggles in which the development process is often a primary arena of social conflict. Working for peace, beyond the goals of mere "stability" or "coexistence," might logically entail helping to defend peasants against landowners in Brazil or the front line states against South African state terrorism. Peace promotion might involve supporting nonviolent resistance to unjust social structures—to the "established disorder," as Emmanuel Mounier called it. At the same time, there are many kinds of conflict—for example, interethnic and religious rivalries—which are inimical to social peace and have no conceivable developmental role. Before CIDA acts in a given circumstance, it therefore needs to understand the roots of the different conflicts and to be able to discriminate among them on developmental grounds.

Bearing this in mind there are several ways in which CIDA resources could be deployed for peace-building purposes within third world conflict situations: First, at a minimum, aid can help the victims of violence: the wounded, the displaced, those who have lost possessions and perhaps their means of livelihood, the refugees forced to flee their own countries.

Second, Canadian policies can stress respect for human rights and the need for political dialogue. Programs can be designed to promote direct participation by the poor in peaceful development, to make them more aware of and better able to defend their rights, and to encourage governments to listen to their concerns. In this regard, CIDA has drawn some lessons from its experience with the ill-fated Negros project in the Philippines. The result is a more genuine partnership involving NGOs in a Philippines-Canada Human Resources Development Fund (PCHRD). A similar fund exists for Sri Lanka.

Third, CIDA can try to identify with and give concrete support to what Brazilian Archbishop Helder Camara calls the "abrahamic minorities" which exist in every country and social situation. These are dedicated individuals and groups who typically operate at the small, grassroots level to bring about change through nonviolent action within their communities. They are courageous civic leaders, speakers for rural and urban workers, educators, church and human rights activists, and many unsung people in all walks of life. They are central to the process of human development. Even in the worst situations of conflict, it may be possible to assist them through the equally courageous work of Canadian and international NGOs in the field. Some of these directly focus on peace work—e.g., International Alert, Peace Brigades International, and—in Canada—the Central American Monitoring Group. Aid could be used to support a wide range of activities from human rights and peace education, developing codes of conduct, and maintaining international solidarity and monitoring networks, to setting up local peace councils and building a base for popular democratic institutions.[19]

Fourth, Canadian aid programs can be designed to complement local, regional, and international efforts at conflict resolution. Areas to be explored include professional training for police forces, alternative socially based civilian defences, instruction in conflict resolution techniques, legal defence and aid funds, and indirect mediation—for example using the churches, on behalf of those caught in or returning to conflict zones. An aid package might follow up diplomatic mediation by donor nations and the sending of multilateral observer or peacekeeping forces—as in Namibia, Central America, and Cambodia. More provocatively, ODA might be explicitly linked to acceptance of peace talks and political negotiations en route to demilitarization, with future commitments contingent on observance of the terms of peace settlements. Former Costa Rican President and Nobel Peace Prize winner Oscar Arias argued for this sort of "peace conditionality".

To date, CIDA has not been, nor I sense wanted to be, in the front lines of peace struggles in the South. The odd small grant through the country focus or NGO channel does not constitute an approach to, much less a strategy for, using aid in conflict situations. Once the conceptual underbrush has been cleared, however, opportunities are exposed to make working for peace part of Canada's aid vocation. CIDA is still being challenged to move beyond the notion of aid as a quantitative transfer from "us" to "them," towards a more holistic (i.e., realistic) and solidarity oriented model of development co-operation which seeks security and justice for all.

Integrating peace objectives into ODA policies and programs

Some Practical Considerations

The analysis to this point suggests that CIDA is not yet ready to assume a substantial peacemaking role and all the risks and burdens which go along with such a role. Moreover, foreign policy, institutional, and conceptual impediments habitually weaken whatever resolve exists to take strong stands rooted in fundamental values. Realistically, that will not change, nor peace promotion become an integral dimension of Canadian aid, without progress on most if not all of the following:

Resources

Implementing new ideas and reorienting existing programs is costly in both financial and human terms. If CIDA is continually fighting fiscal restraint battles, the accent will be on defending rather than acquiring new territory, and on avoiding political risk. ODA growth per se is not the answer, but a supportive and reasonably predictable funding environment is a prerequisite for substantial consideration of peace-building activities.

Political energy

Bureaucratic coolness to using aid as an instrument of values promotion, combined with normal institutional inertia, means that strong ministerial advocacy is essential. The government, and specifically the Secretary of State for External Affairs, must agree that this is an appropriate role for CIDA.

Policy coherence

This applies to Canada's relations with a particular country and to CIDA's priorities. Unless the intended overall effect of Canadian policy is to be peace promoting, support for a few individual projects will tend to remain token and basically passive.

Policy dialogue with recipients

A changed approach must take place within the developing country environment, not just in the realm of vague rhetorical assertion as a public relations response to constituency demands within Canada. Working for peace means CIDA being willing and able to work in solidarity with people caught up in conflict situations and with peace-seeking popular democratic organizations.

Information and analysis

Interventions should not take place without a precise understanding of conflicts and the capacity for proper intelligence gathering and evaluation. It is unrealistic to expect CIDA to play a substantive peacemaking role in Central America, for example, when at times there has been only one Canadian embassy in the region. While it is fine to support multilateral actions, Canada needs a significant long-term presence of its own on the ground to be considered more than a marginal player. Given limited resources, this means choosing carefully where to intervene and how.

Public pressure

It is easier for CIDA not to act than to stick out its neck. Promoting values beyond one's borders is guaranteed to bring on diplomatic and bureaucratic headaches. Public indifference means that difficult decisions can be side-stepped and that the burden of intervention is either not accepted or quietly abandoned.

In sum, overloading CIDA with policy ideas is unlikely to produce beneficial results unless effective means exist which integrate these ideas into the basic operating framework of External Affairs and aid. If peace promotion is perceived by decision makers as merely a troublesome, optional, or superficial activity, it will receive no more than polite attention in the present funding climate. Accepting the challenge of CIDA as peacemaker means convincing the Canadian public and government that a more active engagement in resolving conflicts is necessary to the achievement of Canada's stated ODA goals, and ultimately, therefore, in the Canadian interest.

Conclusions and postscript

Writing in the spring of 1992, much has changed around the globe. The verdict of the preceding sentences stands, however. While the aid program is more politically vulnerable than ever, CIDA is contemplating a major internal restructuring to outfit itself as a leaner, more "strategic" organization, capable of rising to the development challenges of the next century. Surely one of these challenges is building North-South peace and security links in a disorderly, polyglot universe of more states exercising less sovereignty. To leave strife torn societies to their fate would be to turn our backs on hopes for human rights and democratic development. Yet as John Siebert and Menno Wiebe observed in April 1991, surveying the aftermath of the Gulf war and the devastation in the Horn of Africa, CIDA "appears stuck with sending humanitarian aid to war zones while giving little or no thought to contributions it can make to resolving those conflicts. This is a glaring omission in Canada's strategies to fight third world poverty. CIDA requires a policy on conflict resolution to enable it to address conflicts as a root cause of poverty."[20]

Subsequent statements by the Prime Minister and the Secretary of State for External Affairs have seemed strongly to support international interventions, especially by the United Nations, in the name of ending violent conflicts and upholding universal human values. Canadian policy has been carried along by the now flickering optimism about a "new world order" of liberal democracy.[21] Second thoughts have arrived. Canada itself may no longer be a "peaceable kingdom." So what is next, not only for CIDA? The question begs an answer. Can we get our own act together in time to help a troubled world which will not wait for us?

Notes

1. Testimony before the House of Commons Standing Committee on Public Accounts, cited in House of Commons Standing Committee on External Affairs and International Trade (SCEAIT), *Discussion Paper on Issues in Canada's Official Development Assistance Policies and Programs* (Ottawa, July 1986), p. 8.

2. SCEAIT, *For Whose Benefit?*, Report on Canada's Official Development Assistance Policies and Programs (Ottawa: Queen's Printer for Canada, May 1987), p. 12 and 73; Government of Canada, *Canadian International Development Assistance: To Benefit A Better World* (Ottawa: Supply and Services, 1987), pp. 41 and 77.

3. The department added "international trade" to its title in 1989. (In a Freudian misprint, the spine of the department's 1990–91 Part III Expenditure Plan further amended that to "External Affairs and Free Trade Canada!") While trade's star has been rising, North-South concerns have been receding as a focus of bureaucratic attention and energy.

4. Cf. Gerald Wright, "Bureaucratic Politics and Canada's Foreign Economic Policy," in *Selected Problems in Formulating Foreign Economic Policy* eds. Denis Stairs and Gilbert Winham (Toronto: University of Toronto Press, 1985).

5. Victoria Berry and Allan McChesney, "Human Rights and Foreign Policy-Making," in *Human Rights in Canadian Foreign Policy* eds. Robert O. Matthews and Cranford Pratt (Montreal: McGill-Queen's University Press, 1988), p. 62.

6. Nasir Islam, "For Whose Benefit? Smoke and Mirrors: CIDA's Development Assistance Program in the 1980s," in *How Ottawa Spends 1988/89* ed. Katherine A. Graham, (Toronto: James Lorimer and Company, 1988), p. 195–6.

7. Cranford Pratt, "Ethics and foreign policy: the case of Canada's development assistance," *International Journal* (Spring 1988): p. 264–301.

8. C. Pratt, "Canada," in *Internationalism Under Strain: The North-South Policies of Canada, the Netherlands, Norway, and Sweden* ed. C. Pratt (Toronto: University of Toronto Press, 1989), pp. 59–60.

9. Cranford Pratt, "The Limited Place of Human Rights in Canadian Foreign Policy," in *Human Rights, Development and Foreign Policy: Canadian Perspectives* ed. Irving Brecher (Halifax: The Institute for Research on Public Policy, 1989), p. 173.

10. Cf. Raymond Gastil, "Aspects of a U.S. Campaign for Democracy," in *Promoting Democracy: Opportunities and Issues* eds. Ralph Goldman and William Douglas (New York: Praeger, 1988); also Stephen Blank et. al., *Low-intensity conflict in the Third World* (Washington, D.C.: U.S. G.P.O., 1988). For the perverse results, see the Lawyers Committee on Human Rights, *Linking Security Assistance and Human Rights* (New York: 1988 Project Series, no. 3). For a sweeping critique, see Noam Chomsky, *Deterring Democracy* (London: Verso, 1991); also Jack Donnelly, "Human Rights in the New World Order," *World Policy Journal* vol IX, no. 2 (Spring 1992): 249–77.

11. Gerald Schmitz and Victoria Berry, *Human Rights: Canadian Policy Towards Developing Countries* (Ottawa: The North-South Institute, December 1988), pp. 7–8.

12. Martin Rudner, "New Dimensions in Canadian Development Assistance," in *Canada Among Nations, The Tory Record/1988* eds. Maureen Molot and Brian Tomlins (Toronto: James Lorimer and Company, 1989), p. 162.

13. WID's agenda was set out in a five year CIDA action plan, *Integration of Women in Development*, June 1986, which has received a full corporate review and evaluation.

14. See my "Between Political Principle and State Practice: Human Rights `Conditionality' in Canada's Development Assistance," in ed. Brecher, *Human Rights, Development*, p. 467-85; also David Gillies, "Human Rights and Foreign Policy: We've Only Just Begun," *Policy Options*, March 1990, pp. 7–9. Similarly challenging conclusions were reached in a thorough and systematic empirical appraisal of recent Canadian aid performance in light of human rights criteria by T.A. Keeenleyside and Nola Serkasevich, "Canada's aid and human rights observance," *International Journal* XLV, no.1 (Winter 1989-90): 138–69.

15. See Charlotte Montgomery, "Canada decides: who will get aid?" *Globe and Mail*, 22 July 1989; Joydeel Mukherji, "Canada stressing free-market policies in foreign aid programs," *Globe and Mail*, 25 July 1989.

16. Margaret Catley-Carlson, "Aid: A Canadian Vocation," *Daedalus* 117 (Fall 1988): p. 329-30.

17. See Dom Helder Camara, *Revolution Through Peace* (New York: Harper & Row, Publishers, 1971).

18. Cf. *Human Rights and Peace* ed. Michael Hudson (Montreal: Canadian Human Rights Foundation, 1985).

19. See the wealth of suggestions in Edmundo Garcia, "Resolution of Internal Armed Conflict in the Philippines: The Quest for a Just and Lasting Peace in the Period of Democratic Transition," paper for the International Conference on Conflict Resolution, Manila University, the Philippines, December 1988.

20. John Siebert and Menno Wiebe, "Linking economic aid to peace," *Ottawa Citizen*, 25 April 1991, p. A13.

21. For a critical survey see my chapter "Human Rights, Democratization, and International Conflict," in *Canada Among Nations 1992–93: A New World Order?* eds. Fen O. Hampson and Christopher J. Maule (Ottawa: Carleton University Press, 1992). On the underlying issues of democratization, see also Gerald Schmitz and David Gilles, *The Challenge of Democratic Development: Sustaining Democratization in Developing Societies* (Ottawa: The North-South Institute, 1992).

United Nations Peacekeeping in a New Era: Implications for Canada

Gregory Wirick

Parliamentary Centre for Foreign Affairs and Foreign Trade

Suddenly, the world has entered a new era. The Cold War is over. The modern age is passé. But despite brave talk about a "new world order," the shape of this new era remains opaque. It is far easier to define contemporary events by what they are not than by what they are.

The international community may be in for a prolonged period of uncertainty. Some trends—such as the growth of regional trading blocs and the increasing permeability of national borders—point toward increased multilateral co-operation, while others, like the upsurge in ethnocultural conflict, have dramatized the limitations of such co-operation. The result is likely to be considerable experimentation as the search intensifies for different ways of organizing the world and dealing with the multitude of problems which afflict it.

A sentiment widely shared among the Group of Seven and other national leaders is that the United Nations, if altered and adapted, could be applied with greater success than in the past to a number of the more intractable problems. The new found consensus among the permanent members of the UN Security Council has galvanized the world body into taking a far more activist and interventionist approach than ever before in its history.

Such an approach is fraught with considerable peril for UN institutions. The UN has always been an instrument of order, but in the past it was also seen as an instrument of justice. In a new era that may be characterized as much by disorder as order, the UN may find itself favouring one principle at the expense of the other with some regularity. This, in turn, could have a deleterious effect on perceptions of UN objectivity.

Balancing the demands of order and justice may prove to be the central challenge of the new era for the United Nations. Yet striking this balance is of critical importance to one of the growth areas in recent UN activity: peacekeeping, in which objectivity is a cherished principle. What is more, the direction in which peacekeeping has been tending in the new era adds still greater significance to maintaining the balance. More and more, peacekeeping is being considered one element in a continuum of increasingly interrelated UN services which range from preventive diplomacy to economic development.

In the sphere of peace and security, the UN is evolving into a service institution, capable of providing the international community with a host of complementary services to facilitate negotiation, conciliation and—provided there is both luck and will—the actual resolution of various conflicts.[1] This diversity of services argues for examining more closely the actual origins of peacekeeping in order to understand better how it might be effectively adapted to meet new circumstances.

Peacekeeping origins

There have been few trouble spots which have not received the UN's attention, if not always outright assistance. In some instances, developments have permitted the insertion of one of this century's greatest contributions to confidence building: the deployment of peacekeeping or observation troops to the area of hostilities. Peacekeeping was an innovation; its invention was neither provided for nor foreseen in the UN Charter. In that document, the maintenance of peace and security was encouraged by negotiation, mediation, arbitration and judicial procedures under Chapter VI and by military means under Chapter VII. The subsequent development of peacekeeping was "a response to historical necessity."[2]

Between 1945 and 1978, the United Nations set up thirteen peacekeeping and observation missions, followed by a hiatus of ten years. For the most part, according to former UN Under Secretary-General Sir Brian Urquhart, these operations were like a "'sheriff's posse,' mustered at the last minute to prevent the worst." As such they provided "a safety net and an alternative to active confrontation between East and West."[3] Perhaps because of its "extracurricular" origins, peacekeeping has proved to be a quite flexible instrument. Such adaptability is critical to its continuing usefulness.

An integrated approach

The aftermath of a conflict situation can be roughly divided into three phases: stabilization, reconstruction, and development. At first, all that may be attainable is maintenance of the ceasefire. Peacekeeping provides the means to maintain a ceasefire by ensuring "a steady military situation without serious episodes that could easily escalate to large-scale fighting."[4] Although such a situation has also been described as a "controlled impasse," it does permit a period of stabilization which helps to build confidence among the opposing parties. As such, it is normally a precondition of the other phases.

At times, however, economic and social problems are so pressing or so closely related to the breaking political situation that their treatment becomes an essential part of the larger security equation. In the early 1960s, the Operation des Nations Unies au Congo (ONUC) included far more than military security, yet did not extend beyond the initial phase of stabilization. From 1960 to 1964, UN peacekeepers and civilian personnel engaged in both military and nonmilitary operations in the Congo (now Zaire). After the country received independence from Belgium in June 1960, the Congolese army mutinied, and Belgium deployed armed forces in order to protect its citizens. Congolese Prime Minister Patrice Lumumba requested UN peacekeepers to aid in the withdrawal of Belgians and to restore law and order. The resulting operation involved UN soldiers helping to relocate refugees, providing medical and humanitarian assistance, shipping food and medicine to needy provinces, and maintaining law and order, including police operations.

The ONUC had a large civilian component of 2,000 personnel. This was necessary because of the internal disorder caused by conflict within the new state. Moreover, the public service infrastructure of the country had collapsed following the flight of most of the Belgians who had administered the area before independence. Consequently, civilian UN administrators advised the Congolese government on social and economic planning and trained people to fill abandoned public service positions.

> One of the most urgent tasks facing ONUC was to restore minimal essential services.... Hundreds of experts and technicians from various countries were brought to the Congo for this purpose. To supplement the crippled local medical services, the headquarters hospital of the UN Peacekeeping Force and the field clinics maintained by its contingents were open to the population.... The displacement of many refugees and wide-spread unemployment caused ONUC to institute refugee relief and work programmes....ONUC [also] shipped emergency food and medicine...and thus saved the lives of nearly a quarter of a million inhabitants....ONUC also devoted a great deal of time and effort to the protection of the civilian population, especially during the constitutional crisis.[5]

These efforts clearly affected political and military developments. In part because of them, when the last UN troops were withdrawn from the Congo in June 1964, the country "retained the borders it had had at independence, in spite of three major secessionist movements." Brian Urquhart further noted: "We had gone into the Congo at a time of anarchy and collapse to secure the territorial integrity of that country and to help its newly independent government to take over responsibilities for which it had had no preparation whatsoever. Our presence had also prevented the East-West struggle for the Congo from actually taking place on the ground."[5]

The only contemporary experience now complete which approaches the Congo operation in terms of size and breadth was that of the United Nations Transition Assistance Group in Namibia (UNTAG). UNTAG was a year long operation which, under extremely tight deadlines, successfully carried out what the UN itself called "the largest decolonization exercise" in its history.[6] This involved a host of different functions:

The South African military structure in Namibia had to be dismantled and the confinement of SWAPO forces to base in Angola monitored. The South West Africa Police had to be brought under effective monitoring. Discriminatory and restrictive legislation had to be repealed, political prisoners and detainees released, an amnesty for returnees proclaimed, and the many thousands of Namibian exiles, including political leaders, had to be enabled to return.[7]

Above all, UNTAG had the task of ensuring that a major change in political atmosphere took place so that a free and fair electoral campaign culminating in fully democratic elections could occur. This was to occur in a society with no tradition of political democracy, which had been subjected to a harsh and discriminatory system of administration for a hundred years.[8]

To accomplish all this, UNTAG assembled a team which, at maximum deployment during the elections in early November 1989, consisted of almost 8,000 drawn from 120 countries: just under 2,000 civilians (including international personnel), 1,500 police and approximately 4,500 military personnel.[9] It was the first time that a UN peacekeeping operation had involved electoral supervisors and civilian police on a large scale. This massive display of strength—and particularly the efforts of UNTAG's information service, which provided Namibians with relevant and objective information about what was happening—helped the UN to build public confidence in the process. The fact that voter turnout in the November 1989 elections was 97.3 percent gives impressive indication of that confidence.

UNTAG was the first major operation in the new generation of peacekeeping operations which are the offspring of the Cold War's demise. Its lessons are highly relevant to other potential missions which seek to combine elements of peacemaking, peacekeeping, stabilization, and reconstruction—all within a single mandate. A key participant in the negotiating process that led to UNTAG has noted its applicability to "other arenas of peace making": "It underscores the sometimes indispensable role, in situations of deep polarization, of an institution whose involvement can legitimize a political process—in this case, the transition from one political status to another and the selection of a new leadership for that territory."[10]

Peacemaking and peacekeeping should and often do go hand-in-hand. The close link between them, as Chester Crocker has pointed out, can be made still more useful by institutionalizing it:

> During the final stages of the U.S.-led mediation [of the Namibian-Angolan negotiations] in 1988, the parties agreed to create a unique mechanism of their own to monitor and help sustain successful implementation of the settlement: the Joint Commission, the charter of which calls for monthly or bimonthly meetings among the Angolans, Cubans and South Africans for the duration of the settlement and for U.S. and Soviet participation as observers. It is no exaggeration to say that the Joint

Commission saved the settlement in the early days of April 1989. The existence of a forum for the private airing and resolution of problems and the continued participation of those states which built the peace decisively reinforced the UN Secretary-General and his team in their mandate. The Commission signalled the stake of these governments in making the settlement work.[11]

One anomaly of the operation was the underemployment of military personnel who may well have been deployed in excessive numbers. The unwillingness of the force commander to shift any military personnel to police duties when the need was critical may have been sound military practice, but it appears an inadequate response to the multifaceted nature of the mission. The wide range of tasks and responsibilities which UNTAG and similar operations require should have the effect of building an *esprit de corps* that embraces civilian personnel together with the military and police, thus breaking down strict lines of demarcation among the different spheres in an effort to "get the job done."

On the other hand, the difficulties of using military personnel in non traditional activities should not be underestimated. Even policing duties present problems since police are specifically trained to work in and with local communities, unlike their military colleagues. What is needed, however, is for national military establishments, particularly those as dependent on the Cold War for their raison d'être as Canada's has been, to begin contemplating such nontraditional roles and preparing to assume more of them. Likewise, the UN needs to adopt a more integrated approach to peacekeeping which seeks to knit together the myriad strands of responsibilities, narrowly or bureaucratically defined, into the larger whole which the Namibian operation began to reassemble.

It is all but impossible to divorce stabilization from reconstruction in any absolute way. Including peacekeepers in reconstruction efforts is an obvious complement to their involvement in the process of reconciliation. This could entail greater risks for countries contributing peacekeepers, an increased likelihood of becoming embroiled in situations of great danger to the troops, and serious political consequence for the contributing countries. The alternative may be worse, however, if it means continuing hostilities without any prospect of development at all.

Demands on the United Nations

New circumstances have made the demands on the United Nations increasingly burdensome. This is not a problem so long as expectations do not outrun capabilities. Yet the danger of such a mismatch is not speculative; it is already present. The capacity of the United Nations to meet its current commitments is stretched to the limit. Its potential to meet others is open to doubt unless far more resources are made available. In terms of peacekeeping, the pace and scale of operations picked up dramatically with the end of the Cold War in the late 1980s. Eleven new operations have been mounted since June 1988. They are the following:

(1) the UN Good Offices Mission in Afghanistan and Pakistan (UNGOMAP) to monitor the withdrawal of Soviet troops from Afghanistan;

(2) the UN Iran-Iraq Military Observer Group (UNIIMOG) to supervise the ceasefire between Iran and Iraq following their lengthy war;

(3) UNAVEM to supervise the withdrawal of Cuban troops from Angola;

(4) the UN Transition Assistance Group (UNTAG) to supervise the withdrawal of South African troops from Namibia and oversee its transition to independence;

(5) the UN Observer Group in Central America (known as ONUCA, its Spanish acronym), the civilian/military operation created in November 1989 to facilitate a peaceful end to internal and transborder armed struggles in Central America;

(6) the UN Iraq-Kuwait Observation Mission (UNIKOM) to monitor the ceasefire along the Iraq-Kuwait border following the Gulf war;

(7) the UN Mission for the Referendum in the Western Sahara (MINURSO) to enforce a ceasefire between Morocco, which now occupies the former Spanish colony, and the rebel Polisario Front, as well as to organize a referendum on independence;

(8) the UN Observer Group in El Salvador (ONUSAL) to monitor both a ceasefire and the internal human rights situation;

(9) the UN Transitional Authority in Cambodia (UNTAC) to oversee a ceasefire between warring factions, to organize elections for the drafting of a new constitution, and to provide basic civil administration in the interim;

(10) the UN Protection Force in Yugoslavia (UNPROFOR) to monitor a ceasefire between Croatia and the Yugoslav army and to separate the warring factions into protected areas; and

(11) a small operation in Somalia authorized by the Security Council in April 1992 to monitor a fragile truce between warring factions.

The demands that these diverse operations have placed on the UN Secretariat have been enormous. Under changes instituted in March 1992 by the new Secretary-General Boutros Ghali, peacekeeping is now the responsibility of an Office for Peacekeeping Operations headed by an under secretary-general. It will relate closely to the newly created Department of Political Affairs (also headed by an under secretary-general), which will be in charge of peacemaking as well as a range of other issues.

In addition, the executive office of the Secretary-General himself, which consists of roughly a dozen people, plays an active role in dealing with breaking emergency situations. This office is intimately involved in crises in the stages which precede the actual insertion of a peacekeeping force—i.e., diplomatic negotiations and peacemaking. In this respect, the relationship between the executive office of the Secretary-General and the new Department of Political Affairs remains unclear.

More than once in recent years, UN Secretariat resources have been stretched to the breaking point because of the proliferation of demands for peacekeeping, peacemaking, and related services. These kinds of pressures are not likely to diminish in the near future given the increase in ethno-cultural conflict and the new emphasis world leaders are placing on UN modalities. This emphasis was underlined at an extraordinary summit meeting of leaders from the fifteen Security Council states on 31 January 1992, which called on the Secretary-General to report by 1 July on ways to reinforce the UN's capacity for preventive diplomacy, peacemaking, and peacekeeping.

In meeting the plethora of new demands, the human element—i.e., the personnel involved in missions—is critical.[12] For several years during the 1980s the UN was operating under financial constraints largely occasioned by the efforts of the Reagan administration and the U.S. Congress to squeeze a UN system they perceived as politically biased and financially irresponsible. As a consequence, even without the additional demands outlined above, the resulting recruitment freeze at the UN would have left many vacancies as well as significant mismatches between specific posts and people to fill them, while salary and cost-of-living freezes would have compounded the difficulty of finding suitable candidates for those posts which could be filled. When a vast team like that of the UN's Namibian operation (UNTAG) is assembled—which decimated the Secretariat by a huge shift of personnel from New York, with many not replaced until the operation was complete— these financial constraints have a reverse multiplier effect in terms of efficiency.

Another vital element in any peacekeeping operation is logistics but, particularly in those operations which embrace civilian or humanitarian activities, logistics may be the single most important aspect of all. The chief administrative officer and staff of the force secretariat, along with the military logistics staff, are responsible for logistic support, including finances, procurement of supplies, communications between the mission and UN headquarters, and direction and co-ordination of personnel and troop movements in the area of operations.[13]

Unfortunately, the UN has a grossly inadequate supply system. It procures matériel on the world market and transports it to the area of operations. This leads to a variety of problems, which one experienced military officer summarized as follows: (1) the lack of quality control at source leaves the military receiving the supplies with a choice between rejecting them and having their troops endure lengthy delays, or accepting plainly unsatisfactory goods as better than nothing; (2) the frustrations of an antiquated and inflexible system of procurement regulations and procedures; and (3) inadequate staffing arrangements.[14]

An effective logistics system would require a trained staff, sufficient facilities for storage, and adequate financing. Because of inadequate financing, many troop-contributing countries are dependent on countries like Canada for equipment, material supplies and transportation.[15] These constraints and anomalies take on added importance because of the increasing complexity of many of the "new wave" of peacekeeping operations. Large and complex operations like that of UNTAG in Namibia place far greater stress on the UN system than any number of discrete observer missions, which require neither a large deployment of troops nor a wide range of services.

Even UNTAG appears straightforward when compared to the situation in Central America or Cambodia, torn by internal strife as well as external collusion. In the traditional conflict situations between opposing states for which it was initially conceived, peacekeeping is passive, acting as a buffer force or protecting a green line which is the physical manifestation of the truce the diplomats seek to turn into a final settlement. The situation is complicated, however, if there is civil war. In such cases, the demands on peacekeepers are likely to be much greater and more varied since they are really required to become "a surrogate state-builder, monitoring elections, resettling refugees and rebuilding the economy, bureaucracy, and infrastructure."[16]

Brian Urquhart has compared peacekeeping to the work of the police in a nation-state and enforcement to the work of the military.[17] He has prescribed that the UN's four main activities in international peace and security—diplomacy, peacemaking (i.e., the good offices of the Secretary-General), peacekeeping and collective action (or enforcement)—be treated as a kind of seamless web or continuum, one leading automatically to the other. "For example if a peacekeeping operation gets run over by a government, like for example the peacekeeping forces in South Lebanon did in 1982, in the mandate of that peacekeeping operation that should automatically trigger collective action from the Security Council.... If they got trampled on, they would become a tripwire."[18]

One recent report recommended that the UN's peacekeeping capacity should be expanded to encompass deterrence as well as stabilization. Preventive peacekeeping "could be directed towards the dangers of crisis escalation within a country, as well as to threats of external aggression. This implies that social and economic crisis, and not just the collapse of political order, would come under the purview of peacekeeping."[19] The former Soviet Union suggested that missions could be sent to a disputed territory at the request of only one member state in order to safeguard it against external interference.[20]

Before any such drastic restructuring of peacekeeping activities is contemplated, far more resources are needed within the UN for preventive diplomacy. What is required is: "better and more timely information, the greater use of special representatives of the Secretary General and the political courage on the part of the Secretary General to act quickly to bring emerging crises to the attention of the Security Council or to dispatch observers to the scene."[21]

Equipping the UN

The question arises whether the United Nations is equipped. If called upon to assist in some form of nation building, then co-ordinating the immense array of services becomes paramount. Yet international arrangements for assisting in humanitarian emergencies, for example, are apt to reflect the decentralization of international governance. Hence the co-ordination of independent efforts calls for administrative skills of a high order. One model which has been cited is "the concerted international action and centralisation of control and funds" during and immediately after the civil and international war which created the state of Bangladesh in 1971. Sir Robert Jackson, who directed the emergency and rehabilitation program, "insisted on the United Nations system of autonomous agencies and programs speaking, for once, with one voice and acting with a common objective."[22]

At the same time, effective co-ordination will demand trouble shooting—the kind of antibureaucratic skills which can cut through the reams of red tape and get to the heart of the matter as well as the centre of power. UN scholars Gordenker and Weiss comment that "transnational efforts to cope with humanitarian emergencies may be greatly influenced by leadership exerted by well-placed persons" and point to the leadership shown by Bradford Morse and Maurice Strong in the creation and running of the UN Office of Emergency Operations for Africa from 1984 to 1986.

The skills described above might be regarded as a form of political wisdom. The UN also needs intelligence—in every sense of the word. It needs the capacity to see down the road both ways: from where things are coming and where they might be in ten years. One close observer of the UN system has speculated:

> Undertaken as part of a global watch effort, the UN as a world body with social, economic and humanitarian responsibilities as well as a security mandate, could over time develop a comparative advantage over more narrowly based institutions in projecting a broader concept of security. In seeking to establish the conditions for peace, the UN should naturally include issues such as economic and social development, environmental change, human rights, and large-scale migration as factors in its analysis and projections.[23]

Above all, the UN must be equipped with adequate resources. Funding of UN peacekeeping operations rests on a precarious foundation of general revenues and special assessments. The sole exception to this rule is the force in Cyprus, which relies on voluntary contributions—a singular experiment never likely to be repeated because of the immense difficulty of collecting funds from governments on an exclusively voluntary basis. Usually the smaller operations were or are being financed from the regular budget (i.e., from general revenues). The majority are financed by special assessments on all member states.[24]

Because of the plethora of new missions, the UN peacekeeping bill for 1992 is expected to reach U.S. $3 billion, compared to only U.S. $730 million in 1991. As of 29 February 1992, the total of contributions outstanding to UN peacekeeping amounted to U.S. $617 million.[25]

There are many difficulties with the financing of peacekeeping, not least the tortuously complicated formulas the UN has had to devise to smooth over the political unwillingness of various member states to meet their obligations and yet still obtain sufficient funds to cobble together the required forces. In fact, the financial problems of the United Nations are only the symptoms of a political crisis, but a crisis apparently without end or resolution.[26] "It is easy to vote for the setting up of a peace operation," then UN Secretary-General Javier Pérez de Cuéllar observed, "but what has to be understood is that such a vote has to be accompanied by contributions to the effort that the members of the Security Council are themselves asking."[27]

Pérez de Cuéllar noted as an alternative the possibility of establishing a special reserve fund for peacekeeping, supported by all member states. Such a mechanism would help meet the two most pressing financial problems: "(a) adequate cash to meet substantial start-up costs for a large peacekeeping operation before the General Assembly can authorize assessments and Member States pay them in sufficient amounts; and (b) adequate cash to meet significant shortfalls when such assessed contributions are paid with substantial delays or not at all."[28] At present, this idea is wishful thinking; no member state has offered to take the lead in support of such a fund. For an active troop contributor such as Canada to do so would probably be unwise for reasons the Secretary-General himself has provided: "The current financial arrangements are not only dangerously limiting during the period in which a complex operation is being mounted; they also put an inequitable financial burden on troop-contributing countries. In addition, they tend to diminish the perception of collective responsibility, which is psychologically essential to peacekeeping operations."[29]

Given the financial strait-jacket into which the UN has been forced, it must be asked whether extraordinary measures are not called for, even at the risk of diminishing the collective responsibility the Secretary-General is rightly concerned to defend. One possibility might be an endowment fund, which could be launched by appealing directly to those peoples for whom the opening words of the UN Charter presumed to speak. A capital reserve could be raised, especially in the developed countries, by contracting with selected non-governmental organizations to include a checkoff for such a fund as part of their regular fund raising campaigns. Millions are now being raised for public education about regional conflicts, peacemaking and peacekeeping. Perhaps "the peoples" should be offered the chance to contribute directly to a fund that would help offset the miserliness of various member states and might even shame them into meeting their responsibilities.

Options for Canada

Canada's history has made it particularly well suited to act as a catalyst of efforts within the international community to improve the links between peacemaking and peacekeeping and between stabilization and development. Canada has had a traditional commitment to the United Nations and multilateral co-operation. It has had an exemplary record in peacekeeping. In addition it has been a major donor of official development assistance to less developed countries.

Moreover, it is in Canada's interest to encourage a revitalized United Nations which seeks both order and justice in a new era. As a middle power with bigger than middle sized aspirations, Canada has much to offer and more to gain from a strengthened UN system. Much of the impetus for the new optimism surrounding UN institutions has come from the end of the Cold War between the superpowers and the waning of ideology as a major factor in international politics. In a less ideological age, Canada's traditional pragmatic approach suddenly enjoys a comparative advantage among nations.

There is another reason to reemphasize Canada's commitment to a strengthened UN. As the Canadian presence in Europe diminishes, Canada will be seeking new opportunities to play a part and have some influence on the world stage. David Dewitt has argued forcefully: "the traditional residual out-of-area commitment must now become the mainstay of our contribution to international peace and security. ... While the Cold War may have made peacekeeping necessary, the decline of the Cold War in the absence of effective collective security makes it inevitable."[30]

The annual statement of the Minister of National Defence issued in April 1992 acknowledged that, as a result of the UN's renewed legitimacy and effectiveness, Canada "could be asked more frequently than in the past to provide personnel to maintain or restore peace."[31] It also recognized that, as the peacekeeping mandate expands, Canada could be called on to act in a wide variety of roles. An expanded peacekeeping role with greater emphasis on low intensity combat and conflict resolution would involve Canadian specialties which have obvious and increasing relevance in the emerging world order.

Modern military forces have an enormous inventory of capabilities in the engineering, medical, communications, transport, and general logistics fields. These already provide significant assistance in peacekeeping operations. With the active support of contributing countries, their use could be expanded in future operations to embrace a broader definition of security and of the process of stabilization, one that includes and anticipates reconstruction needs. The same capabilities should also be used more frequently in the future for other missions, such as disaster and emergency relief, which have no specifically military function.[32]

The test would come in a situation such as Cambodia or Somalia where there is a possibility of becoming entangled in a web that is either too sticky to permit disengaging or too dangerous not to disengage. Even in the Ethiopian airlift, there was always the risk of a transport plane being shot down. The reaction of the Canadian government to such an incident would depend on circumstances, but considerable planning would need to be done for every sort of eventuality, in part to prepare public opinion so that the government is not besieged to withdraw precipitously should some loss of life occur. The United Nations has a similar responsibility—one wonders how much contingency planning went on in Namibia, for example—for the UN, more than any other jurisdiction, would suffer the consequences should something go wrong.

For those member states committed to multilateralism and to an effective United Nations, the challenge is two-fold. On the one hand, it is essential to maintain a healthy dose of realism and even scepticism about what is doable at the UN, in order to provide both perspective in the face of disappointment and flexibility when the unexpected occurs. On the other hand, a concerted effort must be made to foresee probable demands and to prepare whatever resources may be required.

This dual approach will exact the kind of patient and persistent diplomacy on which Canada has always prided itself. But it may also call for a kind of middle power brinkmanship—a willingness to talk tough and bargain relentlessly, perhaps in concert with other like-minded powers—in order to make the larger point: that an effective world organization requires adequate tools and that they can only come from all of the members acting together and meeting their full responsibilities as members.

At the multilateral level, Canada should continue to press for better financial arrangements at the UN, as well as for a revamped support system to replace the antiquated supply and logistics arrangements which have often resulted in poor supply flow and inadequate stocks.

Canada should also encourage attempts to rethink the conjunction between peacekeeping and peacemaking, and between stabilization and development. Practical ways of co-ordinating large operations which embrace all of these elements must be found: an integrated approach which parallels the broadening of the peacekeeping mandate.

Unilaterally, Canada should reshape its armed forces and employ more of them in peacekeeping pursuits. These could be combined with community based and other nontraditional roles in the absence of specific peacekeeping missions. Ways must also be found to engage more reservists in peacekeeping training and operations despite sometimes limited skills.

Canada should behave as a committed realist. Although peacekeeping is intended as the handmaiden of peacemaking, it "ain't necessarily so"; one can operate without the other. While peacemaking pursued without any resort to peacekeeping is perfectly acceptable, the reverse situation—peacekeepers soldiering on without progress in peacemaking or perhaps even reinforcing the stalemate—breeds disillusion or cynicism with the UN. Cyprus, where peacekeeping troops have been maintained for a quarter century, is the outstanding example of a mandate which seems to have no end, no resolution—despite being duly renewed by the General Assembly every six months!

Again, Canada can play a useful role—in this case simply by explaining the contradictions. While it is possible, as some critics have suggested, that peacekeeping could become an impediment to progress in peacemaking, the alternative is also possible. What would happen if troops were withdrawn? Is a renewal of violence in the absence of a peacekeeping force likely to help the peacemaking or the development process any more? One of the UN Secretariat's wiser heads has written: "We have to face disputes where the parties do not want to reach accommodation, where accommodation is extremely difficult given the present situation and the present interests of the parties. We have to think not so much in terms of solving a dispute "here and now," because it often cannot be done, but in terms of exercising conflict control."[33]

Canadians cherish their record of being present at the creation of the United Nations and active participants in finding ways and means to help the organization function more effectively. Today, when the possibility of recreating or, at least, of rethinking some of the basic concepts about the United Nations is at hand, our presence and participation is taken for granted. The challenge will be whether Canada is able to muster the political will, the imaginative yet practical ideas, and the diplomatic and bureaucratic persistence to make a difference. The answer could have profound implications for the shape of Canada's armed forces, the practice of future peacekeeping, and the evolution of the United Nations.

Notes

1. Edward C. Luck, "Renewing the Mandate: The U.N.'s Role in Peace and Security," in *A Successor Vision: The United Nations of Tomorrow* ed. Peter J. Fromuth, (Lanham, Md., 1988), p. 114.

2. Henry Wiseman, "Peacekeeping in the International Political Context: Historical Analysis and Future Directions," *The United Nations and Peacekeeping*, eds. Indar Jit Rikhye and Kjell Skjelsbaek (New York, 1990), p. 34.

3. Brian Urquhart, "Beyond the 'sheriff's posse'," *Survival*, May/June 1990, p. 197.

4. Kjell Skjelsbaek, "UN Peacekeeping: Expectations, Limitations and Results," in *The United Nations*, ed. by Rikhye and Skjelsbaek, pp. 54–55.

5. F.T. Liu, "The Significance of Past Peacekeeping Operations in Africa to Humanitarian Relief," in *Humanitarian Emergencies and Military Help in Africa*, edited by Thomas G. Weiss, International Peace Academy, (London, 1990), p.26.

6. Brian Urquhart, *A Life in Peace and War* (New York, 1987), p. 195.

7. United Nations, *The Blue Helmets: A Review of Peace-keeping* (New York, 1990), p. 368.

8. *Ibid.*, p. 353.

9. *Ibid.*, pp. 342 and 354.

10. Chester Crocker, "Southern African peace making," *Survival*, May/June 1990, p. 222.

11. *Ibid.*, pp. 231–232.

12. The following paragraph draws from an interview with Susan Mills, deputy UN controller, in New York, September 1989.

13. Robin Hay, "Civilian Aspects of United Nations' Peacekeeping," Canadian Institute for International Peace and Security, Background Paper No. 38, October 1991, p. 1.

14. Colonel J.D. Murray, "The Military Requirements of Peacekeeping: Regular vs. Reserve," in *Canada's Reserves and Peacekeeping*, ed. Calvin Bricker (York Centre for International and Strategic Studies, 1988), pp. 51–42.

15. Rikhye, *The United Nations*, p. 181.

16. Ed Luck, "A Risky Role for U.N. in Cambodia," *Los Angeles Times*, 21 August 1989.

17. Brian Urquhart, "Learning from the Gulf," *New York Review of Books*, 7 March 1991, p. 34.

18. "What Kind of World and Whose Order?" *Peace & Security*, Spring 1991, p. 4.

19. David Cox, Steve Lee, James Sutterlin, *The Reduction of the Risk of War Through Multilateral Means: A Summary of Conference Proceedings*, Canadian Institute for International Peace and Security, Working Paper 18, September 1989, p. 16.

20. *Ibid.*, Appendix A: A Speech by Vladimir Petrovsky, USSR deputy foreign minister, p. 23.

21. Edward C. Luck, *A Successor Vision*, *op. cit.*, p. 114.

22. Urquhart, *op.cit.*, p. 231. Also see Leon Gordenker and Thomas G. Weiss, "Humanitarian Emergencies and Military Help: Some Conceptual Observations," unpublished paper from Harare conference, *op. cit.*, pp. 11-12.

23. Luck, "Renewing the Mandate," in *Successor Vision*, ed. Fromuth, p. 116.

24. Susan R. Mills, "The Financing of United Nations Peace-Keeping Operations: The Need for a Sound Financial Basis," International Peace Academy, Occasional Paper No. 3, pp. 3–4.

25. Paul Lewis, "Pressed by the U.S., U.N. Backs Small Somalia Force," *New York Times*, 26 April 1992.

26. Mills, "Financing of UN Peacekeeping," p. 10.

27. Thalif Deen, "UN head: we need money not applause," *Jane's Defence Weekly*, 30 September 1989, p. 636.

28. Mills,"Financing of UN Peacekeeping," p. 25.

29. "Report of the Secretary-General on the Work of the Organization, *Official Records of the General Assembly, Forty-fourth Session, Supplement No. 1*, September 1989, (A/44/1), p. 10.

30. David Dewitt, "Canadian Defence Policy: Regional Conflicts, Peacekeeping and Stability Operations," *Canadian Defence Policy*, August 1991, p. 41.

31. "Canadian Defence Policy" 1992, April 1992, p. 4.

32. This is already beginning to happen. The 1987 Defence White Paper indicated that the government intended "to be even more active in using the Canadian Forces for humanitarian disaster relief abroad." (p. 86) Ethiopia offered an early opportunity to put the new policy into effect—in contrast to 1984 when it was decided not to airlift food to those African countries suffering from famine, even though a detailed military reconnaissance had been conducted. In 1988 the government reversed itself and an airlift was undertaken ("Operation Nile") to move grain from the ports of entry to the major distribution centres. A professional military officer has recounted of Operation Nile: "There can be few situations which could provide better training for air transport crews than that found in Ethiopia, with the challenging geography and climatic conditions, absence of navigational aids, unimproved airfields and lack of sophisticated infrastructure. Most such operations provide a similar training vehicle, and only a very few could be considered to be of no practical value to the military." Since then the Canadian Forces have been used in a variety of instances abroad relating to emergency or humanitarian assistance. See Colonel Charles Simonds, "External Military Involvement in the Provision of Humanitarian Relief in Ethiopia," *Humanitarian Emergencies and Military Help in Africa* edited by Thomas G. Weiss, International Peace Academy, (London, 1990), pp.61—73.

33. George Sherry, "The Role of the United Nations in Resolving Conflict Situations," United Nations, Department of Public Information, Non-Governmental Organizations Section, DPI/NGO/SB/83/6, 11 March 1983, p. 2.

CUSO and Liberation Movements in Southern Africa: An Appeal for Solidarity

Christopher Neal, David Beer, John van Mossel,
John Saxby and Joan Anne Nolan
CUSO

Introduction

Acting on a personal appeal from Nelson Mandela, just weeks after his release from prison in February 1990, External Affairs Minister Joe Clark, speaking in Toronto, endorsed an all party drive to help the African National Congress (ANC) raise $20 million needed to set up its offices and launch political activities inside South Africa. In June of the same year, when Mandela visited Canada during a world tour, Prime Minister Brian Mulroney pledged $5.7 million in Canadian government aid to help returning exiles in South Africa, most of whom were affiliated with the ANC. It was a dramatic turnaround for Clark and Mulroney, as well as a new approach for External Affairs Canada which had, until then, always avoided declaring such frank support for the ANC.

For almost 20 years, CUSO, one of Canada's largest international development NGOs (nongovernmental organizations), has pressed the federal government to express solidarity with the ANC by providing funds for the liberation movement's nonmilitary work. While Clark expressed determination to adhere to Canadian foreign policy tradition of not offering government financial support for political movements, his appeal for public donations to do so was unprecedented.

To some extent, Clark's appeal vindicated a position long held by CUSO, which has provided staff and financial support for humanitarian and development projects undertaken by national liberation movements in Southern Africa since the early 1970s. This activity, ranging from support for a piggery on a Zimbabwe African People's Union (ZAPU) run farm in Zambia in the 1970s to an African National Congress video unit in 1989, has been criticized by some in Canada as political adventurism, underwriting "violence," embracing of "chic" causes, abuse of aid money, as well as support for "terrorists" and "Communists." It has also attracted considerable support from Canadian churches, development agencies, labour unions, and solidarity groups.

CUSO has always defended its strategy of liberation support as a contribution to peace, justice, and socio-economic development in Southern Africa. CUSO's analysis is that much of the violence in the region can be traced to the apartheid system and the Pretoria regime's unstinting efforts—until recently—to bolster it. That system is the chief obstacle to peace and development. Canadian aid, in this case, can promote peace by contributing to the dismantling of apartheid.

CUSO's policy of support for nonmilitary ANC projects in education and agriculture has been based on the understanding that the most effective way to end apartheid—and the violence it creates—is by supporting the opponents of apartheid. This policy of solidarity with liberation movements has been criticized by some who cite Canada's postwar history as a peacekeeper, implicitly suggesting that Canada has avoided taking sides in many conflicts.

CUSO's position, in the Southern Africa case, has been that Canada *should* take sides by offering solidarity with the just cause. It is a view of peacemaking which differs from the mediation model and has been applied by the Canadian government in several conflicts. It emerges from a recognition that some conflicts must be approached in moral terms and that mediation will perpetuate conflict, in some cases, by meeting villainy halfway. In Southern Africa, CUSO's program managers have determined that the violence is caused by injustice and that the violence will end only when the injustice is corrected. Moreover, the historical record—in which liberation movements have become governing political parties in Mozambique, Angola, Zimbabwe, and Namibia— suggests that liberation support constitutes recognition of the inevitable, as well as a just cause.

In August 1979, the *Globe and Mail* lambasted CUSO for its liberation support policy in an editorial entitled "Taxpayer dollars in guerrilla warchests." It claimed the agency was "splashing about" its 90 percent government funded budget in "highly partisan, extremely dubious ways." The editorial followed a tendentious *Globe* article, "Liberation groups not terrorists to CUSO," in which then reporter Norman Webster wrote after visiting CUSO funded projects on a ZAPU farm in Zambia: "Many Canadians think all members of the Patriotic Front (the alliance of Zimbabwe liberation movements) are terrorists. David Beer (then CUSO's field director in charge of liberation support) has them over for dinner. He also hands over lashings of Canadian Government money to them."

Similar allegations received further play in other media. Maritime poet Alden Nowlan, writing in *The Atlantic Advocate*, compared CUSO's work to financing propaganda for the Irish Republican Army. The far right lobby group, Citizens for Foreign Aid Reform, published a booklet entitled "CUSO and Radicalism," which cites "CUSO's support for terrorist groups in South Africa and radical politics in Canada." These accusations followed a spate of similar ones in 1974, when another *Globe and Mail* article on Canada's plans to help NGOs work with liberation movements in Southern Africa sparked a series of angry newspaper editorials.

If such negative responses to CUSO's liberation support work stopped at fulminations from ill-informed journalists and extreme right fringe groups, they could easily be dismissed. Yet these criticisms of CUSO's activity, couched in more oblique language, have been heard from the highest levels of Canada's government. While reluctant to denounce openly CUSO or the Southern African liberation movements it supports, the federal government traditionally has given both a wide berth. In 1979, for example, CUSO sought a meeting with External Affairs Minister Flora MacDonald for representatives of Zimbabwe's Patriotic Front, then battling the puppet Rhodesian government of Bishop Abel Muzorewa. MacDonald refused. A year later, however, Canada was among the first Western countries to dispatch a trade delegation to meet them—once they had won power in the new nation of Zimbabwe. Seven years later, Prime Minister Mulroney was the first Western leader to visit Zimbabwe, where he basked in praise from the Zimbabwean leaders his party had once spurned.

In May 1989, similar issues resurfaced when CUSO questioned the Mulroney government's decision to fund only one of five modest non-military projects to assist the African National Congress—South Africa's leading liberation movement—with policy research, administration, and education. External Affairs Minister Clark sidestepped a question on the refusals when he appeared before the House of Commons External Affairs Committee 11 May. "CUSO has its perspective," Clark said. "What CUSO is saying…is that CIDA has not funded all five of its requests. Well…every NGO in the country can make that claim. The point is that we have funded one, we are looking at others, and we are prepared to look at ways to work with the African National Congress in a way that is consistent with Canadian policy."

At a time when Canada was seeking to be perceived as a determined adversary of apartheid, the act of turning down four out of five non-military aid projects to the ANC was hardly a stirring gesture of solidarity with the oppressed black majority in South Africa. All the same, it was an improvement over the indifference to African liberation movements of Canadian governments of the previous decade. Accompanied by Mulroney's meeting with ANC leader Oliver Tambo in 1987 and Clark's embrace of Nelson Mandela on the Lusaka airport tarmac in 1990, it showed an evolution in the Canadian position, a movement toward understanding the inevitability of liberation in South Africa.

Canadian editorial opinion towards the ANC has also evolved. After Clark's meeting with Mandela, the *Ottawa Citizen* said in an editorial that, "Canada should not be rejecting appeals from the ANC or other credible black organizations for direct assistance. It should be responding generously to encourage the development of a moderate, nonviolent, viable alternative to white rule."

CUSO Solidarity Work

Origins and rationale

CUSO's history of solidarity with de-colonization and antiapartheid struggles in Southern Africa dates back to the late 1960s. Since then, it has included project funding and administration, as well as political education and advocacy in Canada on behalf of the MPLA of Angola, FRELIMO of Mozambique, ZAPU and ZANU of Zimbabwe, SWAPO of Namibia, the South African Congress of Trade Unions (SACTU) and the African National Congress (ANC) of South Africa. This solidarity emerged from the experience of CUSO volunteers who served two year contracts in Zambia, Tanzania, Malawi, Uganda and Botswana since the mid-1960s. It came from their growing awareness that North-South inequalities of wealth and income were rooted in the exploitation of people and resources in the South by colonialism and neo-colonialism.

In July 1965, CUSO volunteer David Beer, then working in newly independent Zambia as a training officer with the country's Youth Service, met exiled "Zimbabweans," black nationalists from Southern Rhodesia. These members of the Zimbabwe African People's Union (ZAPU), led by Joshua Nkomo, told him of their struggle for a nonracial democratic country in what was then ruled by the white minority regime of Ian Smith. Fifteen years later, they would take power in the renamed capital of Harare, as members of the government of Robert Mugabe's Zimbabwe African National Union (ZANU).

Hundreds of other Canadian CUSO volunteers were exposed to the reality of African liberation movements. In 1967, over one thousand CUSO volunteers were posted around the world, most of them in Africa. Over 200 worked in Southern Africa that year, where many of them met exiled Zimbabweans. They also met exiles from Mozambique and Angola who sought to end Portuguese colonial rule in their countries, refugees from Namibia, and South African nationalists working in exile to end apartheid in South Africa.

Upon their return to Canada, many of these ex-CUSO volunteers, inspired by their experience, pressed CUSO to recognize the political dimension of economic underdevelopment in the South. They were joined by other returned volunteers who had served in Nigeria, where they witnessed the Biafran war, as well as several who had been in the Caribbean and in Southeast Asia, where they were exposed to the impact of the Vietnam war. At CUSO annual meetings in 1968, 1969, and 1970, a group of ex-volunteers proposed that CUSO set up a "political education unit" to disseminate information, organize speaking tours, and raise money in Canada for African liberation movements. Implicit in these proposals was a view that Canadian foreign policy was among the obstacles to necessary change in Southern Africa. Canada, for example, did not repudiate its NATO ally Portugal for its continued colonial rule in Mozambique and Angola; Canada's silence, the CUSO group argued, implied consent.

John Saul, of the Toronto Committee for the Liberation of Southern Africa (TCLSAC), which also included many CUSO Africa ex-volunteers and staff, described the pattern of Canada's position on Southern African liberation struggles as, "rhetorical commitment to the cause of popular freedom on the one hand and 'business as usual' with the oppressive white-minority regimes (in this case, Portugal) on the other."[1]

The "political education" proposals were repeatedly defeated by a majority of members who believed CUSO should steer clear of "politics" and stick to its original, "nonpolitical" vocation as a technical assistance agency. By the early 1970s, these demands resurfaced in modified form with a proposal that CUSO include "development education" in its mandate and create a development education unit. This time, however, the proposal was accepted. A development education unit was approved by the agency in 1973.

The development education unit, along with a Development Charter CUSO adopted at a meeting in Dar es Salaam in 1973, provided a structure for continuing debates over how much emphasis should be placed on "political" analysis, advocacy, and solidarity in CUSO's work both overseas and in Canada. These debates often involved the Canadian International Development Agency (CIDA), which had set up a unit to provide funding to NGOs for their development education activities. CIDA placed restrictions on how CUSO might use these federal funds earmarked for "development education." CIDA specified, for example, that CUSO could not use CIDA funds to criticize Canadian foreign policy or to draw parallels between struggles against oppression in developing countries and struggles by powerless groups in Canada.

Conflicts arose as CUSO perceived international development as an engagement of Canadians in analysis of the political reasons behind underdevelopment and of the roots of poverty and economic exploitation in the third world. This process also implied, in CUSO's view, taking political action in Canada based on that analysis. CIDA, however, wanted "development education" to emphasize Canada's contribution to technical assistance in developing countries and to defend the case for "foreign aid." "We were talking a different language," recalled Beer.

Liberation-support programs

CUSO's Development Charter and the debates over political action marked a philosophical maturing of the organization which paved the way to CUSO's formal adoption in 1976 of a liberation support policy in Southern Africa. That policy was based on the understanding that minority or colonial rule in the region—particularly the South African regime and the social order it protects—remained the primary obstacle to peace and development in Southern Africa. Those who would support development in the subcontinent must, therefore, come to terms with the struggle for social and national liberation and basic human rights for all the region's people. This meant acknowledging the inevitability and legitimacy of armed struggles waged by the liberation movements—an imperative, in CUSO's view, that remains as compelling today as it was during the 1970s.

CUSO's East, Central and Southern Africa (ECSA) staff, which has articulated and implemented CUSO's liberation support program in the field, has maintained a two pronged approach combining work both in Canada and the region. In Canada, this has included a commitment to public education, lobbying, advocacy, and support of other groups with similar goals, such as the Toronto Committee for the Liberation of Southern Africa, Montreal's Centre d'information et de documentation sur le Mozambique et l'Afrique australe (CIDMAA) and the now defunct South African Congress of Trade Unions Solidarity Committee.

In Southern Africa, CUSO has concentrated on building and main-taining working relations with the liberation movements of South Africa, Namibia, and (until 1980) Zimbabwe. CUSO's original plan in 1976 identified several types of support, namely:

- assistance to liberation movements recognized by the Organization of African Unity (OAU) and based in the front line states;
- support for organizations working for change within the minority ruled states (in accordance with liberation movement policies);
- educational assistance, in the form of scholarship aid to members of liberation movements or persons under their care.

In practice, the first of these options has accounted for most of CUSO's work, with an emphasis on support for humanitarian projects with refugees in the care of such liberation movements as ZAPU, ZANU, SWAPO and the ANC. This bias has arisen partly due to urgency of need—in 1980, for example, there were 250,000 Zimbabweans living in Zambia and Mozambique—and partly due to the availability of project funds, through matching grants from CIDA, for this purpose.

CIDA's involvement in liberation-support work undertaken by Cana-dian NGOs began in 1973, when Canada announced at the Trusteeship Committee of the United Nations General Assembly that humanitarian assistance to Southern Africa, "...will be channelled through Canadian non-governmental and international organizations which are assisting the efforts of the peoples of Southern Africa who are involved in the struggle for human dignity and self-determination."[2] This decision emerged from Prime Minister Pierre Trudeau's remarks at the 1973 Commonwealth Conference in Ottawa that Canada was prepared to offer humanitarian support to the liberation movements of Southern Africa.[3]

The issue sprang to public attention with a front page *Globe and Mail* story on 7 February 1974, headlined: "Ottawa to give aid to African guerrilla groups." The story, which noted that CIDA grants would be made through intermediary groups including Canadian NGOs, prompted a minor storm of criticism, with editorials denouncing the policy in the *Ottawa Citizen, Toronto Star, Ottawa Journal, Toronto Sun* and the *Globe and Mail*. Although no money had been disbursed, External Affairs Minister Mitchell Sharp issued a statement defending the policy and outlining criteria for the acceptance of projects. He also insisted that no grants would be approved until the CIDA spending estimates had been approved by Parliament.[4]

CUSO's strategy of liberation support, then, was partly determined by the availability of CIDA funding, but it would be incorrect to depict CUSO in this case as a "vehicle" for a CIDA initiative. The impetus and pressure for federal funds for a liberation support program came from CUSO, Oxfam-Canada, the Canadian Council of Churches, and other groups, including a Toronto based Committee for a Just Canadian Policy towards Southern Africa. This latter group had issued a "Black Paper" in September 1970, urging Canada to provide financial, technical, and medical assistance to liberation movements.[5] The Department of External Affairs and, by extension, CIDA responded to this pressure—and that of leaders of the front line states at the 1973 Commonwealth Conference—in a qualified, circumscribed manner by approving restricted CIDA funding for specific "humanitarian or developmental" projects to assist refugees from Southern Africa.

Following this announcement, CUSO, Oxfam-Canada, the Canadian Catholic Organization for Development and Peace and the United Church of Canada developed several liberation support projects. CUSO was the administrative channel for funding projects, since it was the only Canadian NGO with an office in Lusaka, Zambia, where most exiled Southern African liberation movements have been located.

Projects supported by CUSO, Oxfam-Canada and others through the CUSO aid channel have included schools, nurseries and kindergartens organized by the ANC in Tanzania, by SWAPO in Zambia and Angola and by ZAPU in Zambia. Support was provided in the 1970s for a Zambia based ZAPU print shop, a poultry and piggery project, a research and information centre, a clerical school and two emergency relief projects following a 1978 bombing raid by Rhodesia on three ZAPU camps in Zambia. A ZANU-ZAPU motor vehicle training shop and literacy project in Mozambique were also funded by CUSO.

In June 1979, CUSO—together with Oxfam-Canada, SUCO, the United Church of Canada, the Anglican Church of Canada, and the network of Southern Africa solidarity groups across Canada—also funded and organized a month long tour of Canada by two senior officials with the Zimbabwe Patriotic Front.

By 1979, CUSO had spent over $100,000 on projects with ZAPU and ZANU. It was a significant sum which, together with CUSO assistance to other Southern African liberation movements, amounted to one-third of CUSO's project pool for the region in 1975–80. CIDA had matched this with significant contributions. In 1977–78, the federal government provided a total of $2.7 million for refugees in Southern Africa, of which $269,000 was devoted to NGO sponsored projects. Most of the funds, however, were channelled through UN organizations.[6]

CUSO spending, meanwhile, continued to grow into the 1980s with expansion of CUSO's support program of the ANC and SWAPO; in its first decade of liberation support ending in 1985, CUSO had allocated $500,000 of its own funds to the program and administered another $500,000 donated by other organizations.

CUSO and the African National Congress

CUSO decided in the 1970s to align itself in solidarity with the ANC as the leading force of resistance in South Africa. The ANC has been at the core of the struggle against apartheid since 1912. It has grown in exile since its leaders fled South Africa in 1961, when Nelson Mandela and others were imprisoned and the organization was banned. The ANC has gone through many phases, from the early period of acquiring Zambian government permission to remain, to building a small funding and administration base from which to operate, to the period when young refugees flowed into Zambia after the 1976 Soweto uprising. After the independence of Mozambique and Angola in 1975, new possibilities for support to the ANC were opened up. These were later closed by the 1984 Nkomati Accord between Mozambique and South Africa, which forced thousands of South African exiles and ANC members out of Mozambique.

Another setback occurred when the South African government forced Lesotho and later Botswana to expel ANC partisans from within their borders. Still, a few years after Zimbabwe's independence in 1980, some modest support for the ANC within the front line states emerged, as President Robert Mugabe's ZANU government made overtures to the movement after a long period of ZANU support for the Pan Africanist Congress, which had virtually self-destructed in exile.

Throughout, the ANC survived and grew, in alliance with other members of the antiapartheid movement in South Africa. It emerged during the 1980s as the leading force at the centre of the struggle to overthrow apartheid. It is not alone, with resistance to apartheid coming from youth, churches, trade unions, students, urban and rural women's organizations, township based organizations, and national coalitions such as the United Democratic Front and the Mass Democratic Movement. Practically all of these sectors profess support for the ANC Freedom Charter and most look to the ANC for leadership. This reality has been confirmed and reinforced by the tumultuous receptions accorded Nelson Mandela, Walter Sisulu and the other Rivonia prisoners released in late 1989 and early 1990.

CUSO's relationship with the ANC began informally in the late 1960s, when ANC representatives were routinely asked to brief newly arrived CUSO volunteers on conditions in South Africa and their liberation struggle. The links evolved into project support after CUSO helped organize a 1976 tour of Canada by two women from Soweto, outside Johannesburg, after massacres and repression carried out by South African troops in Soweto and other townships.

In 1978, CUSO developed a package of ANC support projects and raised funds for them from its own sources, as well as Canadian and European churches and NGOs.

These included a research and information centre in Lusaka, to which CUSO contributed $25,000 for office equipment. The centre was expanded to accommodate the ANC's more detailed policy planning for a postapartheid South Africa. It was first set up to document cases of intimidation and repression by the South African regime, research the role of women in the South African economy, and the exploitation of black mine workers, and to counteract South African government propaganda aimed at legitimizing apartheid. The same year, CUSO provided $10,000 for a van for ANC women and $16,000 (over two years) for the ANC's *Voice of Women* magazine. Another project was the construction and maintenance of a youth transit house in Gaberone, Botswana, to accommodate young refugees fleeing the oppression in South Africa.

In 1979, the established practice of obtaining matching grants for CUSO projects with the ANC was shelved by the newly elected Conservative government headed by Prime Minister Joe Clark. It ordered a halt to CIDA matching grants for NGO projects in Cuba, Laos—and with the ANC. CUSO mounted a campaign to have the policy reversed—at least in the case of the ANC projects—but the Clark government stuck to its position.

The decision was announced shortly after the 1979 Commonwealth Conference in Lusaka, at which CUSO field staff had sought to familiarize Canadian officials and journalists attending the conference with Zimbabwean liberation movements by organizing tours of two ZAPU farms for them. External Affairs Minister Flora MacDonald was taken on a private tour of the ZAPU women's Victory Camp, while Douglas Roche, a Conservative MP, toured Freedom Camp, a ZAPU run farm.

Canadian reporters were taken on a third tour. One reporter, Robert MacDonald of the *Toronto Sun*, missed the bus and somehow gained the impression that he—and Roche—had been deliberately denied access to the camp. This was not true; Roche had toured one camp and wrote a favourable report on the basis of that visit. MacDonald of the *Sun* filed a completely erroneous, inflammatory dispatch saying that he and Roche had been denied access to a camp which was partly financed by Canadian funds. CUSO was accused of hiding its CIDA funded ZAPU projects when the opposite was the case. The false charges stuck, however, and likely had some influence on the government's subsequent decision to cut off matching grants for humanitarian support to liberation movements in the region.

CUSO responded by setting up a solidarity fund for ANC projects to replace the lost three-to-one matching grants, but it amounted to only a fraction of the $250,000 planned for the ANC projects. CUSO's Beer returned to Zambia, disappointed, to break the news to Alfred Nzo, the ANC's Secretary-General. Nzo reacted to the loss of Canadian government funding by telling Beer that solidarity expressed by Canadian people through individual donations was more significant to the ANC than federal dollars.

More ANC projects went ahead in 1979 and into the 1980s, as the liberation movement, assisted by CUSO and others, was able to raise funds from SUCO, Oxfam-Canada, Oxfam-America, the Canadian Catholic Organization for Development and Peace, as well as from several European governments. It should be pointed out that by the mid-1980s, the ANC was receiving around $50 million a year in nonmilitary aid. Around $30 million of this was in the form of development specialists, teachers, vehicles, clothing, food, medicines and other in-kind contributions from NGOs, the Soviet Union, and its allies.[7]

Of the remaining $20 million in cash donations, the major contributors were Sweden and Norway, followed by the Netherlands, Austria, the United Nations High Commissioner for Refugees, the Soviet Union, India, and several European NGOs. Other sources include Bishop Desmond Tutu's refugee fund, benefit rock concerts, and China.[8] Britain and Denmark also offer scholarships to ANC constituents through the British consulate.

The ANC's activities in Zambia mushroomed in the 1980s. The organization developed an extensive structure for administration, policy making, budgeting and publicity. Several hundred ANC officials spent years working in over twenty "cabinet" departments, secretariats, and committees in a variety of locations around Lusaka. In threadbare offices with minimum resources, ANC researchers planned for a postapartheid South Africa—exploring options for economic policy, land reform, cooperatives, and mining policy. Here too, the ANC's international relations unit issued directions to its more than forty offices and "embassies" around the world and co-ordinated "dialogue" with other groups in South Africa. Its information and publicity department produced *Sechaba*, the ANC news magazine, later printed in Britain and East Germany. A regular news briefing letter is also produced along with other material.

Until the ANC began moving its operations into South Africa in 1990, the organization's Treasurer-General, Thomas Nkobi, administered its budget from Lusaka, supplying nearly fifteen thousand constituents worldwide with food, clothes, housing, transportation, and health care. Funding was also allocated for scholarships and to maintain the Solomon Mahlangu Freedom College in Tanzania. The ANC raised some of its own food on three large farms in Zambia purchased with Swedish assistance in 1979–80. CUSO, acting on its own behalf and with funds contributed by other NGOs, has also contributed to the farms with donations of water pumps and hardware.

CUSO's strategy

In 1985, CUSO's Southern Africa programs decided to complement their project work with a stronger emphasis on education, information, and advocacy in Canada to advance the cause of liberation in South Africa. This grew from a long-held conviction that regionwide economic development and stability cannot be achieved until South Africa's apartheid regime is replaced. South Africa's economic stranglehold on its neighbours, combined with its direct attacks and backing of proxy armies to de-stabilize the front line states, help to keep these nations in a state of poverty and dependence. The need to emphasize information about Southern Africa's problems was further heightened by Pretoria's imposition of a state of emergency which censored media coverage of events inside South Africa.

CUSO, it was decided, would respond to pressure from its partners in Southern Africa, and stress its role as a platform in Canada to advance the agenda of Southern Africans struggling for freedom and development. "The ANC and other partners see CUSO as a terrain of struggle, a point of openness and sympathy," said John Saxby, CUSO's field staff officer in Zambia in the mid-1980s. "We're not just a conveyor belt for Canadian aid."[9]

While pressing the federal government to adopt a policy more frankly supportive of the opponents of apartheid, CUSO also worked in the 1980s to raise Canadians' awareness of the issues in Southern Africa and the ANC's role. CUSO—along with the Montreal Centre (CIDMAA), International Defence and Aid Fund for Southern Africa, Oxfam-Canada, and the Toronto Committee (TCLSAC)—developed a popular education kit entitled "South Africa on the Move," for circulation among NGOs, solidarity committees, and community groups. CUSO also assisted the ANC's culture department in compiling a poster exhibition incorporating material from community based poster production projects in Southern Africa.

These projects led to a co-operative effort by the ANC's culture and information departments and CUSO to set up a unit to produce video documentaries on the ANC's activities and the situation in South Africa. Again, CUSO sought permission from CIDA to use funding reserved for overseas cooperants to send a Canadian video production teacher to the ANC's Lusaka based information department. The request was refused, on the grounds that development assistance could not be used for what CIDA described as "propaganda." It is ironic to note that External Affairs Minister Clark had no such difficulty when he announced a plan in 1988 to spend $1 million to counter South African government propaganda and disinformation.

CUSO was able to keep the video project alive with funding from other NGOs and, finally, with agreement from Partnership Africa Canada (PAC) to finance the project. This received tacit approval from CIDA through its representative on PAC's board of directors. A CUSO recruited video trainer was sent to help set up the unit and train ANC workers who have now taken over responsibility for it. The unit has produced several mass circulation videos, on subjects such as the Five Freedoms Forum in July 1989 and a meeting between ANC and Afrikaner writers, among many others.

CUSO also designed, with the Rome based InterPress Service, a Harare based biweekly electronic and print information service on Southern Africa for solidarity groups and NGOs in Canada. The service, now under way, also provides training and experience to African journalists in the use and management of information technology and systems. The project is funded by CUSO, which also provides a full time cooperant as project manager, other Canadian NGOs and Partnership Africa Canada.

CUSO has also encouraged "linkages" between Canadian youth, native, church and women's groups and their counterparts in Southern Africa. An example of this is a twinning between Canada's Grain Services Union and the equivalent union, SINTIAB, in Mozambique. A similar linkage has been set up between Zimbabwe's Organization for Collective Co-operatives (OCCZIM) and co-operatives and community centres in Canada. Finally, CUSO has helped promote discussion of South Africa in Canada by acting as cosponsor of two major conferences on apartheid. One called "Taking Sides" was held in Montreal in February 1987, while the other was a parallel conference to the Commonwealth Heads of Government meeting in Vancouver in October 1987.

A challenge to Mulroney

Given Prime Minister Mulroney's determination to press for change in South Africa, expressed with a threat to impose full sanctions in a speech to the United Nations General Assembly in 1985, CUSO decided to challenge the federal government's policy of "no use of CIDA funds for work with the ANC." A proposal was drawn up in 1986 for a Solidarity

Fund, to be disbursed over three years, according to a set of agreed-upon guidelines, for projects and activities of the ANC in Zambia and Tanzania.

After nearly a year of study by External Affairs and CIDA, the proposal was rejected. But federal officials left the door open to specific project proposals. CUSO followed up with three specific project proposals in agriculture, education, and research—all of which were approved under the existing matching funds pool mechanism and cooperant-sending support. These were the first approvals granted CUSO for "liberation support" projects by External Affairs. They were accompanied by a proviso that further approvals would be limited to "humanitarian, in-kind" assistance.

With this apparent encouragement, CUSO went to work in 1987 on a package of five ANC support projects, presented in May 1988, for consideration by CIDA for 100 percent funding. These included the following:

- support for the ANC Treasurer-General's projects' department, which co-ordinates international assistance to the ANC. CIDA funds were to cover office equipment and staff training to improve the department's ability to administer project implementation and accountability;
- support for the ANC's economics and planning department, to cover office furniture, word-processing equipment, and the resources needed for high quality economic research into South Africa's current situation and policies for the future;
- two projects to support scholarships for ANC "constituents" in Canada and in the front line states;
- funding the Dora Tamana child care centre, which cares for 140 children of ANC refugees and exiles in Lusaka.

Of the five proposals, CIDA agreed in 1989—after nearly a year of study—to provide financing for just one, the Dora Tamana day-care centre. The scholarship proposals were refused "due to a shortage of CIDA funds," while the first two, regarded as most significant by both CUSO and the ANC, were rejected as "institutional support" and therefore ineligible for Canadian government funding.

CUSO challenged the rejections in the May 1989 issue of its newsletter aimed at MPs, *CUSO Advocate*, which also noted that the existing limited and voluntary sanctions package had proved ineffective in curtailing Canadian trade with South Africa. In an editorial, CUSO executive director Chris Bryant suggested that "Canada can increase the pressure on Pretoria and make an investment in South Africa's future by supporting, in a much more significant and forthright manner, development and training projects organized by the African National Congress." He urged the government to restore matching grants for projects with the

ANC and expressed support for the ANC's requests for diplomatic recognition and funding for its office in Canada.

Such gestures by Canada would follow those of Sweden and Norway, which were spending $10 million and $4 million a year respectively on ANC support projects. These are significant aid agreements. They demonstrate a willingness to work with and support the leading movement struggling for change in South Africa—as acknowledged by those in the Mass Democratic Movement in South Africa working for an end to apartheid.

Beyond specific material assistance, CUSO program offices and staff have provided administrative assistance to the ANC and previously, other liberation movements. In some cases, this has been substantial, including the development of project memoranda for funding applications; in other cases it is minor. Taken as a whole, the openness of the CUSO offices to liberation movement representatives is both a symbolic and practical gesture of organizational support. In recent years, this type of support has been arguably more significant than the actual dollars CUSO has allocated to ANC projects.

As mentioned earlier, CUSO's office in Lusaka—staffed since 1986 by a fulltime liberation-support staff person—and the warm relationship established with the ANC over the years, have led CUSO to perform an important role as a channel and administrator for funds donated by international agencies to the ANC. When its project funding requests have been shunned by CIDA, CUSO has taken the same proposals to other institutions and NGOs, where they have gained support.

CUSO, while spending only $50,000 a year of its own funds on liberation-support projects plus the cost of a field officer, office, local staff, travel and office expenses, is now administering more than $800,000 in funds for ANC and SWAPO support projects allocated by CIDA (for the day-care centre), Partnership Africa Canada (for the video project), the United Church of Canada, B.C. Save the Children, Oxfam-Canada, the Canadian Catholic Organization for Development and Peace, Community Aid Abroad (of Australia), COSPI of Italy, Socialist Solidarity of Belgium, War on Want (U.K.), and Redd Barna (Save the Children) of Norway. Also, with CUSO having set the precedent of foreign NGO support for the ANC's Zambia farms, a coalition of War on Want, COSPI and Socialist Solidarity applied and received a matching grant of 750,000 ECUs from the European Economic Community in 1987 for CUSO administered ANC farm projects.

CUSO offers its good offices

CUSO has, over the years, offered representatives of the federal government an opportunity to learn more about the ANC by taking advantage of the contacts which have been established. A few meetings have taken place between Canadian High Commission and CIDA officials and ANC representatives, sometimes facilitated by CUSO staff, but Canadian government officials have often shown reluctance to learn more about the ANC. The result is apparently scanty knowledge of the ANC at External Affairs Canada. This was evident when ANC leader Oliver Tambo visited Ottawa in 1987; Prime Minister Mulroney and External Affairs Minister Clark emphasized "ANC violence" in their meetings, showing little understanding of the enormity of South African state terror facing the people of South Africa.

This ANC "violence" and the presence of Communists within the ranks of the ANC were frequently cited by Canadian officials through the 1980s to defend the government's reluctance to provide more extensive support to the liberation movement. CUSO addressed these arguments by supporting the ANC's contention that its "violence" was in fact self-defence and part of the struggle against the much greater violence of apartheid.

Material support for an organization engaged in armed struggle, such as the ANC, may be controversial in some sectors of Canadian society and therefore considered politically risky by foreign policy makers in Ottawa. But the withholding of that support also entails a cost in lost credibility for Canada in black Africa, or indeed, in the postapartheid South Africa likely to be governed by the ANC.

CUSO has urged the federal government to provide nonmilitary assistance to the ANC to strengthen the organization's research, education, publicity, and diplomatic activities, as well as the survival needs of its members and constituents. Canada does not normally require a pacifist policy of countries receiving development assistance; why then should it be demanded of an organization fighting for objectives Canada applauds against a regime whose values Canada rejects, even abhors?

As for the South African Communist Party's support of the ANC, Tambo and others have pointed out that Communists, while significant supporters of the ANC, are not in the majority within the movement's leadership. The ANC's alliance with South African Communists, reaffirmed by Mandela following his release from prison in February 1990, has been the subject of much misunderstanding. In his 1964 Rivonia trial, Mandela, noting that "theoretical differences among those fighting against oppression is a luxury we cannot afford...," recalled that, "...for many decades communists were the only political group in South Africa who were prepared to treat Africans as human beings and their equals."[10] Given that early expression of solidarity with the antiapartheid struggle by South African Communists, the ANC can hardly be faulted for responding in kind.

South Africa expert Thomas G. Karis notes that the Freedom Charter, drawn up in 1955, still expresses the ANC's basic policy which, he says, "is not socialist or Marxist, nor is it anti-capitalist; it envisages a democratic welfare state and a mixed economy."[11] Karis also points out that state control is already extensive in South Africa, with such sectors as telephones, railways, airlines, electricity, iron and steel, atomic energy and the arms industry all owned by the government. This same regime has played up the supposed "Communist threat" posed by the ANC as being worse than the antidemocratic reign of terror and racism which currently prevails. CUSO believes the Communist bogey has been vastly overstated and promulgated by the South African regime for obvious propaganda reasons.[12]

The Communist links of the ANC lose what relevance they may have had in some quarters in the wake of the Mikhail Gorbachev revolution, the collapse of Communism in eastern Europe, and the demise of the U.S.S.R., all of which are exerting a profound reformist influence on the South African Communist Party. This is evident in a paper by South African Communist Party Secretary—and ANC executive member—Joe Slovo, published in January 1990. In it, Slovo calls for "a multi-party post-apartheid democracy" in which "state power must clearly vest in the elected representatives of the people and not, directly or indirectly, in the administrative command of a party."[13]

That Canada has followed the Pretoria regime in raising these disingenuous arguments against the ANC underscores the gulf between the government's analysis of, or interests in, Southern Africa's conflicts and the analysis of CUSO—or indeed, most other Canadian NGOs and churches active in the region, as well as leaders of the front line states. Zambia's then President Kenneth Kaunda, in a meeting with the House of Commons External Affairs Committee in 1989, described the ANC as, "non-racialists who deserve our support."

Canada claims to seek a balanced view of the ANC, with External Affairs representatives describing it as "an important factor in South Africa," and "a part of the solution." The policy has been constructive to some extent, with support being extended by the Canadian embassy in Pretoria to mostly white, progressive-liberal organizations inside South Africa, such as the Institute for a Democratic South Africa (IDASA) and the Five Freedoms Forum. Still CUSO has maintained its argument that Canada needs far more in house experience with the ANC, whose leaders are likely to rule South Africa once majority rule is achieved.

CUSO's perception is that, until recently, this in house experience has been lacking at External Affairs, with the result that analysis of the rapidly evolving situation in South Africa was often faulty, prompting ill-advised policies and ineffective approaches. That analysis, for example, tended to emphasize hoped-for shifts in white South African politics rather than the activities of the more significant Mass Democratic Movement.

The Canadian government, in CUSO's view, seeks a middle ground between white minority apartheid rule and black majority rule in South

Africa which quite simply does not exist. Stanford University's George Fredrickson recently described a dilemma facing liberals seeking solutions in South Africa, which seems to be reflected in the External Affairs position: "The primary question that liberals are now forced to face is: `Where do you stand in the struggle? For freedom or for stability?' They may refuse to choose by calling a plague on the irrationality of both houses and hover around in a fit of sullen irrelevancy. If they do, the struggle for freedom will become the exclusive preserve of the revolutionary, and the maintenance of stability the preserve of increasing repression." [14]

External Affairs Canada's position, as stated in March 1989, was as follows: "Canada's objective is to encourage a peaceful solution that results in a non-racial, representative government in South Africa. We are more likely to achieve both peace and democracy by dealing with the ANC and encouraging it to follow a moderate path. Canada condemns the use of violence by all sides in South Africa, whether aimed at bringing about change or maintaining the apartheid system...."[15] This was reaffirmed by External Affairs Minister Clark in a December 1989 letter, in which he also expressed satisfaction with, "the moderation in the attitude of the ANC" in connection with negotiations.[16]

CUSO's position is that Canada must do more than "deal with the ANC." CUSO also takes issue with Clark's suggestion that the ANC has "moderated" because it is prepared to negotiate with Pretoria, given the right conditions. The ANC, for most of its history, has been ready to negotiate an end to apartheid. Pretoria has steadfastly refused such talks, insisting that the ANC disarm, but continuing its own repression and denial of rights. With the ANC's unbanning and other measures by South African President F.W. de Klerk, it is quite clearly Pretoria which has moderated its extremist position.

Because the ANC, unlike the Pretoria regime, shares Canada's professed goal of "non-racial, representative government," it follows that Canada should express solidarity with the ANC and support its goals in a material way. By refusing to do so, or doing so only with very limited support for minor projects, Ottawa is missing an opportunity to develop links with South Africa's future rulers, links which would stand Canada in good stead in the next century.

In late 1988, Rev. Fumie Gqiba, the ANC's chaplain, said during a visit to Canada, "it is time for Canada to take another historical step with us, a final onslaught." He also expressed puzzlement at what he called Mulroney's "failure to fulfil his promises." [17] An ANC representative in Canada, Peter Mahlangu, has made similar comments. "There has been a lot of goodwill from Canada in terms of sanctions and isolating South Africa," he said in May 1989, "but Canada hasn't done much in terms of practical support for us."[18]

By offering more "practical support" to the ANC—either through CUSO supported projects or another channel—Canada helps the ANC build democratic institutions and develop administrative expertise. Although Ottawa has not specified what it means by "moderate path," one assumes it refers to democracy and nonviolence. If this is the case, the objective is better pursued through seeking greater proximity to the ANC than it is by maintaining distance from it. By providing more material support to the ANC, Canada could assist the movement's leadership to maintain unity behind allegiance to the Freedom Charter, which is founded on non-racialism and democracy—in fact, the moderate path Canada claims to wish for the ANC.

If one accepts the inevitability of an ANC-led or ANC-dominated government in South Africa—as the Mass Democratic Movement in South Africa does—one must also recognize that the ANC's current capacities and policies are inadequate at present for the task of governing. This is another compelling reason for Canada to offer constructive assistance.

A good example of this ANC policy weakness is in the area of land use. At present, 87 percent of South Africa's arable land is owned by whites. Clearly, in a postapartheid South Africa, an extensive program of land redistribution will be required. How will this be done? Although the ANC has conducted studies of South Africa's agrarian situation and how it might be reformed, these have not been widely discussed within the antiapartheid movement, nor have they been translated into policy positions. The ANC, quite simply, was too strapped to devote resources to policy work in this area.

CUSO and other Western agencies currently support research and workshops aimed at developing policy options. CUSO has sought to help the ANC bolster its research by providing funding for an agricultural economist to study land distribution in South Africa, assess alternative approaches to reform, and popularize the results of the research. The study is aimed at providing a basis for policy, so that a free South Africa's rulers will have a chance to avoid the conflicts and pitfalls which have beset land reform in Mozambique and Zimbabwe.

The ANC has now placed a priority on policy research, partly in response to the increasing number of delegations—including Afrikaners and white South African liberals—holding talks with ANC leaders. A postapartheid South Africa governed by the ANC will face challenges of external debt, structural adjustment, and massive unemployment, as well as long-suppressed and therefore urgent demands from the black majority for a redistribution of income and land. Without a policy agenda and strategy backed up by extensive research and debate within the ANC, the movement would be handicapped in its efforts to meet these challenges.

Canada could help to avert such a situation by approving funds—as CUSO has requested—for proposals to assist the ANC's Department of Economics and Planning, the projects' department of its Treasurer-General's office, and the South Africa land study. Such approvals could be a first step, followed by establishment of an extensive program of assistance to the ANC similar to those of the Nordic countries.

Such aid would be an expression of solidarity, a way of hastening the demise of apartheid, an investment in South Africa's future, and a solid contribution to prospects for peace in the region. CUSO will continue to offer the federal government access to the bridges it has built with the ANC—as it has with other Southern African liberation movements in the past. Indeed, CUSO will continue to prod Ottawa into crossing them.

Notes

1. John S. Saul, "Canada and Southern Africa," *Canadian Dimension* vol. 12, no. 1 (January 1977).

2. Paul Ladouceur, "Canadian Humanitarian Aid for Southern Africa," in *Canada, Scandinavia and Southern Africa*, eds. Anglin, Shaw and Widstrand (Uppsala: Scandinavian Institute of African Studies, 1978), p. 93.

3. *Ibid.*, p. 89.

4. *Ibid.*, p. 94.

5. *Ibid.*, p. 86.

6. *Ibid.*, p. 87.

7. Stephen M. Davis, *Apartheid's Rebels*, (New Haven: Yale University Press, 1987), p. 73.

8. *Ibid.*, p. 74.

9. John Saxby, interview by Christopher Neal, 20 October 1989.

10. See Mary Benson, *Nelson Mandela*, (Middlesex: Penguin Books, 1986), pp. 152-3.

11. Thomas G. Karis, "South African Liberation: The Communist Factor," *Foreign Affairs* vol. 65, no. 2 (Winter 1986-87), p. 274.

12. *Ibid.*, p. 275.

13. Joe Slovo, *Has Socialism Failed?*, Umsebenzi Discussion Pamphlet, South African Communist Party (London: Inkululeko Publications, January 1990), p. 27.

14. George M. Fredrickson, "Can South Africa Change?" *New York Review of Books*, 26 October 1989, p. 51.

15. Robert Peck, External Affairs Canada representative, interview by Christopher Neal, 30 March 1989.

16. Letter to Chris Bryant, executive director of CUSO, 18 December 1989.

17. *Globe and Mail*, 8 November 1988.

18. *CUSO Advocate*, May 1989.

Part III: New Forms of Assistance

The International Centre for Human Rights and Democratic Development: A New Approach to Politics and Democracy in Developing Countries?

Andres Perez
University of Western Ontario

Introduction

The adoption by the Canadian Parliament, on 30 September 1988, of the act establishing the International Centre for Human Rights and Democratic Development (ICHRDD) opened a new channel of Canadian assistance to developing countries. The ICHRDD began its operations on 19 October 1991.[1] Since then, it has supported a number of activities intended to promote and defend democracy and human rights in developing countries. The centre has also been confronting the challenge of setting operative goals which respond to its official mission. The distinction that is made here between the official mission of the centre and its operative goals is an important one. Missions are public statements designed to define the raison d'être and the general purposes of an organization. They are "symbolic, frequently not attainable and not even meant to be attained."[2] Operative goals, on the other hand, can be conceptualized as "the ends sought through the actual operating policies of the organization."[3] Organizational missions provide organizations with a general sense of direction and offer "symbolic reassurance to interest groups or the public at large."[4] Organizations can not simply base their existence on general definitions of their purposes, however. They must also identify the concrete and specific objectives which will determine "the main course of organizational behaviour."[5]

This paper analyzes the rationale underlying the creation of the ICHRDD and explores some possible alternative operative goals and strategies which the centre may adopt to respond to its mission. More specifically, this paper argues that the formal justification for the creation of the ICHRDD is based on an ahistorical and legalistic view of democracy and politics in developing countries. The selection of the centre's operative goals and strategies constitutes an opportunity both to overcome these deficiencies and to articulate a Canadian approach to democratic development and human rights which is compatible with the history, needs, and aspirations of developing countries.

The ICHRDD: the rationale underlying its creation

The study of organizations requires an examination of the rationale that justifies their creation and mandate. The rationale that underlies the creation of an organization constitutes a theoretical explanation of the nature of the social issues and problems which the organization is expected to confront in the fulfilment of its mandate and objectives. These explanations are based on "postulations" and "background assumptions."[6] Postulations are explicitly formulated statements that express a particular understanding of the causes and implications of social phenomena. Background assumptions, on the other hand, are "unpostulated" and "unlabelled" interpretations of the essence of social reality. Alvin Gouldner explains: "Background assumptions are embedded in a theory's postulations. Operating within and alongside of them, they are, as it were, "silent partners" in the theoretical enterprise. Background assumptions provide some of the bases of choice and the invisible cement for linking together postulations. From beginning to end, they influence a theory's formulation and the researches to which it leads."[7] The formal rationale underlying the creation of the ICHRDD is based on three postulations:

(a) Social conflict and human rights violations in developing countries are the result of both economic and political inequality, and the failure of political institutions to defend and protect the citizens of those countries.[8]
(b) Democratic institutions are effective mechanisms for the protection of human rights.[9]
(c) Canada's democratic experience can be useful in assisting developing countries to establish their own democratic institutions.[10]

There are conceptions of social and political reality underlying these postulations that constitute the "background assumptions" upon which the formal justification for the creation of the ICHRDD is based. These assumptions are "unpostulated" and "unlabelled", but they are traceable and ultimately recognizable. Very frequently, they lie hidden behind the use of undefined concepts.

Concepts are left undefined when it is assumed that their meaning is universal and/or self-evident. From this perspective, undefined concepts are not devoid of meaning; rather, they constitute "data containers."[11] The documents that comprise the theoretical foundations of the ICHRDD discuss the importance and value of democratic practices and institutions without discussing and defining the concept of democracy itself. The concept is left undefined, but it works as a "silent partner" in shaping the centre's mandate and objectives. Occasionally the undefined concept of democracy "speaks out" and reveals the content of the background assumptions that form part of the theoretical underpinnings of the ICHRDD.

Three background assumptions can be identified as a result of a critical analysis of the documents that justify the creation of the ICHRDD: democracy is liberal democracy;[12] democracy is a formal-legal mechanism for conflict resolution; liberal democracy can be reproduced in developing countries with the technical support of democratic countries like Canada. The following is an examination of these assumptions.

Assumption # 1: Democracy is liberal democracy

The Special Joint Committee of the Senate and the House of Commons on Canada's International Relations recommended the establishment of an "International Institute of Human Rights and Democratic Development" in June 1986. The objective of the proposed institute was to contribute to "the long term development of political, civil, and cultural rights" in developing countries.[13] The report recommended that the modus operandi of the institute should be "practical and primarily technical in nature, careful to avoid advocacy, propaganda and the most sensitive or controversial areas of democratic development."[14] Examples of the activities proposed for the institute include election monitoring, technical and financial support to workers' organizations, and research in the areas of human rights and legislative institutions.[15]

The government of Canada accepted the committee's recommendation for the creation of the institute. The Secretary of State for External Affairs subsequently commissioned a report to explore ways of proceeding with "the creation of an institution which would have as its objective, the development, strengthening and promotion of democratic institutions and human rights in developing countries...."[16] The *rapporteurs* responsible for this exploration consulted a wide range of individuals and representatives of Canadian and international institutions, who were generally supportive of the Canadian government's initiative; however, the *rapporteurs* were also warned about the dangers associated with any attempt to transfer Canadian democratic institutions and practices to other countries:

> Many of our interlocutors, notably those working in the area of cooperation with developing countries, and those involved in the protection and promotion of human rights internationally, have cautioned us against the use of the word "democracy" and its derivatives in the formulation of the name and the mandate of an eventual institution. This terminology, they have reminded us, has acquired an ideological, political and cultural meaning which differs profoundly from one region of the world to another. Coming from a western industrialized country, it risks being interpreted as an intention to impose on our cooperation programs in this area our own concept of democracy.[17]

Unfortunately, the *rapporteurs* did not explore and explain the implications and substantive problems associated with the use of the concept of democracy in the rationale that justified the creation of the ICHRDD. They proposed instead the elimination of the word "democratic" in the name of the Center; that is, they proposed the name International Centre for Human Rights and Institutional Development instead of International Centre for Human Rights and Democratic Development. The ultimate objective of this centre would be "the promotion, development and strengthening of institutions, programs and practices which serve to give effect to the rights and freedoms enshrined in the International Bill of Human Rights.[18] The proposed removal of the concept of democracy was bureaucratically convenient but intellectually inadequate. By replacing the concept of "democratic" with "institutional," the report failed to explore both the nature of political phenomena in developing countries and Canada's capacity to contribute to these countries' democratic development.

The act that established the centre retained the word "democratic" in the name of the new organization and stated that the objective of the centre was the promotion, development and strengthening of democratic and human rights institutions and programs in developing countries in accordance with the tenets of the International Bill of Human Rights.[19] Democracy was defined by default as liberal democracy in the absence of a substantive exploration into the essence of politics in developing countries. This may be seen in the way in which the International Bill of Human Rights is politicized in the act that created the ICHRDD.

The International Bill of Human Rights is an attempt to establish some principles of social life as inalienable characteristics of the human condition.[20] The bill of rights does not endorse any particular political system as a means to achieve, promote, and defend those rights. The formal statement of objectives of ICHRDD reduces the political scope of the bill by imbedding a preference for *pluralistic political systems* as the proper means to preserve and promote human rights in developing countries. Officially, the objectives of the centre are:

> To initiate, encourage and support cooperation between Canada and other countries in the promotion, development and strengthening of democratic and human rights institutions and programs that give effect to the rights and freedoms enshrined in the International Bill of Human Rights, including, among those rights, the right to an adequate standard of living, the rights of persons not to be subjected to torture or to cruel, inhuman or degrading treatment or punishment, the rights of freedom of opinion and expression and the right to vote and be elected at periodic, genuine elections *in pluralistic political systems* [emphasis added]. A major object will be to help reduce the wide gap that sometimes exists between the formal adherence of states to international human rights agreements and the actual human rights practices of states.21

The concept of political pluralism helps to clarify the way in which the concept of democracy was used and interpreted in the documents that contain the rationale underlying the creation of the ICHRDD. Political pluralism is a concept that claims to represent and describe the way in which political conflict and competition is organized in liberal democratic societies.[22] Pluralist analyses of liberal democratic societies suggest that power is distributed among a plethora of interest groups. These groups are associations of individuals that organize their actions to defend their interests. The demands articulated by interest groups are aggregated by political parties, which translate them to the state. The pluralist perspective of society conceptualizes the state as an institution that represents the general interest of society; hence, it is supposed to respond to the demands of interest groups while it upholds the public interest.[23]

An argument could be made that the concept of pluralism may be used according to its "valuational" meaning—that is, as a concept that simply refers to the existence and tolerance of "disagreement and dissension within the political community."[24] The statement of objectives of the ICHRDD, however, refers to pluralism as a system—that is, it uses the concept of pluralism according to its "functional" meaning. Charles Davis explains that "while valuational pluralism concerns political culture, functional pluralism refers to political structure."[25] Thus, functional pluralism refers to a system of interest representation in which "the constituents units are organized into an unspecified number of multiple, voluntary, competitive, non-hierarchically ordered, and self-determined (as to type or scope of interest) categories that are not specifically licensed, recognized, subsidised or otherwise controlled in leadership selection or interest articulation by the state and that do not exercise a monopoly of representational activity within their respective categories."[26]

By linking human rights and political pluralism, the formal statement of objectives of the ICHRDD does not contemplate the possibility that some human rights such as "the right to an adequate standard of living" could be achieved by means of a nonpluralistic political system (Cuba is an example of this possibility). It also ignores the possibility that the promotion and endorsement of political pluralism in countries characterized by high degrees of social and economic inequality can lead to the preservation of the status-quo and the continued exploitation of the poor (Guatemala is an example of this). Finally, the Centre's mandate contradicts some aspects of the formal rationale underlying the creation of the ICHRDD because it links human rights with political pluralism. This formal rationale opposes the idea of interpreting democratic development as the export of Canadian values and institutions into developing countries.[27]

Assumption # 2: Democracy is a mechanism for conflict resolution

The documents that led to the creation of the ICHRDD emphasize the formal and legal dimensions of democracy; that is, democracy is conceived of as an institutional mechanism for the organization of political competition. This approach fails to recognize that democracy is both an institutional arrangement for conflict resolution and the expression of a political consensus.[28] These two dimensions of democracy are interdependent in so far as the effectiveness of democracy as a mechanism for conflict resolution depends on the existence of a social consensus regarding the basic organization of political life. This consensus does not lead to the elimination of conflict, but allows conflict to be regulated and managed within socially accepted boundaries. Thus, it is important to distinguish between political conflict *within* the regime, and political conflict *about* the regime.[29] Maurice Duverger explains that the difference between these two forms of political conflict "resembles the distinction between a game played according to the rules, and a contest that is waged against the rules in order to establish new rules."[30] Conflict within the regime is marginal in the sense that it does not affect the fundamental principles and institutions of a political system. Conflict about the regime, on the other hand, is fundamental because it questions the very basis of political life.

Elections and other formal democratic mechanisms for conflict resolution deal with marginal rather than fundamental social issues. They are effective only when political disputes can be resolved with changes of government rather than changes of political systems; thus, fundamental political differences must be settled before elections can be used effectively. From this perspective, elections are democratic not because they are *about* democracy, but because they occur *within* democracy.[31] Put in a different way, elections and other democratic mechanisms for conflict resolution are functional only when they deal with conflict within the regime. They are effective as long as their legal and formal application is sustained by a legitimized view of the fundamental nature of the regime. Robert Dahl explains:

> In a sense, what we ordinarily describe as democratic "politics" is merely the chaff. It is the surface manifestation, representing superficial conflicts. Prior to politics, beneath it, enveloping it, restricting it, conditioning it, is the underlying consensus on policy that usually exists in the society among a predominant portion of the politically active members. Without such a consensus no democratic system would long survive the endless irritations and frustrations of elections and party competition. With such a consensus the disputes over policy alternatives are nearly always disputes over a set of alternatives that have already been winnowed down to those within the broad area of basic agreement.[32]

In many, if not most, developing countries political instability and turmoil express the absence of a minimum consensus regarding the political organization of society. Terry Lynn Karl explains that achieving this consensus requires agreement among social forces and political actors at least with regard to "the permanent rules governing the competition for public office; the resolution of conflict; the reproduction of capital; and the appropriate role of the state, particularly the military and the bureaucracy."[33]

Promoting the use of elections and other formal democratic mechanisms of conflict resolution in socially fragmented and politically polarized societies is putting the cart before the mules. A legalistic and formal approach to democratic development in developing countries might even be counterproductive in that it could promote the legalization of illegitimate regimes. In his analysis of legitimacy and ethnicity in South Africa, Hebert Adam has shown how legality can become a substitute for legitimacy and an effective guideline for the enforcement of order. According to Adam, "the separation of legality from legitimacy makes it possible to rule illegitimately with the aid of the law."[34]

Assumption # 3: Liberal democracy can be reproduced with technical support from democratic countries like Canada

Attempts to promote the development and consolidation of democracy in developing countries are not new. Many efforts were made by the West during the 1950s, 1960s and 1970s to explore ways of inducing the political evolution of developing countries along liberal democratic lines. Richard A. Higgott has pointed out that this was a period of optimism, when it was believed that "the growth of "scientific" social science would form the basis for rational exercises in social engineering."[35] A similar optimism seems to lie behind the rationale that underlies the creation of the ICHRDD. It follows that an assessment of the theoretical foundations of the post-World War II attempts to promote democratic development in developing countries is required to facilitate an understanding of the possibilities and obstacles that the ICHRDD will face in its attempt to promote the development and consolidation of democratic institutions in developing countries.

The developing world was caught between the hegemonic tendencies of the United States of America and the Soviet Union in the aftermath of the World War II. In these circumstances, the theory and the practice of development were introduced into developing countries to promote their evolution according to the political and economic priorities of the capitalist and industrialized countries of the West.

During the postwar years, development was simply equated with economic growth as it was measured by traditional economic indicators such as Gross National Product (GNP) and income per capita.[36] In the 1960s, the sociological, psychological, and political dimensions of development began to be identified and studied. Joseph La Palombara used the concept of political development to argue that external inducements were necessary to facilitate the evolution of developing countries "in the direction of freedom rather than tyranny."[37] Freedom was equated with liberal democracy and tyranny with anything that resembled fascism or Marxism.[38] Political development entailed the development of liberal democratic political systems in the third world by means of external inducements.[39]

Political development represents an historical approach to politics and democracy in developing countries. Liberal democracy was used by the proponents of political development as a normative model for the South, without considering the historical factors which determined the emergence and consolidation of political processes and institutions in present liberal democratic societies. Furthermore, liberal democracy as a normative model was introduced in developing countries without due consideration to the historical factors which have shaped the political evolution of these societies and which condition their future political possibilities.

The rationale that justifies the creation of the ICHRDD is also ahistorical in that it assumes that the practice of liberal democracy can be replicated in developing countries and that Canada's experience can be useful in the institutionalization of those practices. At the root of this ahistorical interpretation of democracy lies a confusion between what Dankwart Rustow calls the genetic and the functional dimensions of democracy. Briefly stated, Rustow argues that the conditions which are required to maintain an established democratic system are not the same as those required for the development and consolidation of a new one.[40] Canada has a great deal of experience in the maintenance of institutionalized democratic practices. These democratic practices, however, are the outcome, not the cause, of the political evolution of the country. To assume that the knowledge and expertise required to maintain an institutionalized democracy are the same as the competence required to create one is to ignore the historical processes that determine the nature, structure, and function of political institutions in both developing and developed countries.

Democracy, legality, and legitimacy: alternative operational strategies

There are at least two possible courses of action for the ICHRDD. The first is to conceive of democratic development as the promotion of *legally* established democratic institutional arrangements for the resolution of

political conflict. Unfortunately, this is the orientation that can be naturally and logically derived from the rationale that underlies the creation
of the ICHRDD.

A second option is to regard democratic development as the promotion of national democratic social consensus regarding the system of
rules that govern political conflict and competition. This approach does
not ignore the value and importance of formal-legal democratic processes, but it sees the legitimacy of these processes rather than their
legality, as the cornerstone of democracy.

A law is a prescription to regulate human behaviour. The application
of the law requires the use of power, which can be exercised through
relations of coercion or through relations of domination. Relations of
coercion are based on force, violence, repression and threat, while
relations of domination are based on the acknowledged legitimacy of the
rulers by the ruled.[41] From this perspective, the legitimization of power
relations is vital to the maintenance of social order and to the effective
functioning of political institutions. The stability provided by political
institutions is not simply based on formal and procedural adequacy but
on society's acceptance of their role. The functional effects of liberal
democratic rules and institutions in democratic societies are not simply
due to their legal foundation but to society's recognition of the legitimacy
of those rules and institutions. Democratic institutions can be legal but
not legitimate in the absence of this social acceptance.[42]

Most current approaches to democratic development follow a legalistic approach to politics in developing countries. These approaches
involve activities such as political party training, legislative training,
management of local governments, programs of civic education, and
above all, election management and election monitoring.[43] This formal
and legalistic approach to democratic development ignores the fact that
the effectiveness of elections and other democratic mechanisms of conflict resolution is largely dependent on the existence of a minimum social
consensus regarding the rules that govern political competition. Giuseppe
Di Palma argues that in Europe,

> elections were never used as a tool to bring about democracy. Similarly,
> they were never used to arrest liberalization at the threshold of democ-
> racy, by artfully constraining electoral participation and procedures. Nor
> were they ever successfully used to go beyond democracy, towards some
> kind of radicalizing utopia. As a tool for democracy, they were not
> needed; as a tool against it, they were late and insufficient. Instead,
> elections were knowingly used to legitimise after the fact, and even with
> some delay, a democratic choice that had already been made by and
> through the revival of civil society and of state/institutional autonomy.[44]

The revival of civil society as a condition for the consolidation of
democracy provides an important entry point for the formulation of a

nonlegalistic operational strategy to promote democratic development in developing countries. The emphasis of this approach is on the conformation of a democratic social consensus concerning the rules that govern political life and political competition in developing countries rather than on the promotion of legal institutions and procedures.

This approach seems to be the one being followed by the first administration of the ICHRDD. In a recent speech Edward Broadbent, the Centre's President, explained that "...the key to democracy is the building of a civil society. It gives meaning and importance to elections. A well developed civil society both requires free elections and ensures that elections are not meaningless. The building of a civil society, therefore, ought to be seen as the major element in democratic development."[45] In this approach, the promotion of human rights is not seen as a task that is separated from the promotion of democratic institutions. According to Broadbent, "each human right is a brick in the edifice of democracy."[46] From this perspective, the building of a civil society entails "...setting up institutions, organizations and practices which encourage people to take responsibility for their own destinies. For workers, it would involve the right to organize a union; for national minorities and indigenous peoples, the right to their language and their culture; for farmers, the opening of a credit union; for children, the opening of a school, and for citizens at large, the opportunity to create a new political party or to publicly express their opinions."[47]

ICHRDD's current approach to human rights and democratic development implies that the promotion of democracy involves the development of people's capacity to influence the social structures and the political processes within which they live. More specifically, it involves the empowering of the marginal sectors of society to facilitate their capacity to influence the orientation, organization, and functioning of the state. The orientation of the ICHRDD coincides with the operational strategy formulated by the International Development Research Center (IDRC) for its experimental research program on representative institutions, participatory processes, and public policies. A brief review of the rationale, objectives, and operational strategy of this program may expose alternative avenues through which the ICHRDD can further develop its strategy of democratic development through the revitalization of civil society.

IDRC has explored ways of ensuring that the results of the research projects it supports contribute to the solution of problems facing the marginal social sectors of developing countries.[48] IDRC viewed public policies as important mechanisms for the use and implementation of research results in these explorations and for this reason, IDRC concluded that "the discussions of research impact should include an analysis of the nature of the processes of public policy formulation and implementation in developing countries."[49] IDRC established the experimental research program on representative institutions, participatory processes and public policies in 1987 to facilitate this analysis. The central objective of this program was "to explore the possibilities to facilitate the participation of the most disadvantaged sectors of developing countries in the processes of formulation and implementation of public policies."[50] The program and its objective were based on the assumption that "the capacity or willingness of social institutions to formulate and implement policies that address the problems of the most disadvantaged social groups of developing countries largely depends on the capacity of these groups to influence the processes of formulation and implementation of public policies. The influence of these groups is made effective through a variety of mechanisms of political representation such as political parties, unions, interest groups, etc."[51]

Two research areas were established: "Political Analysis of Processes of Formulation and Implementation of Public Policies" and "Analysis of Political Actors and Institutions." The first research area was intended to include research activities exploring the role of different political and bureaucratic actors in the formulation of public policies. The second research area aimed at supporting research activities which would study the functions, structure, and evolution of actors and institutions involved in policy making and policy implementation in developing countries.[52]

IDRC consciously avoided a formalistic approach to politics in developing countries when it designed its research program on representative institutions, participatory processes and public policies. Researchers in different developing countries received support to explore possible ways of achieving the participation of the marginal social sectors in the formulation and implementation of public policies that affected their lives. They were free to propose the level of analysis (national policies or local policies) and the policy area that they wanted to study. More significantly, IDRC's experimental program did not have as its ultimate goal the promotion of any particular type of political system or institutions. The program was based on the assumption that the definition of the form and nature of the political institutions of developing countries was the sole right and responsibility of the people of those countries. For this reason, research projects exploring avenues of political participation in policy formulation were supported in countries representing a wide variety of political systems and orientations. They included countries that had recently moved from military to democratically elected regimes (Argentina, Uruguay, and Brazil); a country that was undergoing a process of institutionalization of a socialist-oriented revolution (Nicaragua); a country with a long tradition of liberal democratic practices and institutions (Costa Rica); a socialist country with a political system based on the Leninist principle of democratic centralism

(Cuba); a country subjected to one of the most brutal military regimes in the history of the world (Chile); finally, the country considered to be the largest democracy in the world (India).

ICHRDD could benefit by studying the IDRC's experience in the area of participation, representation, and public policy. ICHRDD might even propose to absorb some of the program's activities since the democratization of policy making and policy implementation is central to the construction of democratic civil societies in developing countries.

Conclusion

The purpose of this essay was to analyze the rationale underlying the creation of the ICHRDD and to explore alternatives to the institute's operational strategy. The arguments presented here clearly favour the formulation of a strategy which transcends the ahistorical and formalistic approach contained in the reports that provide the Centre's theoretical foundation. The ICHRDD's current strategy of promoting democratic development through the revitalization of civil society is one that can avoid the limitations and obstacles inherent in the organizational rationale of the Centre; however, this strategy involves long, difficult, and sometimes frustrating efforts whose results might not be evident to many politicians and bureaucrats looking for quick and visible results.

There will be a strong temptation in a new organization like the International Centre for Human Rights and Democratic Development to take the easy path of promoting and diffusing the political technology of democracy in the name of democratic development. The modus operandi required to follow this path is well known. Moreover, the product of this operative strategy is visible and it enjoys legitimacy at home. Undoubtedly ICHRDD's future relevance will be determined by the way it balances its own domestic pressures and constraints with the imagination, creativity, and long-term involvement required for work in the difficult political conditions of developing countries.

Notes

1.   International Centre for Human Rights and Democratic Development, *Annual Report 1991* (Montreal, 1991), p. 1.

2.   Florence Heffron, *Organization Theory and Public Organizations: The Political Connection* (Englewood Cliffs, N.J.: Prentice Hall, 1989), p. 90.

3.   Charles Perrow, "The Analysis of Goals in Complex Organizations," *American Sociological Review* vol. 26, no. 6 (1961): 855.

4.   Heffron, *Organizational Theory*, p. 90.

5.   R.L. Blumbers, *Organization in Contemporary Society* (Englewood Cliffs, N.J.: Prentice Hall, Inc., 1987), p. 76.

6. For a full explanation of the concepts of "postulations" and "background assumptions," see Alvin Gouldner, *The Coming Crisis of Western Sociology* (New York: Basic Books, Inc., 1970), pp. 29–35.

7. Gouldner, *Coming Crisis*, p. 24.

8. See the Special Joint Committee of the Senate and of the House of Commons on Canada's International Relations, *Independence and Internationalism* (Ottawa, June 1986), p. 104.

9. *Ibid.*

10. *Ibid.*, pp. 103–105.

11. See Giovanni Sartori, "Concept Misinformation in Comparative Politics," in *Comparative Politics: Notes and Readings* eds. Roy C. Macridis and Bernard Brown, (Homewood, Ill.: The Dorsey Press, 1977), pp. 24–49.

12. The concept of "liberal democracy" is used here to refer to: "a political system in which (1) virtually all adult citizens are entitled to vote; (2) major policy-making officials are selected by the votes of citizens in elections in which more than one candidate has a reasonable chance of victory; and (3) there is substantial freedom for citizens to organize or join political parties and interest groups and to act individually or collectively to influence public policy." John A. Peeler, *Latin American Democracies* (Chapel Hill: The University of North Carolina Press, 1985), p. 5.

13. The Special Joint Committee, *Independence*, pp. 103–104.

14. *Ibid.*, p. 105.

15. *Ibid.*

16. Gisele Cote-Harper and John Courtney, "Report to the Right Honourable Joe Clark and the Honourable Monique Landry: International Cooperation for the Development of Human Rights and Democratic Institutions," 30 June 1987, p. 1.

17. *Ibid.*, pp. 24–25.

18. *Ibid.*, pp. 27–28.

19. See Canada, Parliament, The International Centre for Human Rights and Democratic Development Act, 35-36-37 Elizabeth II, Chapter 64, 1988.

20. For the purpose of the act, the International Bill of Human Rights includes:

    a) the Universal Declaration of Human Rights;

    b) the International Covenant on Civil and Political Rights;

    c) the Optional Protocol to the International Covenant on Civil and Political Rights; and

    d) the International Covenant on Economic, Social and Cultural Rights. See Canada, Parliament, The International Centre Act.

21. The International Centre for Human Rights and Democratic Development Act, Chapter 64.

22. Corporatism represents the most important alternative explanation of the political dynamic of advanced industrial democratic societies. See Reginald J. Harrison, *Pluralism and Corporatism: The Evolution of Modern Democracies* (London: George Allen & Unwin, 1980).

23. Robert Alford, "Paradigms of Relations Between the State and Society," in *Stress and Contradictions in Modern Capitalism*, ed. L.N. Lindberg (Massachusset:

HEAT, 1975), pp. 146–147. See also *Comparing Pluralist Democracies: Strains on Legitimac*, ed. Mattei Dogan (Boulder: Westview Press, 1988).

24. Charles Davis, "The Philosophical Foundations of Pluralism," in Antonio de Abreu Freire et al., *Le Pluralisme* (Montreal: FIDES, 1974), p. 225.

25. *Ibid.*, p. 224.

26. Philippe Schmitter, "Still the Century of Corporatism?" *The Review of Politics* vol. 36, no. 1 (January 1974): 96.

27. See the Special Joint Committee, *Independence*, p. 104 and Cote-Harper and Courtney, "Report to Right Honourable Joe Clark," p. 350.

28. For in depth analyses of these two dimensions see among others, Robert A. Dahl, *A Preface to Democratic Theory* (Chicago: The University of Chicago Press, 1956); Robert A. Dahl, *Polyarchy: Participation and Opposition* (New Haven: Yale University Press, 1971); Dankwart A. Rustow, "Transitions to Democracy: Toward a Dynamic Model," *Comparative Politics*, April 1970, pp. 337–366; Terry Lynn Karl, "Democracy by Design: The Christian Democratic Party in El Salvador," in *The Central American Impasse*, eds. Giuseppe Di Palma and Laurence Whitehead (London: Croom Helm, 1986), pp. 195–217; C.B. MacPherson, *The Life and Times of Liberal Democracy* (Oxford: Oxford University Press, 1980); Jose Nun, "La Teoria Politica y la Transicion Democratica," in *Ensayos Sobre la Transicion Democratica en Argentina*, eds. Jose Nun and Juan Carlos Portantiero (Buenos Aires: Puntosur, 1987), pp. 15–56.

29. See Maurice Duverger, *The Study of Politics* (New York: Thomas Y. Crowell Company, 1972), pp. 207–211.

30. *Ibid.*, p. 207.

31. Giuseppe Di Palma, "The European and the Central American Experience," in *The Central America Impasse*, eds. Giuseppe DiPalma and Lawrence Whitehead, p.35.

32. Dahl, *A Preface*, pp. 132–133.

33. Terry Karl, "Imposing Consent? Electoralism vs. Democratization in El Salvador," in *Elections and Democratization in Latin America, 1980–1985*, eds. Paul W. Drake and Eduardo Silva (San Diego: University of California: 1986), p. 10.

34. Hebert Adam, "Legitimacy and the Institutionalization of Ethnicity: Comparing South Africa," in *Ethnic Groups and the State*, ed. Paul Brass (London: Croom Helm, 1985), p. 265.

35. Richard A. Higgott, *Political Development Theory* (London: Croom Helm, 1983), p. 16.

36. See J.B. Nugent and P.A. Yotopoulos, "What Has Orthodox Development Economics Learned from Recent Experience," *World Development* vol. 7, no. 6 (1979): 542, in Bjorn Hettne, *Development Theory and the Third World*, SAREC Report R 2 (Swedish Agency for Research Cooperation with Developing Countries, 1982), p. 19.

37. *Bureaucracy and Political Development*, ed. Joseph La Palombara (New Jersey: Princeton University Press, 1963), p. x.

38. Higgott, *Political Development*, p. 16.

39. See Ralph Braibanti, "External Inducements of Political Administrative Development: An Institutional Strategy," in *Political and Administrative Development*, ed. Ralph Braibanti (Durham: Duke University Press, 1969), pp. 3–106.

40. Rustow, "Transitions to Democracy", p. 346.

41. Max Weber, *Economy and Society: An Outline of Interpretive Sociology*, eds. Guenther Roth and Claus Wittich, trans. Ephraim Fischoff et al. (New York: Bedminster Press, 1968), vol. III, p. 946.

42. See Joseph LaPalombara, *Politics Within Nations* (Englewood Cliffs, N.J.: Prentice Hall Inc., 1974), pp. 48–50.

43. See, for example, the activities of The Centre for Democracy, The National Endowment for Democracy, and the National Democratic Institute.

44. Di Palma, "The European," p.35.

45. Edward Broadbent, "Democratic Development: Beyond Election Monitoring," speech delivered at the Canada Latin-America Forum, Washington, 4 March 1991, p. 6.

46. *Ibid.*, p. 5.

47. *Ibid.*, pp. 6–7.

48. International Development Research Centre, Social Science Division, "Experimental Research Program on Representative Institutions, Participatory Processes and Public Policies," Internal Document (Ottawa, 1987), p. 1.

49. *Ibid.*

50. *Ibid.*, p. 3.

51. *Ibid.*, p. 2.

52. *Ibid.*, pp. 3–4.

Immunization and Cease-fires

Robin Hay and Clyde Sanger*

Canadian Committee, Days of Peace

Introduction

Two remarkable phenomena are taking place in the world today: one is the campaign to immunize all children of the developing world; the other is the trend toward the resolution of regional conflict. While these are unrelated events, it is possible for them to be linked in a way that would augment the chances of success for both. The means of this linking, we propose, is the immunization cease-fire—a cessation of fighting for a predetermined time, for instance five days, in order that children can be immunized. Such cease-fires have happened in El Salvador and Lebanon. A humanitarian cease-fire with an immunization component has taken place in the Sudan. This paper presents case studies of these cease-fires as workable examples of the "aid as peacemaker" idea; it argues for the application of this concept in other regional conflicts.

This chapter was drafted in mid-1989 and does not therefore take account of the following events: the overthrow of the Mengistu regime in Ethiopia, the breakdown of peace negotiations in the Sudan, and the level of child immunization actually reached by the UNICEF-WHO target date of 1990. Nor does it mention the ambitious and successful conference on humanitarian cease-fires mounted by the Days of Peace organization in Ottawa in November 1991, attended not only by a strong UNICEF contingent headed by Jim Grant, but also by delegations from eight conflict zones. The general argument in this chapter is not overtaken, so much as reinforced however, by such events.

---

* This paper draws from the study, "Humanitarian Cease-fires: An Examination of their Role in the Resolution of Conflict" by Robin Hay (September 1989). This study was commissioned by the Canadian Committee of Days of Peace, an Ottawa based group of organizations and individuals working in the fields of health, development, and conflict resolution. The committee's purpose is to promote the holding of cease-fires in war zones to allow children to be immunized. Financial assistance for Robin Hay's research was received from the Canadian Institute for International Peace and Security.

The context

Universal immunization by 1990

The world is in the midst of what UNICEF has termed the "Child Health Revolution." One part of this is immunization. In 1977 fewer than 10 percent of the children of the developing world were immunized against the main fatal childhood diseases. In that year, UNICEF and the World Health Organization set 1990 as the target date to achieve universal child immunization. Their programme aims to immunize 80 percent of the developing world's children against measles, polio, diphtheria, whooping cough, tetanus, and tuberculosis. As of 1989, more than 60 percent of the world's children have been immunized. Canada strongly supports this goal. The Canadian government has given $44 million towards universal immunization in developing countries. Nineteen Canadian NGOs have contributed more than $13 million and implement the program with host governments in forty-two countries.

Movement toward the resolution of regional conflict

In 1988 and again in 1989, the number of wars decreased. For the first time in thirty one years, no new wars (armed conflicts with deaths over one thousand) were started. This halted a trend in the 1980s of an annual rise in the number of conflicts. It had reached a peak in 1987, with twenty-seven individual wars under way. By July 1989 the annual count had dropped to fifteen wars—300,000 people died in them that year, compared with 477,000 in 1987. There was a marked increase over previous years in the number of armed conflicts resolved through dialogue. Several reasons account for these developments, including a new importance accorded to the United Nations, the resort to regional negotiations, and the reduction in Cold War tension between the Americans and the Soviets. Whatever the causes of this peaceful shift, it is important for this trend to be supported and strengthened in coming years.

Immunization cease-fire proposal

Health as a bridge to peace

One main obstacle to achieving universal immunization is war. War impedes or completely blocks access by health workers to children. As a result, children in war zones are being killed by vaccine-preventable diseases. While immunization levels in many developing countries are approaching 75 percent, in war zones rates can drop below 15 percent.

Immunization cease-fires can increase child immunization levels in war zones and can provide a reason for short-term peace which could help build the momentum for the negotiation of lasting peace. To meet this challenge is the goal of the Canadian committee of Days of Peace. The committee is less an organization than a network of representatives of organizations and agencies, as well as of well-connected individuals. Taking advantage of the campaign to immunize the world's children by the end of 1990, this group proposes the negotiation of five day "humanitarian cease-fires" in zones of conflict in order to immunize the children living there.

Not only will this bring health protection to children who, because of the war, would otherwise have lacked it, but it also provides a reason for peace. Stopping a war for five days, in aid of such a laudable cause, can ideally serve as a first step in bringing about a permanent cease-fire.

Let no one think that, just because it is such a simple and immediately attractive idea, negotiating a cease-fire in order to deliver humanitarian aid is an uncomplicated business. On the contrary, it is an arduous and politically delicate process. The delicacy, arising from the political sensitivities of both the disputants and the intermediary, has usually meant that the few successes there have been so far are not well documented. This lack of documentation is explained by the fact that the organizations involved are (to their credit) action rather than research oriented. "There is no time to record what is being done," is how Luis Rivera, UNICEF's chief of communications, explained the situation in an interview in July 1989. Nevertheless, there is adequate material to describe cease-fires that were established for humanitarian purposes in El Salvador in 1985 and subsequent years, in Lebanon in 1987, and in the Sudan in 1989.

Case Studies

El Salvador

On 3 February 1985, at 8 A.M., the people of El Salvador embarked on the first of three scheduled "days of tranquillity." This term was used to describe the series of informal one day cease-fires between rebel forces and government troops which UNICEF and the Roman Catholic church in El Salvador had managed to arrange. The cease-fire days took place one Sunday a month for three consecutive months. The purpose of the cease-fires was to allow the International Committee of the Red Cross (ICRC) and local health authorities to enter the war torn areas and immunize up to 400,000 children against five main childhood diseases: diphtheria, whooping cough, tetanus, polio, and measles.

The idea was discussed in July 1984 during a conversation in New York between UNICEF Executive Director James Grant and the president of El Salvador, José Napoleon Duarte. During their talk, Grant reminded Duarte that some twenty thousand Salvadoran children were dying every year, a loss far exceeding the total number of deaths caused by the war. He also pointed out that most of these deaths could have been prevented with fifty cents worth of vaccine. Persuasively, Grant added that the benefits of a concerted immunization program would be swiftly visible within, for instance, the span of one presidential term. This final point may have clinched the agreement, though Duarte agreed not to use the vaccination campaign for partisan politics.

UNICEF stipulated that a campaign must involve all the children in El Salvador and, therefore, must cover all the conflict zones. Duarte objected that it would be too dangerous to try to enter territory controlled by the guerillas. Grant then raised the idea of a temporary cease-fire throughout the country; in this way the whole plan for immunization cease-fires was born. In October 1984, an evaluation team, made up of people from the Pan-American Health Organization (PAHO), UNICEF, and El Salvador's Ministry of Health—started a feasibility study of the proposed program. They drafted a three year Plan of Action, recommending three immunization days each year, starting in 1985 on 3 February, 3 March and 23 April.

The next step was for the government to negotiate a cease-fire with the guerillas of the Farabundo Marti National Liberation Front (FMLN). This was not a straightforward business. The problem was that the government, and particularly the military commanders, felt that negotiating even a temporary cease-fire for humanitarian purposes with the guerillas would imply some formal recognition of the FMLN. It was solved by getting two leaders of the Roman Catholic church in El Salvador—Monsignor Arturo Rivera Damas and Monsignor Gregorio Rosa Chavez—to act as interlocutors with the FMLN. This was an ideal choice, for the church had been for years a staunch defender of human rights—propounding moral principles and arguing for uniform national standards of behaviour. It had thus kept active contact with the opposing factions.

The FMLN leaders told the church team they were interested in the scheme. One guerilla commander commented: "The vaccination is of great importance for our people. We cannot be in disagreement in any way." So a complicated procedure for negotiations was established. Health ministry officials took to UNICEF representatives their proposals for immunization in various parts of the country. These were passed on to one or another church leader, who presented them to the guerillas. The guerillas made modifications and returned them to the government through the same channels. In this manner the government maintained the fiction that it was not negotiating with the rebels.

The outcome of this "nonnegotiation" was an unsigned agreement in which each side undertook not to carry out armed activities on the immunization days. UNICEF took great care not to refer to the agreement as a truce or cease-fire; instead, it coined the phrase "day of tranquillity." An idea of how tentative the arrangement was can be gathered from the fact that the guerillas did not give the church leaders final confirmation they would respect a cease-fire until late in the afternoon of 2 February. At that point an FMLN representative telephoned Monsignor Chavez to say simply, "It is our policy to let the children be vaccinated," and then hung up.

A huge social mobilization campaign prepared the way for these days of tranquillity. A media drive began six weeks before the first such day in 1985. It included more than eleven thousand announcements on television and radio. Before the opening day the main newspaper reported plans daily, while one million leaflets, thirty thousand brochures and ten thousand posters were distributed. Catholic and Protestant leaders preached from the pulpit the importance of vaccination and told their congregations to go straight from the church—the "days of tranquillity" were all Sundays—to the vaccination posts with their children.

True to the commitment they had made in New York, neither Duarte nor Grant sought any advantage from the campaign. Grant made sure that credit for its success was broadly shared: a February 1985 UNICEF press release acknowledges the participation of, among others, the government and the guerillas, the Catholic leadership, the ICRC, PAHO, the UN Development Program (UNDP), the US Agency for International Development (USAID) and also the Rotarians, the Lions Club and the Boy Scouts. For its part, the government took care not to describe the campaign as an exclusive initiative of its health authorities, or of any other department.

Lebanon

In the heady days which followed the first successful campaign in El Salvador, James Grant proclaimed that it had set an example for many other conflict zones. Two years later it was followed in Lebanon and, again, UNICEF initiated the move. In Lebanon, however, there was no obvious mediator like the Catholic church in El Salvador to deal with the several warring factions. The task fell to Grant himself and to Richard Reid, the regional head of UNICEF in the Middle East.

For almost a year they held painstaking negotiations with the different concerned parties, including Israel, Syria and the Iranian-backed Hezbollah. Their tactic was similar to that used in El Salvador: they called attention to the damage done to medical services and health precautions for children by twelve years of civil war and pointed out that, almost certainly, more children were dying from malnutrition and disease than from the actual violence of war. They argued that the only way to tackle the scourge of disease was to institute a series of cease-fires lasting three days each in September, October, and November 1987.

They convinced all factions. As Richard Reid said later, everyone was willing to unite for a single humanitarian effort. As in El Salvador, a campaign of social mobilization prepared people for the immunization program. Television and radio stations alerted the people, and Lebanon's Islamic mullahs helped spread the word from the minarets of their mosques.

The immunization program was a co-operative process in every particular. UNICEF was the chief organizer and also provided syringes and vaccines. The World Health Organization supplied the cold chain equipment (the storage and transit facilities which ensure the vaccines are kept at the required temperature). The Lebanese government and the ICRC produced the health workers. The different military factions supplied transport and communications equipment to the vaccination teams. So, on 23 September 1987, the gunfire stopped and vaccinations took place in 762 centres across the country. It soon became apparent that three days were not enough, and the cease-fire was extended for a fourth day. Reports from all sectors indicated that no fighting occurred during this time.

The Sudan

In the grip of widespread famine, nearly 250,000 women, children, and men perished in southern Sudan in 1988. This tragedy prompted the UN Secretary-General, Javier Pérez de Cuéllar, to urge the Sudanese prime minister, Sadiq Al-Mahdi, to call a high level conference of donors and UN agencies in order to work out a plan of action which might prevent a repetition of that disaster. Sadiq Al-Mahdi took his advice, and a two day meeting was duly held in March 1989 in Khartoum. It focused on the need to preposition food stocks at various points in southern Sudan before the rainy season began in May, which, until November, would cut off much of the region from outside help. The primary task was to streamline procedures for the delivery and stockpiling of supplies on a massive scale. It was calculated that to prevent a famine in which, perhaps, 100,000 people would die of starvation, up to 172,000 tons of food relief was required, costing U.S. $121 million. Nonfood aid, including an immunization component and kits of emergency drugs, would cost another $11 million.

Planners at the Khartoum meeting concluded that the whole of April would have to be observed as a "month of tranquillity," in order to transport supplies to the needy area by road, train, barge, and airplane. This would require a commitment by both government and rebel forces not to attack the transport and, in effect, recognize the neutrality of humanitarian relief. They also had to guarantee free access to all relief personnel to reach civilians in need throughout the Sudan. Beyond this, all who took part in the Khartoum meeting agreed on the paramount need for a permanent peaceful solution to the conflict which has been devastating the country for more than thirty years. All speakers placed a first priority on meeting the humanitarian needs, but equally they stressed the urgent importance of cease-fire and peace negotiations. The prime minister assured them his government put the highest priority on achieving peace.

On 23 March, the UN Secretary-General appointed James Grant as his special representative charged with implementing the Sudanese relief effort. Grant and Reid had spent the previous two weeks securing the agreement of the rebel Sudanese Peoples Liberation Army (SPLA) to a cease-fire. At first the Khartoum government refused them permission to make direct contact with the SPLA, but, under pressure from international agencies and the media, Sadiq Al-Mahdi eventually relented.

In the spirit of the Khartoum meeting's desire for long-term peace, the UNICEF pair urged the rebels to accept an earlier government offer of a six month cease-fire. Not only was this rejected, but the scheme for a single "month of tranquillity" throughout the Sudan was also turned down. The most the SPLA would agree to were eight corridors of peace along which, for one month, relief supplies could be delivered without hindrance. The UNICEF leaders decided that this offer, in effect, met the requirements of the Khartoum Plan of Action.

These "corridors of tranquillity" have been kept open by both sides several times beyond the original period of one month. Many observers have, in fact, cited this expandable arrangement as directly contributing to the process of establishing a long-term peace in the Sudan. Indeed, the arrangement paved the way for peace negotiations which began in June 1989.

Not only do the "corridors" constitute a humanitarian cease-fire of a different order, they also set other precedents. One writer in the *Washington Post* remarked in May 1989 that Operation Lifeline Sudan, as the UNICEF initiative is called, has established the right of civilians caught up in war to have access to relief aid, as well as the right of outside humanitarian agencies to supply it. Sudan has also been cited as the first country where two warring parties agreed on a common plan of action to protect and feed civilians on both sides of a conflict. In neither Lebanon nor El Salvador was there any formal agreement on the cease-fires.

Lessons of the humanitarian cease-fire cases

The cases of El Salvador, Lebanon, and the Sudan show, at the very least, that humanitarian cease-fires are feasible. They also demonstrate other possible effects of such cease-fires:

1. Cease-fires provide a concrete experience of co-operation. In all three cases, parties to the conflict actively co-operated in the relief effort. This included logistical and other forms of assistance. The agreement to stop fighting required the establishment of some form of constructive communication between the belligerents. This is an example of the concept of conflict resolution being changed into the notion of

conflict transformation. The conflict has not been resolved by the cease-fire, but it has been to a degree transformed in character.

2.   Humanitarian cease-fires can strengthen the hand of moderate factions who facilitate the cease-fire agreement. In El Salvador, for instance, the immunization campaign provided the church with a concrete, universally recognized mandate to increase its mediating role and hence its credibility with both sides in the conflict. It has provided the church with an additional means to strive openly for peace and reconciliation in that country.

3.   Humanitarian cease-fires can provide an opportunity for discussions leading to real peace. In Sudan, the "corridors of tranquillity" and the associated relief effort have been judged instrumental in paving the way for the peace talks which began in July 1989. Both parties to the conflict have acknowledged that Operation Lifeline Sudan has contributed to peace. This direct contribution to the peace process has been seen in other cases also. In 1965, in the Dominican Republic, during the fighting that followed the election of Juan Bosch to the presidency, a humanitarian cease-fire was arranged by the International Committee of the Red Cross to allow for the removal of the wounded and sick from the conflict zone around the capital, Santo Domingo. The cease-fire, intended only to allow the Red Cross to accomplish its mission, was extended by agreement between the belligerents and eventually helped bring an end to the fighting.

4.   Humanitarian cease-fires demonstrate the recognition by parties to a conflict that child health and other goals are held in common. The cease-fire requires the recognition that despite the dispute, both sides do share some values. Realization of this common goal is, for that period at least, more important than the goal of continuing the combat. Participation in a humanitarian relief effort may also lead to a greater recognition of the rules of warfare concerned with the rights of civilians as outlined in the Geneva Conventions. This recognition sometimes can lead to more humanitarian behaviour, even if the dispute is ended by military means, instead of a negotiated settlement. For instance, when the Nigerian civil war ended in 1970 with the military defeat of the Biafran forces, Quaker relief action, which had been carried on throughout the war, helped imbue both sides with a spirit of reconciliation. The Nigerian leader, General Yakubu Gowon, especially expressed this spirit. In accepting the Biafran surrender, he ordered all measures to be taken to effect a peaceful transfer of power without vindictiveness, and he went on to salute the soldiers who had "fought so bravely on the other side and welcomed all back as brothers." His actions were reported by Mike Yarrow in his 1978 book, *Quaker Experiences in International Conciliation* (Yale, 1978).

While not documented, it appears likely that the gesture of peace inherent in any humanitarian cease-fire could serve as a model for other countries. Writing to President Duarte, after the success of the first El Salvador immunization cease-fire in February 1985, UN Secretary-General Pérez de Cuéllar said: "The [immunization] coverage achieved, as well as the climate of tranquillity and peace during the immunization process, represents an example for the world of what really can be obtained when the will and the wish to do it exists." In this case, however, if it was an example for the world, the lack of publicity about it in other zones of conflict lessened the opportunity of making it a model for them.

Beyond these points, it remains to be demonstrated the full extent of the contribution that a humanitarian cease-fire can make to the ultimate resolution of conflict. The most common objection to the notion of a temporary abatement of hostilities in order to fulfil a humanitarian need is that the recipients of the aid are immediately afterwards flung back into the path of conflict. This irony is well understood by those negotiating cease-fires. That is why the Khartoum Plan of Action called for a commitment by the Sudanese government to seek ways to negotiate a long-term peace with the SPLA. Yet in other cases the negotiators may feel that to ask for such a commitment from the warring parties would be counterproductive to the goal of the negotiations, because it might compromise their claim to political impartiality and neutrality.

Key international players

Role of UNICEF

As the three cases indicate, UNICEF often has been the lead agency in negotiating humanitarian cease-fires. In fact, the linking of immunization to cease-fires was the idea of Nils Thedin (now deceased) who was the leader of the Swedish delegation to UNICEF. Thedin promoted this idea regularly at UNICEF meetings and according to Jim Grant, "made my life miserable until I acted on the idea." In each of the above cases, however, the cease-fire idea grew out of circumstances unique to the local situation. UNICEF has not attempted to investigate application of this idea across the board in war zones.

World campaign on the rights of victims of war

The twenty-fifth International Conference of the Red Cross in October 1986 recommended "a universal campaign to make known to all, not only to the armed forces but to the civilians, the right of the latter to international law." The conference faced the ugly fact that today nine out of ten war victims are civilians, and it resolved that, in order to give civilians better protection during armed conflicts, action had to be taken to enhance the understanding and respect for humanitarian law.

According to a Red Cross brochure, these actions may include "family reunification, exchange of prisoners, dissemination of international humanitarian law, relief operations and inoculation campaigns."

It is, in fact, a broad-fronted campaign in which an immunization program is one element, but not necessarily the primary one. An international joint committee of the Red Cross was set up to design the campaign, and Princess Christina of Sweden became its chair. Members of the Canadian Days of Peace Committee have spoken with Princess Christina about campaign plans and have also met in Geneva with Leon Davico, recently appointed world co-ordinator of the Red Cross and Red Crescent campaign.

Achieving Days of Peace

The Committee

Dr. Ed Ragan, who is director of Canada's International Immunization Program, came to realize that war was a main obstacle to achieving universal immunization. He learned of the El Salvador case and other examples, and was surprised to learn that no one was working concertedly to immunize children in war zones by arranging temporary cease-fires. War was being treated like a natural disaster, something beyond human control, and not like the exercise of human choice that it is. In early 1988 he and Murray Thomson, a long time worker for international development and for the resolution of conflict, convened a meeting of people concerned about child health in conflict zones. This group grew, during several months of discussion, into the more formal Canadian Committee of Days of Peace. The committee decided to promote the concept of immunization cease-fires with international and Canadian agencies and organizations, and to establish a network of contacts so as to be able to introduce the concept to combatants through trusted intermediaries.

Choice of conflict areas

The committee decided that, if it were to play any more active a part than simply supporting, in a general sense, the Red Cross and WHO efforts, it had to decide on which countries and conflict areas it should concentrate to be effective. So it drew up a list of criteria to help choose priority countries. It compiled the following list (without putting the criteria in any strict order of priority):

1. Need for immunization.
2. The presence of embassies of the combatant countries in Ottawa, and of Canadian embassies in their countries.
3. Canadian NGO and other connections.

4. The possibility of actually achieving some progress toward a cease-fire and peace negotiations. Factors here include how long the war has gone on and signs of war-weariness; whether this is a new idea to the conflict; whether the conflict was likely to be resolved before the idea could be introduced.

5. The potential of reaching influential actors in the conflict. Clearly it is important that there be a structure on the insurgent side of the conflict, with which it is possible to deal.

6. The possibility of finding allies in a particular campaign.

7. The existence of actors who can mobilize immunization support for the region.

8. Strategic factors of various sorts.

On this basis, the committee identified three areas for priority consideration: El Salvador, Sri Lanka, and the Horn of Africa. The possibility of applying some leverage from a Canadian base seemed promising in all three countries. There were fourteen other conflict areas on which it seemed wise to keep active files but where there were often already "big actors" involved. Three of these were in West Asia, four in South and Southeast Asia, and seven in Africa.

The committee soon learned that almost any area offered its own peculiar, and not always predictable, difficulties. A prime example was the Horn of Africa, where Eritrean and Tigrayan forces had been fighting the Ethiopian government troops with somewhat different objectives. The needs were enormous: there had been no immunization done in Tigray from 1974 to 1988, when a British team from the Health Action Group was invited. A registered nurse, Christine Brown, spent five months there as a team member, working with the Relief Society of Tigray (REST), and her last activity was a pilot project to immunize three thousand children against measles. She told the Canadian committee that there were no problems in training the REST health care workers to do the immunizing, but no cold chain had existed, and there was no electricity and few vehicles. (They used Oxfam emergency equipment during the project.) With the fighting continuing, they could not gather people for immunization during daylight for fear of attracting the attention of Ethiopian bombers; so it was done at night or else along thickly forested river banks. This created major logistical problems. They sometimes had to walk for five hours each way to a location for immunization, carrying the cold chests. The result was that, in an operation lasting a month, they managed to immunize 2,139 children against measles.

If a cease-fire were negotiated, of course some of these difficulties—but by no means all of them—would disappear. But how realistic are the hopes of achieving a cease-fire for humanitarian purposes? Is there, after all these years of fighting (twenty-five years, in the Eritrean case), a nearly equal amount of war-weariness on both sides? Possibly, but this is always a difficult judgement to make. The Tigrayan Peoples' Liberation Front believes (as does its Eritrean counterpart) that it now has the upper hand in its struggle and may think that even a short cease-fire might be of advantage to the hard-pressed Ethiopian forces. Meanwhile, on the Ethiopian side, WHO and UNICEF have been involved in immunization programs; so the need there is less insistent. The Canadian Committee of Days of Peace has made contact with the Carter Centre in Atlanta, Georgia in the hopes of introducing the immunization cease-fire concept into current negotiations.

The role of CIDA

Through the International Council for Adult Education, the Canadian International Development Agency (CIDA) has already contributed $17,500 toward the work of the Canadian Committee for Days of Peace. CIDA's energetic preparations for the World Summit for Children in New York in September 1990 raised hopes that the link would be firmly made between child immunization and conflict transformation.

In general, CIDA has played a limited role in the area of aid related to peacemaking in conflict situations. The Canadian government has tried to reduce actual or potential conflicts by participation in various UN peacekeeping operations, by sending police trainers (to Grenada) and police monitors (to Namibia), by giving electoral and legal assistance in various countries, and by offering "nonlethal" military assistance in the form of spare parts and training and balance of payments support related to security expenditure (Mozambique in September 1988). The issues surrounding such assistance have been thoroughly discussed in many of the papers in this book.

Conclusion

It is clear that such work at peacemaking in conflict zones requires special care and sensitivity. Knowledge of the hazards and of the route to take in a particular situation, is essential and takes time to accumulate. It is also clear that there is a current flowing in the direction of linking the activities of peace building and of humanitarian assistance; the further linking with development assistance is bound to strengthen the process. It cannot be a question of "hands off" when there is so much demonstrated need. Immunization cease-fires present an opportunity for meeting a defined world goal of universal immunization, while they also have a very small but potentially important impact on the ability of belligerents to move toward a peaceful settlement of their dispute.

Food for Guns—When Foreign Aid Helps to Stop the Fighting

Brian Hanington
CARE

ADDIS ABABA — Situation deteriorating with armed robbery and extortion. Expatriates may be the next targets. Individuals refusing to turn over assets are being shot.

ASBETEFERI — Ambushed and shot full of holes.

DIRE DAWA — Situation tense. Morale affected by continuing insecurity.

GARAMULETA — Fifty of our staff isolated with garrison under siege and attack.

KARAMILE — Heavy exchange of fire while vehicles passing through town. Major bridge over river completely cut.

MASSAWA — Convoy fired upon on arrival. Escorts returned fire with heavy mortars.

They read like highlights from military after-action reports, but the quotations above are actually excerpts from the regular situation reports filed back to headquarters by CARE Canada field staff. CARE Canada is the autonomous Canadian wing of a federation of CARE organizations around the world—organizations which pool their resources and energies and, operating as a relief and development agency, have gained a reputation for going to great lengths to get food, water, medicine, and other essentials to people in need.

In the past decade, CARE's involvement in conflict zones has been intensive and effective. From the Horn of Africa to the heart of Cambodia, the fifty year old NGO has assisted the homeless, the starving, the destitute, and the displaced. With 361 or more wars begun since 1946 when CARE was born, it is understandable that much of CARE's work has been done in the midst of conflict and violence.

CARE deals with people in war zones because its fundamental mandate is the alleviation of human suffering, and war is the chief architect of agony. Aside from natural catastrophes (CARE's initial expertise was in relief and disaster management), it is in the heat and aftermath of armed conflict that the highest levels of suffering occur.

With the end of the superpower conflict in the past few years, the numbers of smaller conflicts in the third world have risen steeply.

Contestants in dozens of small scale battles have filled the vacuum created with the ending of the Cold War.

As situation reports attest, CARE staff members generally approach the horrors of war (at least in their writing) with businesslike objectivity. The goal is to get relief through, whether food, water, medicine, blankets or tents, and their reports matter-of-factly outline their successes and failures in achieving the objectives.

In six years of supplying water to Somalian refugees in Ethiopia, CARE water tankers have only failed to make their deliveries six days out of two thousand. How this is achieved is difficult to assess, sometimes even for CARE staff members themselves. Even in stable conditions a fleet of heavy machines will normally require down time for regular servicing—if not for engine rebuilds then at least for flat tires, boiled radiators and lack of oil. Still the CARE vehicles have kept on rolling, and the determination of the drivers and staff to keep the critically important supply lines open has been mentioned in major media throughout the world.

The routes over which these drivers take their cargo include roadless desert and heavy bush, flooded plains, and rocky foothills across great distances in extreme heat, through often hostile territories where military control can shift from one group to another in the space of a one night battle.

In the last fifteen years, this sort of work has taken CARE fleets throughout the South. In 1978 they set up operations on the Thai-Cambodian border, providing relief to refugees from the Pol Pot regime, who were fleeing for their lives into Thai camps. In 1981 they moved into Somalia in the wake of the Ogaden war, providing relief to the 700,000 Ethiopians who had drifted into Somalia in search of security. Three years later they established themselves in Mozambique, where 1.5 million people had been displaced in a bloody war. Then Ethiopia. Then Sudan. By 1989 they were back in Somalia full time, this time aiding refugees once more flowing in from Ethiopia.

Then in 1991, as the world learned about genocide in Iraq, CARE moved into South Turkey to support the ousted Kurds. Within months it had set up camp in Iraq proper, the first group to move into the postwar declared *safe haven* zone. Since then, it has become one of the few relief agencies to convince the Iraqi government that it should have entry to the unaided *southern* parts of Iraq.

Today, CARE has added refugee camps in both Kenya and Zambia to its responsibilities and has recently moved back onto the Thai-Cambodian border, this time to aid in the resettlement of refugees who, after a homeless decade, will at last be returning to Cambodia.

In all CARE's operations, moving fast, staying low to the ground, and being totally flexible have been the keys both to operational success and minimal loss of life. The wisdom of these principles has been well demonstrated in the Horn of Africa where supplying desperately needed water to refugee camps is often a major trial. Subjected to gunfire and bombings, CARE drivers have learned to be fully flexible in how they navigate their way cross-country. Sometimes they seek escort by the reigning military authority, but this is not always wise, for the very presence of that escort can unintentionally raise the status of the CARE convoy to that of a key military target. Many CARE trucks have been fired on by snipers and some subjected to mortar and grenade attack.

Then, even when they make it safely to their destination, fleets are still at risk. Rival factions within camps will often compete for limited resources. When water or food arrives in an area in which people are both starving and dying of thirst, emotions run high. CARE water tankers have been hit by grenades lobbed from camp sectors which were not scheduled for water stops that day.

In addition to the obvious physical risks of operating in or near war zones is the frequent accusation of bias. CARE is doggedly nonpolitical. Sometimes accused by one side of supporting the other, or charged with delivering aid to nations whose human rights records prove they don't deserve it, CARE refuses to make judgements about the right of a people to aid, and will not compromise the premise that CARE works for all people in need regardless of their affiliations.

Mike Mispelaar, head of Food Security for CARE Canada says:

If a government should be changed, someone is going to have to change it. Those who are starving in the desert are never going to be able to engineer change. People in these situations are in a state of utter exhaustion. Even though they may see the corruption and mismanagement of the governments whose decisions affect their lives, they have no capacity to react. People must be fed; they must have peace, long before they can work for change. By providing food, water, medicine or clothing, we help them meet their primary needs. Often, if we don't, no one will.

Unlike many NGOs working in relief, CARE is not simply a fund raising agency or clearing house for relief goods. CARE has always believed that having trained, paid staff on the front line is the only way to ensure the level of success which disaster and conflict situations demand. This willingness to be *in the fray* has led to a number of experiences which have in turn forced the CARE leadership to reexamine the relation of aid and conflict.

In places such as Somalia, long-term efforts to bring the necessities of life to a war torn region have sometimes changed the focus of the combatant's battle to that of controlling an area in which the aid resources are delivered. In a perverse turnabout, the multimillions spent on food, clothing, and medicine have given competing factions an enduring reason to fight.[1]

That the presence of foreign aid may aggravate conflict, then, is increasingly appreciated. Still the reverse can be true, and CARE plans to use its experience to turn the tables and experiment with using foreign aid to motivate truce.

The thinking springs from the observation that in almost all situations in which CARE has become a target, the issue is that its trucks are carrying precisely what the war seems to be about—food and water. The reality, of course, is that food insecurity often masks underlying problems of ethnic and political difference.

In the seemingly endless round of bush wars in the Horn of Africa, the objective is usually control of limited food resources. When food supplies are adequate, fighting abates. When supplies are scarce, fighting intensifies. If one graphs the progress of a conflict such as this, plotting intensity of fighting against time, it might look like Figure 1.

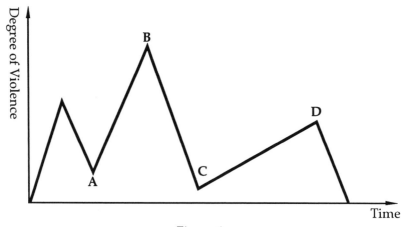

Figure 1

In the continuum of this conflict, point A is a time of minimal violence. Point B is the moment of greatest violence. CARE's thinking is that if, at any trough, one makes available the kinds of resources over which fighting has been taking place, then the subsequent crest may be much lower than expected. If at trough C the CARE tankers roll in with food and water, it may be that crest D will be significantly lower than otherwise and much human suffering may be averted. The notion is that aid delivery can have tactical as well as strategic components.

How does one accomplish this? The limitations of simply trucking in food and water, which CARE already does, have already been noted and include the lack of true sustainability of the program. Extra measures are required which might both move people toward greater security and lessen their desires to raise arms against each other.

The CARE Food Security team has developed a creative approach which advocates the exchange of food and supplies for armaments but, to understand its potential, one must reexamine the nature of contemporary conflict. When two major forces meet head to head on the battlefield, there isn't much to be done until the fighting has stopped. Heavy fighting is usually brief, however; in modern warfare the cost of ammunition and the rapid exhaustion of troops have made battles necessarily shorter.[2] For the most part, therefore, what is actually occurring in conflict zones is a form of posttruce banditry in which soldiers demobilized from organized combat apply their soldiering skills to objectives closer to home. Using weapons stolen, bought, or taken as spoils of war, they continue military aggression at the community level, defending their villages or ravaging the land in search of food for their families. Trained to apply military force to achieve their objectives, displaced militia in Africa and Asia regularly become the highwaymen of the postbattle era.

It has been estimated that for every rifle turned in after a war, another is stolen and hidden for later use. At the time of writing, one can acquire an AK-47 Kalashnikov rifle in Mozambique for U.S. $5. In Angola, it is believed that every family is now armed with an average of two weapons. CARE staff argue that the very existence of these weapons and the accompanying ammunition makes peace more and more difficult both to achieve and to sustain. Just having the guns is a major problem. In Somalia, it is rumoured that more people are killed from stray lead raining down from the sky than from direct fire. Indeed, so many accidental deaths are caused there by rifle fire that the most common Somalia nickname for *rifle* is a word which means "the gun that killed my friend."

CARE is about to address that issue in a practical way. Called FOOD FOR GUNS project plan, CARE will offer a long-term donation of food and supplies to anyone willing to turn in weapons. For a single AK-47, for instance, the FOOD FOR GUNS program will offer as much as fifty-five kilograms of maize, with beans, oil, and canned meat each month for a total of eighteen months.

In other words, any family which hands in a gun will be able to feed itself for a year and a half, which CARE Food Security people think could be hard to resist. The exchange rate, of course, holds no economic logic. It isn't meant to. It simply serves as a way to get firearms out of circulation and reduce the need for a family to turn to banditry to survive. The eighteen month period is sufficient time, given a peaceful environment, for a family to plant and raise crops and, to that end, the program also provides an eighteen month agricultural pack containing seeds, fertilizers, and tools. The program also leads people into an eighteen month relationship in which other development possibilities such as education and employment might be explored.

FOOD FOR GUNS has many logistical complexities. Local traders will have to be subcontracted to distribute the food every month. A large number of gun collection centres will have to be established in consultation with the local governments of whichever nations agree to the program. Destruction facilities must be set up, and security at these sites will be of paramount importance.

Will it work? Can such a simple tactical manoeuvre make an impact on the rate of violence and the level of conflict in any locale? That remains to be seen, but CARE has already had positive results from approaches that were once considered radical and are now accepted as everyday practice. As long as CARE can convince its donors to back the initiative, it will go ahead. CARE Food Security Staff are already searching for a location to launch a pilot program. It will have to be a location which is relatively secure and isolated, not subject to repeated military interference from outside forces. Cambodia, Ethiopia, and Angola are all possible choices. Given, however, that the long-term objective of FOOD FOR GUNS is the development of food self-sufficiency through a return to agriculture, a major stumbling block will be the countless land mines which lie in the soil of nations whose lands have been battlegrounds for decades.[3]

Other problems, such as political interference and the possible disenchantment of influential donors such as the Canadian International Development Agency (CIDA) with the profile of one nation or another may make an initial selection difficult. Still a test site will be found and, before long, CARE teams will be once again knocking on donors' doors, this time to offer a creative alternative to violence.

_____

Notes

1. This phenomenon of dependence has been observed elsewhere. Canadian peacekeeping operations, for instance, hailed by some as a great contribution to global security, are criticized by others as being of such day-to-day economic benefit to any feuding community that opposing forces soon agree that it is economically unwise to get along lest the peacekeepers and their high disposable incomes be withdrawn.

2. Before the break-up of the Soviet empire put them out of business, military strategists predicted that, if World War III were declared, it would have to be fought and won within seven days, for troops would be irrecoverably exhausted after a single week of warfare.

3. Cambodia, for instance, has an estimated one million land mines buried, and the charting of mine locations was long ago abandoned. In this nation, which understandably has more amputees per capita than any other, the prospect of a smooth return to farming is unrealistic.

The Horn of Africa Project: Modelling Alternative Conflict Resolution

Ronald J.R. Mathies, Harold Miller and Menno Wiebe
University of Waterloo

Purpose

This paper reflects on the Horn of Africa Project (HAP)—a conflict resolution venture based at the Institute of Peace and Conflict Studies, Conrad Grebel College in Waterloo, Ontario. The project was begun as an effort to test the ability of the voluntary agency community to address, in a sustained way, conflict as a root cause of hunger. For the Horn of Africa, the obvious response was to exercise whatever talents the NGO community held in order to contribute to the larger task of building peace as opposed to the typical emphasis on the job of logistics and the urgencies of relief aid.

The context of this initiative is found in the circle of Mennonite[1] educational and international service institutions. This paper follows the project from its inception through the formative period, and proceeds into a description of the major activities. Within the Mennonite community the experience confronts the issue of humanitarianism in a conflict setting, providing some new territory to probe and critique, and is a precedent against which some other ideas are tested. Beyond this community, relationships exist with a range of voluntary coalitions and independent actors.

The project is still active, (though renamed and recast with a wider mandate as the World Order and Regional Conflict project) and thus final conclusions are difficult to establish—particularly as the Horn of Africa experiences rapid changes in its own local/regional dynamics, and as international attention focuses on the complexity of resolving the region's conflicts. Still the project can quite confidently state that its sustained commitment to addressing conflicts brings unexpected results for which preparation is often impossible. Therefore flexibility, as both a precedent and an antecedent to this concern, and an ongoing commitment to pursue the concern are vital elements of this project. Recognizing these elements should make clear how the NGO community is ideally placed to use its global understanding, expand its existing networks, and rise to the challenge of speaking to "popular" (i.e., relating to the people) issues previously left to states and state informed bodies.

Background

The "Great African Famine" took centre stage in 1984–85. Around the world, images of hunger and starvation relentlessly filled television screens. In equally unprecedented fashion, responses to the tragedy mobilized. The world remembers LIVE AID, the global television benefit concert, and BAND-AID, one of the more illustrious relief efforts mobilized in response to the Ethiopian drought. There were many other responses to the tragedy, coalescing within the Northern/Western world into a vastly expanded awareness of the African continent.

But the depth of this awareness and, more critically, its cost, deserve honest discussion. In many respects Ethiopia was presented to the typical media "consumer" as an archetype for Africa—awash in misery and devoid of hope. "Consumers" were assuaged, realizing their indispensability and the potential of their largesse. The debate continues, unresolved, as to whether the disaster could have been avoided by a more timely response, and with a lesser assault on African sensibilities.

Context of conflict[2]

During the past century Ethiopia was recognized by black peoples everywhere as a lone outpost of independent black African rule. (Liberia also has a long history of independence but has been viewed usually as an ex-slave settler country, whose establishment had been initiated from North America.) Thus Ethiopia was a unifying symbol for the whole of the continent. Although occupied for a short time by the Italians (1935–1941), Ethiopia was not colonized by metropolitan powers in a manner similar to the remainder of Africa. During his forty-four year reign (1930–1974), Emperor Haile Selassie played exceptional roles in world forums, projecting the image of a world class statesman and African nationalist. With his overthrow in 1974, Ethiopia's mystique faded quickly to reveal deeply rooted cleavages, fuelled on the one hand by the imperial tradition of the emperors and resisted on the other by increasingly self-aware, armed opposition groups.

Ethiopia as an historical symbol, as well as Ethiopia the contemporary state, is at the centre of many competing claims over territory and governing legitimacy. The Ethiopian government faced a succession of opposition forces which contended that the territory of Eritrea (on the Red Sea coast) was illegally denied the chance to pursue its postcolonial fate as an independent nation as did Libya and Somalia.[3] The colonial period is also the locus of Somali and Oromo grievances. These groups accuse Ethiopia of having pursued European style colonialism at the turn of the century, a process which helped secure the Somali-speaking Ogaden region in the east and the predominantly Oromo regions in the

south for the empire. As the Ethiopian government has looked north, it
has encountered the vestiges of an ancient rivalry between Tigrayan and
Amhara rulers now played out by another armed opposition group
which has built on this historical Tigrayan homogeneity to challenge the
legitimacy of the government to govern on behalf of all Ethiopians.

In the face of all this, Ethiopia maintained the primacy of its long
history of centralized, unified rule in the Horn as a basis to struggle
against forces perceived to threaten that heritage. Following the removal
of Haile Selassie by a committee of junior officers in 1974, hopes ran high
that the military rulers would enable new possibilities for peace, replacing hated feudal structures with socialist categories.[4] Efforts were made
but to no avail.

In neighbouring Sudan, regional disparities, sanctioned and magni-
fied by colonial rule, brought the country to war just as it forged
independence. Perceived primarily as an African/Arab conflict, it found
a resolution in 1972 through the World Council of Churches. Before a
decade elapsed, however, this federal arrangement unravelled and
brought a resumption of conflict. The constitutional arrangement of
government and the role of religious organizations in governing are
central to the debate.

During the formative period of the Horn of Africa Project (1984–86),
conflict situations in the Horn[5] were essentially characterized by stalemate. On the one hand, sovereign governments insisted on territorial
integrity and noninterference from outside actors as a sine qua non in any
negotiations, while on the other an array of opposition movements
armed themselves in order to command attention within and without, in
the hope of correcting perceived injustices.

A certain reciprocity existed in which virtually each conflicting party
received from or gave support to the struggle of the "enemy's enemy."
Nonstate protagonists usually benefited from a sympathetic state. At the
very least Ethiopia turned a blind eye to activities of the Sudan People's
Liberation Army (SPLA) and a number of Somali opposition movements, while governments in the Sudan and Somalia responded in kind
by hosting fronts opposed to the Ethiopian government. Sustained
conflict throughout the Horn was the obvious result, causing civilian
populations from every conflict zone to seek shelter—most often where
the international community could take responsibility.

This configuration was reinforced by strong support from the USSR
for the Ethiopian government, while the United States provided support
for the border states of Somalia, Kenya, and the Sudan. Thus, in addition
to the interlocking complexities of national and regional politics, the
bipolar East/West dynamic served to position the region's conflicts in a
global context. *Perestroika* was still in its infancy.

NGOs in context

Finally, a comment on the nongovernmental organization (NGO) scene. Since 1984, when proposals for HAP were initially discussed, the NGO community's focus has shifted dramatically. In Somalia, during the period under consideration, NGOs were relatively few in number and took very low profiles. In Ethiopia, where NGOs had extremely high visibility during the famine relief period, the government imposed stringent regulations regarding their presence and function, bringing them closer to the country's declared development goals. For the Sudan, much of the NGO energy has been expended on crossborder relief efforts—again relatively high profile—attempting to meet the needs of the war ravaged south of the country.

The "Great African Famine" exposed the sometimes misguided ideals and euphoria within the NGO enterprise, along with the manipulative and insensitive aspects of a lopsided power relationship between donors and recipients. Many new NGOs were born as a result of this experience, and many were brought up short by the situation's complexity and the seeming futility of an aid blitz which took no account of the ongoing concern and attention necessary in the region. The experience of 1984–85 was thus a key contributor to debates over NGO roles. It challenged practitioners and theoreticians to explore a wider range of issues which would place the NGO agenda tentatively on a path toward greater political innovation.

The Horn of Africa as project

During the mid-1980s within the NGO community generally, and within the Mennonite Central Committee (MCC)[6] particularly, some disquieting questions required answers. Was drought the only cause for the famine? Did continuing armed conflict between the Addis government and armed opposition bode ill for longer term food security and political stability? Could these longer term questions be addressed in any way by the NGO community?

Together with staff members of the Institute of Peace and Conflict Studies (IPACS), MCC urged that greater attention and effort go into exploring conflict in the Horn and into discerning avenues open to the NGO community to contribute to peace. There was of course an awareness that no single undertaking could bring the desired peace. But participants felt, nonetheless, that something could be done and that a beginning needed to be made. A graduate student was employed to assemble an initial survey report on Ethiopia, identifying relevant historic factors, outlining the current political/social conditions, and offering suggestions for the NGO agenda.

The resultant report offered a variety of action proposals for the Mennonite Central Committee. According to the introduction, the report was intended to (1) present a synopsis of the conflict in Ethiopia; (2) discuss the need for reconciliation; (3) discuss possible options for North American Mennonites in reconciliation and conflict resolution; and (4) provide a resource list of persons with expertise relevant to the situation in the Horn of Africa.

When the project took shape, the emphasis was twofold: public education in North America about the close connection between hunger and conflict in the Horn of Africa, and, secondly, the offer of a private disinterested discussion forum for people from the Horn of Africa with conflicting perspectives on the region. This forum, having evolved into a process of consultations, encourages lines of discussion to occur among Horn participants, more than *from* them to the project. Consultations are understood as an exercise in trust-building among individuals who are outside of decision-making roles, albeit holding strongly to their convictions. The hope is that participants might relay some personal observations to associates with the same convictions, and thus incrementally erode some of the misunderstandings and misperceptions which have festered over the years.

Organizational Background

Mennonite presence in Ethiopia long predated the famine. Having functioned in both the so-called development mode and in the traditional mission/church-planting mode, that presence continues in modified form to this day. This larger Mennonite tradition provides a context for HAP's concern which has, interestingly, given a firm basis for developing trust. One participant commented on the Mennonite tradition: "Because we share with Anabaptists a history of persecution, I believe they, more than any Western community, are uniquely qualified to speak to us as a suffering people without shame, embarrassment, or guilt."[7] Mennonites have no corner on the market of suffering (particularly not of late), nor of integrity and trust, but their claim on an identifiable heritage (despite its parochialism) provides useful handles for scrutiny of their motives and activities. For this reason alone faith communities have the strength of possessing a heritage and envisioning a future which is mediated by the present. This type of stability speaks volumes in situations of conflict.

HAP itself is a minimalist operation, occupying a two by five metre space with only one fulltime staff person. A second person, seconded from Mennonite Central Committee, gave part-time service to the project from 1987–1989. A local advisory committee acts as a sounding board for the activities of the project. Conrad Grebel College, which houses the Institute of Peace and Conflict Studies (IPACS) and in turn the Horn of

Africa Project, is sponsored by the Mennonite Conference of Eastern Canada and academically affiliated with the University of Waterloo. HAP is accountable to Conrad Grebel College by sharing copies of significant documentation and by the presence of the IPACS Director on various administrative committees of the College. The project, which began with a two year schedule, has been solely supported by and has direct accountability links to the Mennonite Central Committee. It was expected that the project would either run its course or prove its ongoing viability and seek funds from other sources during those two years.

Funding

HAP's fund-raising experience reflects the diverse character of the project and its relationships. Initial core funding provided by the Mennonite Central Committee was intended to cover only the first two years of the project's life. Thus the search for funds from other sources soon became part of HAP's ongoing agenda.

In 1987 HAP submitted a major funding proposal to Partnership Africa Canada (PAC), essentially making application for access to Canadian government funds via the Canadian International Development Agency (CIDA). HAP's application went through a lengthy process including consultations with PAC staff who were eager to continue an initiative making explicit links between conflict and development. HAP was eventually informed that its application was approved, but PAC went on to say that, "constraints external to the PAC process do not allow PAC to fund the project...[since] a CIDA policy...states that projects dealing with militarism/peace issues will not be accepted for funding by CIDA."[8]

In response to this refusal, HAP sought the assistance of Canadian Council of International Cooperation (CCIC) staff in appealing the rejection and expressed its astonishment regarding CIDA's (unpublicized) powers to overrule PAC decisions. HAP's disappointment was particularly acute in view of PAC's encouragement and guidance in the preparation of HAP's application. Meanwhile a strange ambivalence prevails—the PAC Board's approval of the HAP submission is still part of the official record and only awaits CIDA approval to disburse the funds.

This surprise rejection forced HAP to seek alternative funding sources. The PAC decision came at the close of 1987 and almost closed the project, since MCC's two year commitment was finishing and the staff person was completing her term. MCC filled the gap for 1988, convinced that the project was worth continued support and deserved a chance to check alternate funding avenues, particularly other NGOs. In anticipation of its November 1988 consultation (outlined below), HAP directed an appeal to more than fifty Canadian NGOs. Considering the project's uniqueness, the advisory committee thought the best chance for success was to pursue funds based on concrete events rather than expect response for the more difficult core administrative costs. Contributions from ten Canadian organizations eventually arrived, adequately covering the projected costs of the November event. A grant was also received from the Canadian Institute for International Peace and Security (CIIPS), which is at a similar distance from government as Partnership Africa Canada, and was recommended to HAP as the appropriate channel for assisting a "militarism/peace" program.

A major grant from PAC was approved in mid-1990 and funds were disbursed for the first of two years, but renewed confusion concerning CIDA's funding and PAC's degree of independence from it necessitated the cancellation of the second year funding and a return of a portion of the disbursed first year support. The project's financial difficulties provide adequate grist for the analytical mill. An obvious question must be directed at government agencies which maintain the policy that the development agenda does not intersect with conflict. Is it any longer possible to delude ourselves that the spheres of development and conflict exist independently? If this is a delusion, what means can bring them within shouting distance at the policy table? One would be forgiven for suspecting that governments are not eager to see NGOs (possessing informed and committed constituencies) explore a wider scope of activities.

Accountability

Accountability for both core and event funding was undertaken in a deliberate fashion. Donors were advised on details of the consultation meetings, but were not expected to attend. For purposes of accountability they were subsequently sent copies of the proceedings and invited, additionally, to convenient locations for detailed briefings. This pattern of detailed briefing with the several donors was itself considered integral to the networking character of the project process.

The merits of this approach are clearer in retrospect. HAP is not exclusively academic in its character, nor is it altogether an NGO venture; it is a hybrid that incorporates aspects of and maintains links with both. For the donor community this has been problematic. Clearer project designations would possibly elicit more ready funding. Like other projects of ambivalent category, HAP is easily attracted by the security which lump sum grant funding would offer. On the other hand, it is recognized that a leaner existence acts to discipline both the direction and the content of the project. Necessity has to some degree become a virtue.

Consultative and open-ended process

From its inception, HAP was intent on the goal of contributing toward reconciliation or peace in the Horn of Africa. The means and the activities through which such a goal could be realized have been open to experimentation. One of the first HAP activities focused on a survey of five major print media and their reporting on conflict in the Horn. The findings of that research survey provided the initial data upon which people from the Horn of Africa were invited to reflect.

The term "academics" is loosely used to describe those present at this first consultation; possessing a doctorate was not the criteria as much as having a personal and professional connection to the region. All were emigrés now living in North America. The actual discussions of the 21–23 November 1986 consultation appeared in the form of published proceedings. These exhaustive proceedings were distilled, edited and finally vetted into a public education document entitled *War and Famine: Indigenous Perspectives on Conflict in the Horn of Africa*.

A second consultation was called for 22–24 April 1988. Its purpose was to explore avenues toward peaceful resolution of conflict and to identify some of the obstacles en route. Considered during the consultation were the nature and the validity of voluntary associations' operations in Africa—opportunities and problems inherent in external initiatives toward conflict resolution—and the relevance of traditional (African) approaches to conflict resolution. As in the previous consultation, transcripts of the proceedings were submitted to participants for editing. The proceedings were subsequently published in April 1989 under the title, *A Review of Conflict Resolution Agenda in the Horn of Africa*. A supplementary educational document entitled *Facing the Enemy: Conflict Resolution Rooted in the Horn of Africa* was completed in 1989.

Between 24-27 November 1988, HAP organized a third consultation under the rubric "Conflict Resolution in the Horn of Africa: Envisioning Alternative Futures." In addition to repeat invitations for people who had attended previous consultations, special invitations were sent to persons living in Africa. The intent was to enliven the discussion with comment and insight informed by the realism of current conditions in the Horn of Africa. The edited proceedings and papers contributed to this consultation are published under the title of the consultation and dated October 1989.

This gathering and listening process generates some very creative discussion which begins to go beyond the "safe" boundaries of discourse on the Horn. Yet much of the discourse reverts to defensive posturing consistent with the lack of trust which pervades most contentious discussions. In discussions with particular "sides," HAP is usually confronted with a thorough description of the problem "as it is." One cannot become cynical or dismiss this "preaching," since it can be expected that much lies below the sermon.

These encounters prompt some people to accuse HAP of being used, even just by listening to the propaganda. While this is the case, no party in any encounter is less prone to this than any other conflicting party. It should be considered a strength to be open to being used, all the while fully aware of that fact. In dealing with a conflict situation it is wise not to assume that one is privy to a special relationship or unique information. It is a truism that conflicting parties will keep whatever is necessary to themselves. So one must be prepared for contacts and relationships founded on pragmatism. This isn't meant to be cynical or critical, but is intended as a sober comment on the station of "third parties" in a conflict. To be "used" is not necessarily a malicious act, but is something which should be graciously accepted as part of the process by any third party. If anything, to be used is a mark of respect and/or value. In such a case one would hope that all parties are using the third party so that some communication and information is travelling between conflicting parties.

The second major segment of the HAP process is public education—primarily through publications. These are noted in the previous paragraphs. Originally perceived as the major contribution to be made by this project, public education is predominantly a complementary vehicle for the consultation process. Nevertheless, this area remains as the one tangible reference point through which the project can interact with a wider audience. This interaction through print is also helped by the media as it picks up articles on the Horn written by HAP staff. The third plank of HAP's work is networking. A rather nebulous commodity, networking activities are intricately linked with the consultation process which in turn feeds back into networking.

The importance of being connected and moving information has increased as the number of organizations and coalitions forming around the Horn of Africa has grown. Aside from a multitude of conferences dwelling on various issues affecting the Horn, longer term initiatives (HAP among them) mushroomed as the NGO community appropriated conflict concerns as crucial to development efforts. A well-organized coalition of NGOs in the U.S. and another in Europe gave useful direction for NGOs to approach governments on policy questions concerning the Horn. A looser coalition of NGOs provided co-ordination on the Canadian scene through the Canadian Council for International Cooperation (CCIC).

More similar to HAP is another Horn of Africa Project at the Life & Peace Institute in Sweden. Its research program is quite extensive and its networking links are wide. In the same category is a noninstitutional peace group in Nairobi, Kenya, which has over the past years organized lectures and seminars and has attempted to be a reference point for nongovernmental thinking on peace issues for Africa.

At HAP's prodding, these various initiatives came together for the first time in a one day meeting in early 1989. No "action plan" was drawn up at the meeting, but the links established on this occasion have been variously exploited since then. The mysteries of networking are in evidence. Because of connections fostered through HAP consultations and related activity, events have taken place and connections have been made which otherwise would not have occurred.

Product: prolific intangibles

Many of us, because of the kinds of differing views we had about this issue, probably would have found ourselves trying to kill each other. But we are fortunate to have this kind of opportunity to come together and see each other as human beings.[9]

HAP has provided a sustained forum around which representatives of the most diverse opinions gather to discuss, debate, and ultimately to take the risk of transforming images and even building trust. Despite the intangible appearance of such a process, HAP is convinced that much has (and will continue to) take place as a result of this sustained forum and reference point; the nature of what takes place, though, is decidedly serendipitous and catalytic rather than direct. The lesson learned from this conviction about outcomes is that "results" and "effectiveness" must not be the ultimate test of the project's efforts. "Results" are very ephemeral in a context where strategic military fortunes constantly shift. What was once an acceptable approach or offer by a particular party can quickly turn sour if, for example, fortunes turn and a show of strength is considered critical.

Obviously there must be some means to validate the project's work and maintain the conviction that value exists in these efforts. In this case, ideas like "results" and "effectiveness" need broader definitions. It is difficult to reconcile the patience necessary to encourage constructive discussion with the urgency of a war that kills instantly and starves people slowly. Yet if there is one thing that all involved agree upon, it is that the process of resolving conflicts in the Horn will be painstakingly long; thus the situation demands concerned constituencies whose energies will not flag in the face of little apparent change.

The tension between careful patience and immediate urgency is constant but creative. One of the unique aspects of the project is its insistence on being both "NGO" and "Institute" without settling into the self-assured routine of either. Where many NGOs expend all their energy in moving food at the expense of critical reflection, and Institutes (read "conferences") run circles around critical reflection with few handles to alleviate suffering, HAP has modestly tried to find a way between them which takes each seriously but keeps them in tension. It should be clear that "results" are found more easily in one or the other of these two streams, although neither is guaranteed to have staying power. It is on this account that one hears the challenge, in effect—"where are the people (organizations, institutions, etc.) who will stay the course with those of us who must endure these conflicts to their conclusion and beyond?" Reference points are needed to distil and focus information while at the same time constantly exercising new ideas for peace.

The most important factor in this initiative is the mercurial commodity of integrity and trust. There is some amount of influence that people can wield on behalf of their own integrity, but trust almost defies attempts to develop it.

With time the project has noticed a gradual increase in its stature and a corresponding increase in the expectations as expressed by the Horn Africans who are connected to the project. For HAP this gradual shift, though not completely unforeseen, was unintentional and certainly not seen as a requirement for the project's earliest plans. A tentative conclusion is that the absence of intention in seeking trust was a major factor in assuring people that aims were modest, above board, and responsive to changing needs rather than preprogrammed toward institutional aggrandizement—a strong concern expressed in early conversations.

Again, the qualities of trust and integrity bespeak the necessity of time and patience. Conflicts waged in the Horn of Africa take on a similarly vitriolic (and occasionally even armed) character in expatriate communities. Therefore reactions to third party concern are variously shaded with suspicion; are there other implicit interests which favour a particular "side"? Time and patience allow "good intentions" to be verified by more than just rhetoric.

It has been beneficial that HAP's specific heritage (i.e., MCC) has longer roots in the Horn. There are countless instances where people from the Horn stop short and exclaim (in effect): "Oh! You mean the Mennonites who ran the hospital and school in Nazret!" The mission tradition involved much of what was sinister in "Europe's" relationship with Africa, but it also established some remarkable bonds which provided (and still provide) a basis for people from the Horn to validate their trust. In the absence of high level people who can command doors to open, or governments who can use international protocol to approach some conflicting parties, unofficial actions must rely on the conflicting parties' knowledge and trust. This default situation is fortunate since it gives a more lasting and committed foundation for overcoming obstacles to peace. Clearly in such a context, churches are well placed to play supportive roles in establishing some trust where it is absent and in assuring conflicting parties that a path of dialogue to "the enemy" is possible without fear of protocol and sanctions implicit in official interchange. To be sure, fostering trust is never a completed task. Setbacks occur with disappointing ease when careless comments or lack of clarity cause misunderstandings. HAP has learnt some difficult lessons in this regard, all of which reinforce the need for careful yet frank communication.

HAP also has numerous tangible credits to claim, and among them are:

- As a direct consequence of HAP's networking links with East Africa, Dr. Hizkias Assefa—a consultation participant—was a resource person to several conflict resolution seminars in East Africa during mid-1989. Dr. Hizkias' book: *Mediation of Civil Wars: Approaches and Strategies—The Sudan Conflict* (Westview, 1987), was widely distributed in East Africa by HAP.

- Through various circumstances, HAP staff have had the opportunity of meeting with highly placed officials of the Ethiopian and Sudanese governments.

- HAP has had opportunities to host visitors from the Horn of Africa region, including a delegation from the Ethiopian government, representatives from the Ethiopian Orthodox Church, a professor—long outspoken on conflict issues—from the University of Khartoum, and a mission from the Sudan Council of Churches.

- In a variety of conferences and academic institutions, HAP has had opportunity both to highlight the conflict issues from the Horn of Africa region and reflect/report on initiatives taken by HAP to address those conflicts.

- Occasional coverage on HAP activity in local and regional media has introduced the public to the intricacies of conflict issues in the Horn of Africa.

- For Conrad Grebel College and the University of Waterloo's Peace and Conflict Studies Program, HAP has provided a window onto active conflict situations.

- Documentation produced by HAP circulates in the Horn of Africa and within the exile and expatriate Horn community in North America, thus providing access to opinion and conversation taking place within a deeply divided community.

HAP as model: a peace tradition and beyond

As a model, HAP can be viewed in two ways. Firstly, it is heir to the Mennonite peace tradition which strives to live out radically the peace witnessed by Jesus Christ in the Christian gospel. This is certainly not solely Mennonite territory but is also exemplified (arguably, in a more consistent manner) in the Society of Friends (Quakers). Secondly HAP is a specialty project, eclectic in its institutional and relational arrangements, which serves as an example of increasing diversity and creativity within the larger NGO community.

There is little evidence from HAP files of focused reflection either by the staff or by the host institutions regarding the ideological or theoretical bases for initiatives taken. Rather, there is the sense that the project was—consciously and unconsciously—infused with Mennonite peace theory and praxis.[10] The Mennonite Church is widely acknowledged as an "historic peace church," both by the religious community and by the respective North American governments. Within Mennonite theological circles much has been written on the Mennonite "peace position," and from the history of Mennonite Central Committee activity, beginning in 1920, there are repeated examples of Mennonite peace initiatives.

In the Mennonite tradition, armed conflict is not accepted as a means of settling either communal or national disputes. Indeed much of the Mennonite peace effort during this century has addressed issues related to conscientious objection to war. Only in recent decades has the "peace testimony"—as it is sometimes referred to—coalesced into specific peace or conflict resolution skills. Within the Mennonite Central Committee, trained staff offer mediation skills under the rubric of Mennonite Conciliation Service (MCS). MCS addresses a wide range of issues both within and outside the Mennonite community, from the traditional "fence line" disputes to marital problems, from legal disputes to confrontations between the Miskito Indians and the Nicaraguan government. The last experience begins to approximate the nature of the issues addressed by HAP—issues of international relevance, implementing specific conciliation skills for their resolution.

HAP functions quite self-consciously in the networking mode, situated deliberately within a world of conflicting constituencies. Early in its formative period, MCC felt that its concern for conflicts in the Horn of Africa could best be addressed by an informed Mennonite constituency or, on another level, by an informed Canadian public. HAP would therefore be designed to educate the several constituencies accordingly. Therefore, the focuses of HAP included a strong documentation/education component. As the project proceeded, a second focus developed on networking with a variety of specialist coalitions whose concerns also centred on the Horn of Africa. On a tertiary level the project also interacts with a donor constituency, with HAP providing orientation and debriefing on project activity. With the dynamics among the actors in the Horn region changing weekly, sometimes daily, a fourth level focus has centred on monitoring negotiation possibilities and fine tuning HAP plans for future activity accordingly. In its directional shifts and changing focuses, HAP has followed the Quaker pattern that starts with a specific concern and proceeds—often intuitively—with that concern in ways which demonstrate their potential to advance the possibilities for peace.

HAP's institutional arrangements reflect a certain logic; there is easy access to communication facilities, to conference facilities, to resource libraries, and there is the possibility of interaction within a climate of common concern. In addition there is a sense that the institutional base provides legitimating links with the Canadian Mennonite constituency—HAP functions, after all, as part of the Mennonite family. It can be debated whether the institutional arrangement is a necessary or sufficient condition for the success of a project like HAP. Certainly the institutional links have proved useful.

Still the absolutely indispensable ingredient, which in the final analysis carries the project along, has been the quality of flexibility. At every point where the project touches institution, structure, dynamic, or precedent, the persons or institutions involved prove themselves totally flexible and accommodating. There is no "right way of doing things"— everything is an experiment, everything is precedent.

Future parameters of HAP will be determined by a number of factors. Already the Mennonite Central Committee has given notice that its contribution of core funding will be discontinued at an agreed date, this in keeping with MCC's principle of supporting catalytic action rather than long-term institutional activity. There is discussion within the NGO network regarding the most useful support roles to be played by projects of this kind. Careful planning around continued exchange of views within the coalition community becomes a critical variable to the future of the project. Effectiveness of the project may be enhanced by critical mid course changes or by its timely termination.

Finally, there is merit in examining the original goal of the project— "peace for the Horn of Africa." Given the complexities of the issues at work in the Horn region, the goal as originally stated could be taken as naive at best and cavalier at worst. The journey from that original formulation to present understandings has become complex and diffuse, as those involved have encountered a variety of realities. Expectations for an informed constituency may in fact have been achieved, but is difficult to quantify and even more difficult to mobilize. More readily realized have been the active networking linkages with coalitions and institutions related to the Horn.

Aid as peacemaker: a broader NGO agenda

In his introduction to this volume, Robert Miller refers to the theme of the book as encompassing newly recognized agenda items for donor governments and nongovernmental organizations. The impact of conflict on development was only recently a peripheral concern; it is rapidly becoming a critical test case for relevance among most governmental and private agencies.[11] One statistic should suffice to indicate the level of frustration in agencies with the cycle of war, famine, and relief: during the decade of the 1980s, two-thirds of Canada's $480 million to Ethiopia and 57 percent of the $220 million to Sudan was committed to food and emergency assistance.[12] A total of $447 million was essentially spent on picking up the pieces. While picking up pieces is a virtuous act, questions must be asked when needs continue unabated for over a decade. Of the remaining $253 million of Canada's money which presumably went to longer term development work, one can be sure it wasn't unaffected by the conflicts. When Canada can make $447 million available over a decade to combat famines largely caused by war, alternative ideas are necessary to challenge those priorities and provide specific peacemaking ideas which could make use of even a fraction of that amount.

With the advent of each new disaster such as war or famine, additional NGOs are born. In 1907 there were by one count approximately 200 international NGOs. Today the figure is said to be in the neighbourhood of 18,000.[13] NGOs move through several recognizable phases: (1) relief and welfare, (2) small scale development, and (3) sustainable systems development (catalytic networking).[14] This sequence is perceived to be a shift from single-minded NGO activity toward open-ended interaction with a wide range of issues, including latterly, questions of equitable access to resources and the related conflicts. This NGO pattern, working generally from the "top down," is complemented by many grass roots groups emerging in countries around the world from the "bottom up."[15]

The chronic emergency needs in the Horn keep many agencies focused on the first of the stages noted above. Increasingly, agencies responding to that stage are much more cognizant of the third stage and wrestle with the tension. This happened quite quickly after the mid-1980s when it became clear that longer term development could not easily follow from the emergency response. The result was that NGO coalitions began in the United States and Europe with a focus on peace concerns for the Horn of Africa.

The NGO community sees aid as a tool for peacemaking through "second track," alternative diplomacy and policy advocacy. Lobbying for policy changes is familiar to NGOs, though not without contention and division within the community over particular policy issues; more active peacemaking, on the other hand, is new territory for individual NGOs, even more so for the collective community.

A search of current literature on second track or alternative diplomacy leads almost invariably to the Quaker experiences in international conciliation. Like Mennonites, Quakers are usually included in the historic peace church category. Within the peace church community and within the larger NGO world, Quakers have played pioneering roles. Their efforts are associated with the negotiations between East and West Germany during the building of the Berlin Wall, with the mediation of the India-Pakistan wars,[16] and with the negotiations leading to the establishment of Zimbabwe as a modern nation. Thanks to their extraordinary vision and determination,[17] they have for years kept an alternative agenda alive for NGOs more cautious than themselves.

As a case study, this paper points to some new directions for aid as a peacemaker. To help sharpen the discussion with specific peacemaking categories for aid donors, a few themes will be helpful: (a) social empowerment; (b) trust building; (c) peace advocacy; and (d) social reconstruction.[18]

The first category—social empowerment—assumes a broader understanding of peacemaking. Here, aid with a concern for peacemaking attempts to forestall the most destructive effects of conflict by building skills of conflict analysis and conflict resolution prior to the onset of desperation leading to war. This is no easier than activity in the midst of full-scale confrontation, since it often addresses a significant power difference which the more powerful are loath to rectify. Social empowerment comes very close to partisan advocacy. More case studies and experiential reflection will help indicate where the opportunities are for social empowerment to be a peacemaking tool.

The trust-building category is about as unfamiliar as social empowerment; in many respects they should exist alongside each other. Building trust is not so much to be defined or programmed as it is to be recognized and applied. NGOs build relationships at many levels within a community where, as outsiders, they are often looked to as disinterested observers better able to fairly weigh a situation. These relationships that NGOs have, particularly in the midst of overt conflict, are seldom exploited for bridge-building potential. Familiarity, even trust, are hard-earned accomplishments with valuable opportunities in conflict situations, even if they result from partisan sympathy. Without betraying familiarity or trust, relationships can be used creatively by NGOs to raise new issues, recall old ones, suggest an unpopular option, or lend support to an uncertain initiative which reaches for peace.

The third theme, peace advocacy, is probably less familiar than the previous two, but is well within the purview of most NGOs. Advocating for peace aims to influence public opinion as well as decision makers with the conviction that armed conflict will not resolve disputes, but rather that serious negotiation is required. Whether prior to peace discussions or during negotiations, the goal is to build momentum that will make it increasingly difficult to repudiate a peace process without incurring broad criticism. Peace advocacy speaks for the victims of conflict and criticizes, in an impartial manner, all who take up guns to resolve disputes.

Making aid dollars conditional on a serious peace process would be a practical instance of peace advocacy at work. It would send a signal that the aid community sees little worth in committing money in a context where war directly or indirectly undermines intended goals. A similar statement could be made with emergency aid, if donors are again convinced that there is little logic in providing food to people who will quite likely die because of war, or suffer starvation when the war and famine cycles meet again. Peace advocacy insists that the obligation for suffering and starving people rests squarely on conflicting parties; it also insists that governments and NGOs not lose sight of this and make every effort to create or sustain a peace process.

The realm of reconstruction is the most comfortable for the aid community. From the perspective of aid as a peacemaking tool, reconstruction plays a substantial role, particularly when it also takes account of the more difficult task of reconstructing the social fabric of a war shattered region. The distinction is noted by a close associate of HAP. "This is more than physical reconstruction of people's lives, communities and countries or the task of monitoring the implementation of peace accords. It is the reconstruction of the broken social and human fabric. The goal is the further solidification of dialogue, understanding and cooperation that characterizes sustainable and positive peace."[19]

Support for reconciliation efforts, exchanges, and similar initiatives is at least as critical as physical reconstruction programs. While it may appear slightly late to focus on conflict resolution in a reconstruction phase, there is an acute need to explore the rudiments of conflict resolution in order to build a lasting peace.

In summarizing these four categories, some comments regarding integration and co-operation are necessary. Though agencies will have varying strengths in these categories, integrity, consistency and balance are exemplified when they follow through from social empowerment and trust-building (which often lead to some suspicion), to peace advocacy (which might be uncomfortable for all parties), and finally to social reconstruction (which gains the acceptance of all). Co-operation is also important since the challenge of peacemaking, particularly at broader levels, can hardly be undertaken by a single actor. As NGOs involvement in peacemaking gains acceptance, unco-ordinated activities will be mediocre at best and exploited for partisan gain at worst. Co-operation does not imply coalition, however, but rather demands greater networking.

Before we leave the theme of aid as contributor to peacemaking, some specific suggestions might be useful:

1. Aid funds could sponsor all manner of "research" projects related to conflict resolution in the third world, such as:
    (a) explore the experiences and future possibilities of peace "zones" or corridors.[20]
    (b) compile an inventory of conflict resolution efforts in the South, regardless of success—what was discussed, how did it proceed, etc.
    (c) collect and catalogue various peace agreements, peace plans, regional cooperation plans, etc., as a resource to show that options exist.

    (d) research NGO experiences in conflict resolution.

    (e) study and catalogue the consequences of war—for a village, a district, a country, a region.

2.   Field workers could have a specific mandate to find, understand, and gather together traditional modes of resolving conflict.

3.   Funds could be committed towards colleges or specific instructors in the South who wish to initiate a course or program in peace studies.

4.   The aid community could tax itself five cents on every dollar of emergency relief in a conflict region. This five percent would fund the suggestions listed above.

The current inventory of ideas is not vast, but this is a consequence of an unimaginative aid community consumed with the logistics of moving emergency items in a conflict setting. Once a commitment is made to the peacemaking necessity, the list will grow in quantity and creativity.

Conclusion

As this narrative indicates, HAP has developed its own expertise and trajectory as a project. It has also fine-tuned the project process to include close networking relationships with other support groups; it acts as a reference point for liaison and contact between both primary (conflicting parties) and secondary (NGOs and institutions) actors; it has become fine tuned to the weekly, almost daily changes in the Horn region. The line between reflection and action has become blurred. Some portions of the enterprise normally categorized as "field experience" have been effectively bent to intersect with HAP; in other words "field experience" has visited HAP's institutional base. On the other hand, HAP staff have paid visits to the "field," to a variety of fields related to the Horn of Africa.

Can such a diverse activity in any sense be seen as a model to be emulated? Similar attempts around conflict issues in other settings, by other institutions, would almost certainly take their own distinct trajectories. Broad patterns would be generally recognizable, while details could be expected to vary enormously. As a category of second track diplomatic activity, HAP's efforts function amid a variety of opaque designations, none of which fully captures the range of nuances at work.

Political scientists who observe and analyze from a distance offer generous recognition of the NGO contribution toward a reordering of the African political configurations. They write tentatively of a "Second Liberation" for Africa, facilitated and informed by an engaged, organized citizenry, both inside and outside the African continent.[21] HAP plays its role in the midst of that enterprise, an enterprise still awaiting definitive christening.

Notes

1. Mennonites are from the left wing of the sixteenth century radical reformation, as much dissatisfied with the reforms of Luther as with the church of Rome.

2. Substantial literature exists to explain various grievances. *War and Famine: Indigenous Perspectives of Conflict in the Horn of Africa*, Waterloo, Ontario: Institute of Peace and Conflict Studies, 1988, is a summation of five distinct perspectives on Ethiopia. A very helpful bibliography is presented by Tekeste Negash, "Toward a Bibliography on Conflicts in the Horn of Africa," *Life and Peace Review*. (Uppsala, Sweden) vol. 12, no. 3 (1988).

3. Along with Libya and Somaliland, Eritrea was Italy's colonial responsibility.

4. Virtually every armed movement opposed to the Ethiopian government appeals to formal socialist principles.

5. For purposes of this project, the Horn of Africa is defined as Ethiopia and its neighbours. A United Nations initiated agency known as the Inter-Governmental Agency against Drought and for Development (IGADD) includes Uganda. This grouping acts as the only officially constituted African entity which conforms in general terms to what is accepted within HAP as the Horn of Africa region.

6. A church sponsored service agency of the Mennonite and Brethren in Christ Churches.

7. *Consultation on the Horn of Africa, 21-23 November 1986: Edited Proceedings.* (Waterloo: Institute of Peace and Conflict Studies, 1988), p. 33.

8. Letter from Anne-Marie Lambert (Associate Director of PAC) to HAP, 20 October 1987.

9. One participant's comment at the conclusion of the April 1988 HAP consultation.

10. Literature on the subject is extensive. One of the classics written by a Mennonite author is by Guy F. Hershberger, *War, Peace, and Non-Resistance*. (Scottdale, PA.: Herald Press, 1944).

11. Cf. Larry Minear, *Helping People in an Age of Conflict: Toward a New Professionalism in U.S. Voluntary Assistance* (New York: Interaction, 1988).

12. "Report of the Parliamentary Delegation to Ethiopia and Sudan, January 1991," p. 8.

13. Elise Boulding, "The Rise of INGOs: New Leadership for a Planet in Transition," *Breakthrough* (Fall 1987/Spring 1988): 14.

14. David Korten. "Third Generation Strategies," *World Development* vol. 15 (Autumn 1987): 147–149. Cf. David Korten, *Getting to the 21st Century: Voluntary Action and the Global Agenda* (West Hartford, CT: Kumarian Press, 1990), 113–132.

15. Alan B. Durning, "Action at the Grassroots: Fighting Poverty and Environmental Decline," *World Watch Paper 88,* January 1989, p. 10.

16. C.H. Mike Yarrow, *Quaker Experience in International Conciliation* (New Haven, CT.: Yale University Press, 1978). This book features an excellent essay on the range of conflict resolution theory in addition to the extensive case studies.

17. Sydney D. Bailey, "Non-Official Mediation in Disputes: Reflections on Quaker Experience," *International Affairs* (1985): 208.

18. John Paul Lederach, "Conflict Transformation: the Case for Peace Advocacy," in *NGOs Making Peace: A Prospect for the Horn* (Waterloo, Ontario: Institute of Peace and Conflict Studies, 1991), p. 814.

19. *Ibid.*

20. One such example is Larry Minear et. al., *Humanitarianism Under Siege: A Critical Review of Operation Lifeline Sudan* (Trenton, New Jersey: Red Sea Press, 1991).

21. "The State and the Crisis in Africa: In Search of a Second Liberation." *Development Dialogue*, Dag Hammarshjold Foundation, Uppsala, Sweden (1987:2): 5.

Findings and Conclusions

Aid as Peacemaker:
Concluding Observations
and Reflections

Robert Miller

Parliamentary Centre for Foreign Affairs and Foreign Trade

The editor of a collection like this may sometimes provide, or attempt to provide, a framework into which all of the cases can be fitted. Those who look for this in *Aid as Peacemaker* will be disappointed. We have invented no such framework, which is not to say one cannot be invented. We invite others to try.

The words "observations and reflections" suggest the different intent behind this concluding piece. Our purpose is to share thoughts concerning four different points that we found ourselves returning to time after time in the course of this study: the first point is that, contrary to the conventional wisdom, development and peace are an odd and fractious couple which can be reconciled only with great difficulty; second, that we should be very modest about our ability to promote reconciliation, but also undeterred by our limitations; third, that we should be imaginative about identifying and developing a wide range of peacemaking tools; finally, that Canada should seize the opportunity to develop its capacity as peacemaker. On the latter point, we offer a modest proposal which may or may not appeal to those who make policy.

The odd couple of development and peace

Among the major obstacles to developing aid as peacemaker is the entrenched skepticism of senior government officials, captured so beautifully in the withering putdown by one of them that this peacemaking task was just another decoration on the Canadian International Development Agency (CIDA) Christmas tree. The implication was pretty clear: whereas development is serious business, peacemaking is faddish and ornamental, attractive only to those who are more interested in the appearance than the reality of things.

The dismissal of peacemaking arises from the conventional wisdom that in supporting economic development—for example by helping to build dams and roads—the Canadian aid program is already doing everything it can or should to contribute to a prosperous and peaceful third world. This widely held notion simply assumes the neutrality or beneficence of economic development in relation to political forces. As we pointed out in the introduction to the book, this belief refuses to come to grips with the evidence that development, even the most innocuous and benign forms of development, inevitably disturbs the status quo and the balance of power among groups and individuals. If the ripple effect of change reinforces waves which are already rolling though society, the results may include steadily rising levels of conflict and violence.

Canada's own recent history should disabuse us of the notion that economic development is the necessary and sufficient cure for conflict. Quite the contrary. In addition to the rising levels of anomic violence which seem to characterize advanced postindustrial societies, political conflict in Canada has risen right along with Gross National Product (GNP) per capita. In what seems a paradox to many people around the world, the growing prosperity of Canadians has been accompanied by an unprecedented resurgence of Quebec separatism. To many, though by no means all Quebecers, economic development has been interpreted as the final proof that the province not only should but can go it alone.

These and other examples we could cite merely confirm that it is time for Canada to abandon the innocent conceit that international development assistance is apolitical. Each time that we provide assistance to another country, we become part of its equation of political forces. By effect, if not by intent, we act politically. The appearance of violence throughout much of the South has simply made this more apparent, for violence is a kind of litmus test of politics gone awry. Since the essence of morality is to accept responsibility for the consequences as well as the intentions of our acts, Canadian policy makers must take into account the political consequences of development decisions, which means especially the consequences for conflict and peace.

If this is so, what is to guide us in calculating the effects of our actions? What is the relationship between development and peace? Is there a model which can lead us unerringly towards peaceful forms of development? There is not. We know of none. Certainly we cannot claim that development and peace are invariably complementary. One can cite examples—modern Central America, Mozambique—where peace would almost certainly improve the prospects for development but there are other examples where conflict has accelerated social and economic change and boosted development. As we interpret it, the evidence of the causal connection between development and peace is inconclusive, just as the link between democracy and development remains unproved and perhaps unprovable.

Instead of assuming a happy marriage between development and peace, we should recognize the difficulty of their relationship. We should accept that they are an odd couple with regard at least to values, driven by different impulses and often acting at cross-purposes to one another.

Development expresses the human restlessness which has grown hyper-active over the past several hundred years. It is forever challenging the status quo by pitting one interest against another. While deploring violence, development may often encourage it and accept it as just another cost of doing business. By contrast, the search for peace represents the human desire for reconciliation and harmony, both among people and between people and creation. For much of this century, peace has served as a rather ineffectual opposition to a world run by and for development.

For reasons that were spelled out in the introduction to this collection, there is an emerging concern to find ways of reconciling development and peace. The world has become frightened by its own rapidly expanding capacity for violence and senses that it is linked in some fashion to the same forces which drive economic and social development. We have seen that reconciliation will not be arranged automatically by "history" which leaves only one other candidate for the job—us.

If reconciliation is to take place, it will be through the discovery and expression of values in which both development and peace can find their roots, for neither can or will be sacrificed to the other. Gerald Schmitz describes peacemaking as "a call to nonviolent action to transform social structures" and David Wurfel writes about "growth with justice" and "empowerment of the powerless." Canada—together with many other aid donors, both bilateral and multilateral—has recently "discovered" democracy and human rights as the missing link between development and peace. In applauding the general direction of this new policy, we nonetheless echo the warning issued by Andres Perez in his essay on the International Centre for Human Rights and Democratic Development. Human rights and democratic institutions must be rooted in a framework of values which nourishes a sense of community.

On modesty

If the first of our reflections is that development and peace can be reconciled only with difficulty, the second follows naturally—we should be modest about our ability to play peacemaker. Aid as peacemaker says that, where possible and appropriate, Canadian development assistance should be used to help avert, ameliorate or reduce large scale violent conflict in developing countries. Unlike peacekeeping which seeks to treat the immediate symptoms of conflict, peacemaking tries to alter the underlying causes, be they economic, political, or social. The reader can hardly have been surprised to find that the ability to influence third world conflict in this way is about as limited as our ability to change individual behaviour successfully. The collection of papers illustrates that the chances of making peace may be slightest when the need is greatest.

Apart from the elusiveness and complexity of the relationship between development and peace—which we have already described—parties to violent conflict rarely appreciate the attempts by outsiders to resolve the dispute. Where the conflict is a domestic one—within the family or borders of a country—the resentment of outside interference is apt to be intense and particularly risky for the outsider. For a small to middle sized power like Canada, the difficulties of trying to mediate simply multiply. No doubt that is why "quiet diplomacy," which tries to downplay the appearance of influence, continues to be the folk wisdom of Canadian foreign policy.

The difficulties of peacemaking arise from more than the ingratitude of those we seek to help. Bearing in mind that the aim is to alter the underlying causes of conflict, peacemakers are limited by the formidable ignorance they bring to their task. One of the cautions that runs throughout these papers is that Canada is often so "thin on the ground" that it is in no position to know what is going on, let alone why, let alone do anything constructive about it. The one merit of violent conflict is that it induces modesty through fear of getting one's fingers burned. There is, unfortunately, no such hesitation when it comes to prescribing economic and other medicine for ailing countries in the South, although the risks for the people directly involved may be as high.

As Andres Perez points out, the danger of unguarded ignorance is that it will substitute technique for understanding. Such ignorance may assume that if only the third world adopts our institutions and practices, its conflicts would be resolved or much reduced. Of course, if agreement were so easy on institutional solutions the conflicts would not have arisen in the first place. The issue being hammered out in many countries—Canada included—is both maddeningly simple and hard to resolve: in whatever institutions we create, who will have what kinds of power? To that, there is no simple technocratic solution.

So there is every reason to be modest about aid as peacemaker, but there is no reason to be deterred. Even when there are no opportunities to do good, one must strive to avoid doing harm. In his paper on Sri Lanka, David Gillies warns us that large scale development projects may stir up, if not create, powerful communal tensions. He argues that Canadian aid workers, whose eyes may be blinded by the glare of Canadian exports, should watch for the dangers.

The papers give practical, if modest, examples of how we can use aid as a peacemaker, provided we have the wit, will, and imagination to do so. It is pointed out more than once that Canada's lack of clout may confer advantages, for if we are not trusted more than other countries, at least we may be less mistrusted than some. The papers, by implication, urge us to stand on guard against the perverse Canadian habit of exaggerating our *lack* of influence. As David Wurfel points out in his essay on the Philippines, the quality of peacemaking may matter more than the power of the peacemaker. "Peace or conflict are not social conditions or processes which can be measured quantitatively. Interventions which are quantitatively small can, if they are seen as morally right and based on an accurate assessment of the situation, have a significant impact on peace and conflict resolution."

The appeal of designing new tools of peacemaking rests finally on the high costs of the alternative. To take a recent spectacular example, the war in the Persian Gulf cost Canada, a minor player, an estimated $90 million per month. The Canadian government paid the bill promptly and enthusiastically, although for years it had pled poverty when it came to funding the aid program. The conflict itself was enormously destructive, accomplishing in a matter of months the devastation of Kuwait and the reversal of Iraq's economic development. Nonetheless, the war might well have been justifiable had the international community reasonably concluded that the nonviolent alternative—economic sanctions—would not and could not work. Instead that option was brushed aside as the appeal of war proved irresistible. In this instance, the war seemed remarkably fast and efficient. By the time the high costs came rolling in, the deed was done and the world's attention had moved elsewhere.

The tools of the trade

If peacemaking is an important but imprecise science at best (the understatement of the day), its tools are correspondingly rough and ready. On the other hand, there are more tools and a greater variety of them than is commonly supposed, and new ones are being developed every day. This means that the choice facing Canada is not always the stark one of doing peacemaking or not; rather it is a question of choosing the right tools—or the most acceptable tools—to do the job.

We would divide the possible methods of Canada using aid to make peace into two sets of options: the hard options and the soft. In using these terms, we do not mean to equate hard with difficult and soft with easy, nor hard with principled and soft with opportunistic. The difference is only that the hard options are more likely to involve confrontation between Canada and another country, and therefore the sacrifice of other Canadian interests, whereas the soft options attempt to achieve the same objectives through one form or other of cooperation. It is not our purpose here to assess these tools of the trade but simply to describe them and succinctly pose questions about their use.

Hard options

(i) Solidarity

By far the hardest of the hard options for Canada is that of unequivocally coming to the support of some party in the world struggling for justice. Chris Neal argues in his essay on CUSO in Southern Africa that solidarity "emerges from a recognition that some conflicts must be approached in moral terms and that mediation will perpetuate conflict by meeting villainy halfway." Both Neal and Linda Freeman are sharply critical of Canada's unwillingness to commit itself fully to the African National Congress (ANC) while at the same time professing support for its cause. Why? Was it because the government chose to approach the conflict in an amoral way or because—as the government claimed—it could not support the ANC so long as it retained armed conflict as an option for change in South Africa? Whatever the explanation, it seems clear that Canada is powerfully averse to taking sides in armed conflict, except where—as in the Persian Gulf—major allies are similarly engaged.

(ii) Aid conditionality

If solidarity is the harder of the hard options, aid conditionality is the commoner. It involves providing aid or not and varying the amount of aid according to some criteria having to do (usually) with the behaviour of recipient governments. It is the tool that Canadians are most likely to ask their government to use because it is simple and direct and therefore has political resonance. The government has recently become far more responsive to considerations of this kind. On the other hand, aid conditionality as practiced by Canada faces some serious limitations. As David Close argues in his essay on Central America, effective use of such an instrument demands an in country presence to provide politicians and civil servants in Canada with informed, seasoned judgements about the policy alternatives. "Unfortunately we do not have this presence in Central America." Despite the political sex appeal of bold, unilateral action, this option is more likely to be effective for Canada when it is exercised in co-operation with other countries and based on careful multilateral monitoring.

Soft options

(i) Alternative channels

As suggested above, aid conditionality is more likely to be effective when co-ordinated internationally, although it then faces the considerable obstacle of having to obtain a consensus among numerous governments.

David Gillies in his essay on Sri Lanka indicates just how difficult that can be and Greg Wirick in his paper on the United Nations argues that, despite its recent successes, the world body suffers from many infirmities. Nonetheless, the point remains that Canada has a variety of channels open to it to play the role of peacemaker. In their essays on the Philippines and Central America, David Wurfel and David Close explore the advantages and disadvantages of supporting nongovernmental organizations when Canada does not want a government-to-government aid program. The advantage is that Canada keeps channels open without too overtly extending the hand of friendship. On the other hand, as Wurfel argues, the Canadian government must then be prepared to back up the NGOs when, as is likely, they eventually offend the local powers-that-be.

(ii) Alternative forms of aid

David Close makes the point that Canada can and sometimes should provide assistance even when development as such is clearly impossible. This amounts to a kind of "soft solidarity" with struggling people inasmuch as it identifies Canada with the need for political change without overtly challenging the government in question. The assistance given to black groups in South Africa is a variation on this form of assistance, an investment in the day when development would be possible. Similarly, Canada may use emergency food aid or other forms of humanitarian assistance to send a political signal, while also helping to keep people alive.

(iii) Promoting democracy and social justice

The Canadian aid program has now recognized the importance of democratic development by identifying "political sustainability" as one of the five pillars of development. But as Wurfel and others make clear, Canada should not equate democracy with the formal apparatus of electoral institutions alone. If democracy is to work in a country like the Philippines, it must be "infused with justice" for the poor. In turn, foreign aid "cannot be neutral; it either reduces social justice or it enhances it." Wurfel applauds CIDA's eventual insistence that all new projects should include an element of permanent land reform as an example of enhancing social justice.

(iv) Development dialogue with the recipient government

At the heart of all the soft options lies the judgement that it is possible to change a situation of conflict though positive engagement of one kind or other. Another form of engagement recommended by our contributors is development dialogue between the Canadian government and the recipient government. While insisting on the importance of this kind of frank exchange, Gerry Schmitz casts doubt on the Canadian government's capacity or willingness to do it. As he notes, productive dialogue requires that Canada first be clear about its own development objectives and purposes, a requirement betrayed by "the muddled policy on conditionality and values promotion."

(v) Consultation and dialogue among stakeholders

David Wurfel's paper on the Philippines illustrates that if the spirit is willing, it is possible for Canadian aid officials to learn from their mistakes. In this one instance, CIDA responded to sharp criticism of its Philippine Development Assistance Program (PDAP) by formulating an entirely new structure after lengthy consultation involving an ideologically diverse group of Filipino NGOs. By bringing together people who had never previously spoken to one another, the consultation itself "indirectly promoted peace," Wurfel concludes.

(vi) Using aid projects to build the momentum for peace

The paper by Hay and Sanger and the one by Mathies et al. illustrate the possibilities of using aid projects to help break up logjams of conflict or to reinforce a momentum for peace. Recalling our earlier point that peacemakers should not be deterred by the modesty of their accomplishments, it can safely be acknowledged that projects of this sort are tiny and seemingly inconsequential on the third world battlefield. Mathies notes, however, that behind the modesty of conflict resolution and other techniques there lies the "hope that participants might… incrementally erode some of the misunderstandings and misperceptions that have festered over the years."

Canada as peacemaker

In describing a few of the tools of aid as peacemaker, we have become conscious of two things: first, that there are many other techniques and approaches which might have been mentioned or which await discovery; and second, that none of these tools of the trade will ever be put to much use unless Canada—and Canadians—are seized by the challenge of peacemaking. This would involve going well beyond—conceptually, politically and organizationally—mere tinkering with peacemaking as an adjunct to development assistance. It would involve a redefinition and revitalization of Canada's role in the world.

Specifically, Canada should now unite its two great foreign policy vocations—peacekeeping and development—by creating a new Department of International Security. This would consist of the transformed remnants of the Department of National Defence and of the Canadian International Development Agency. Its mandate would be to reconcile the very different and sometimes conflicting goals of international development and peace. To the task of development, it would bring an understanding that conflict resolution is an essential part of change; to conflict resolution, it would bring an understanding of the imperatives of development. From this complex mixing of different foreign policy goals could come a very rich Canadian perspective on the problems of the world.

The possibilities that lie in blending the military role of peacekeeping and the civilian role of development were illustrated during a visit to Namibia in the fall of 1989, a few months prior to that country's achievement of independence. The parliamentary delegation which the author accompanied spent a day in the north of the country near the Angolan border where much of the fiercest fighting in the civil war had taken place. By the time we arrived, South African troops had been replaced by United Nations Peacekeeping troops, specifically FINNBATT—a Finnish battalion. Much of its activity consisted of patrolling the area and investigating alleged violations of the cease fire agreement, but the Finnish soldiers played another important role as well—in development.

It was explained to us that following the studies of a Finnish anthropologist who had been assigned to headquarters, the battalion had devised a series of aid projects—mainly having to do with water and food supply—for the people in the surrounding villages. It was quite apparent from the amount of time and care that went into briefing the visitors about this activity that FINNBATT regarded it as an essential part of its mission. When asked why, the commanding officer explained very simply that the effectiveness of the battalion's work in peacekeeping depended on gaining the trust of the people and there was only one way to do this—by showing practical concern for the basic problems of their lives such as food and water.

There is a fairly large step to be taken from this insight to the creation of a Department of International Security which would throw civilian developers and military peacekeepers together in bureaucratic intimacy. Yet it is a step that can and should be taken. With the end of the Cold War, the Canadian armed forces are a solution in search of a problem. Bernard Wood, the President of the Canadian Institute for International Peace and Security, suggests in his annual statement for 1992 that the problem is the proliferation of ethnic and other conflict throughout the world, much of it in the South. He observes that "for Canada UN peacekeeping may represent primary—as opposed to ancillary—defence challenges. It is time to recognize that UN peacekeeping is a global 'growth industry' in which Canada is the world leader. It is a source of healthy national pride and extraordinarily strong public support for Canada's armed forces."

Growth industry or not, there is a danger that peacekeeping will come to be seen as just another band-aid solution which fails to address the underlying political, economic, and social problems that give rise to conflict in the first place. The UN operation in Namibia was both successful and interesting precisely because it insisted that peacekeeping was only an element in a broader process of economic and political— mainly political —change. Similarly, in persuing the primary defence challenge of peacekeeping, the Canadian armed forces need a creative partnership with international development, through close working relations with CIDA, the International Development Research Centre (IDRC), other governmental development agencies, and also with nongovernmental organizations (NGOs).

For the time being, we can only catch glimpses of the future. CARE Canada has recently begun a collaboration with a retired senior officer in the Canadian armed forces to advice the agency on how to manage development projects in conflict situations in the Horn of Africa. The officer, who commanded peacekeeping operations during his military career, was fascinated by the challenge of applying his specialized knowledge in an entirely new field. The example suggests the possibility of creating a register of ex-peacekeepers who might be interested in undertaking peacemaking assignments for development agencies, in effect an NGO for peacekeepers.

Conclusion

As we bring these reflections to a close, a question intrudes: doesn't all of this seem a bit bizarre and irrelevant in early 1992, with Canada clinging to life by its constitutional fingertips? Maybe, but the future (and extent) of the country will depend in part on a sense of national purpose, on a sense that Canada has important things to do in the world. In the midst of our national gloom, it is time to start dreaming again.

MARQUIS
Montmagny, Qc
November 1992